STAY HUNGRY & KICK BURNOUT IN THE BUTT

Also by Dr. Steven Berglas

The Success Syndrome:
Hitting Bottom When You Reach the Top

Self-Handicapping:
The Paradox That Isn't

Your Own Worst Enemy:
Understanding the Paradox of Self-Defeating Behavior

Reclaiming the Fire:
How Successful People Overcome Burnout

STAY HUNGRY & KICK BURNOUT IN THE BUTT

DR. STEVEN BERGLAS

Foreword by Marshall Goldsmith

CENTER STREET

Nashville New York

Center Street
Hachette Book Group
1290 Avenue of the Americas, New York, NY 10104
centerstreet.com
twitter.com/centerstreet

First edition: September 2018

Center Street is a division of Hachette Book Group, Inc.
The Center Street name and logo are trademarks of Hachette Book Group, Inc.

The publisher is not responsible for websites (or their content)
that are not owned by the publisher.

Scriptures taken from the Holy Bible, New International Version®, NIV®.
Copyright © 1973, 1978, 1984, 2011 by Biblica, Inc.™ Used by permission of Zondervan.
All rights reserved worldwide. www.zondervan.com The "NIV" and
"New International Version" are trademarks registered in the United States
Patent and Trademark Office by Biblica, Inc.™
Scriptures marked "KJV" are from the Holy Bible, King James Version.

Library of Congress Cataloging-in-Publication Data

Names: Berglas, Steven, author.
Title: Stay hungry & kick burnout in the butt / Dr. Steven Berglas.
Other titles: Stay hungry and kick burnout in the butt
Description: First Edition. | New York : Center Street, [2018] |
Includes bibliographical references and index.
Identifiers: LCCN 2018011994| ISBN 9781478921493 (hardcover) |
ISBN 9781549194559 (audio download) | ISBN 9781478921509 (ebook)
Subjects: LCSH: Job satisfaction. | Motivation (Psychology) | Career development.
Classification: LCC HF5549.5.J63 B447 2018 | DDC 650.1—dc23
LC record available at https://lccn.loc.gov/2018011994

ISBNs: 978-1-4789-2149-3 (hardcover), 978-1-4789-2150-9 (ebook)

Printed in the United States of America

LSC-C

10 9 8 7 6 5 4 3 2 1

In loving memory of my father, Jerome K. Berglas:

Ancora imparo.

Contents

CONTENTS

Foreword

One of the most popular current dictums in career and life—often attributed to Confucius, though many others have been credited with similar words over the years—is that if you find a job you love, you'll never work a day in your life. The idea is that when you are fully engaged in the work you do, it won't seem like work at all. Indeed, it will be so fulfilling that work and life will be forever intertwined in one long and happy continuum. Your job will be your life, and it will lift your spirits and fulfill you in ways that most of us could never imagine possible.

What happens, however, is that when you start a job you like it just fine, but over time—not too long a time for most—you find yourself dreading the commute to work in the morning, or you notice that you cannot wait for 5:00 p.m. to arrive so you can leave your workplace as far behind as possible. Sure, some folks stay late, but you're not one of those drudges. You wanted uplifts from that job, you're not getting them, so all you want now is out. This feeling, by the way—feeling so psychologically empty that you can barely function—is not limited to the office; you notice that it has encroached upon your personal life as well.

Now what do you do?

In his very insightful book, Steven Berglas turns the conventional wisdom of work and career on its head, taking the reader on a thought-provoking journey through the psychology of what brings us happiness in our work and why it's so difficult for most of us to avoid succumbing to career burnout. We all know people whose work has made them utterly miserable, relegating them to the never-ending hell of being trapped in "golden handcuffs." They have tried switching jobs before—probably several times—only to end up depressed, dejected, and totally distressed once the honeymoon period ends, and asking themselves, "Why bother?" I have seen it in my own coaching practice: executives and managers— all very smart, all very hardworking—whose careers have crushed their spirits and left them wanting to do anything other than what they were doing before "a job they loved" failed to give them the emotional rewards they expected it would.

Research shows that 80 percent of all workers feel stress on the job, 40 percent report that their job is either very stressful or extremely stressful, and 25 percent consider their jobs to be the number one cause of stress in their lives. All this stress takes an enormous toll on the people who feel it, and on the organizations that employ them. Stress on the job can result in relatively mild physical ailments such as fatigue, headaches, back pain, nausea, and frequent colds, but it can also be deadly, leading to high blood pressure and heart attacks. It's estimated that stress costs US companies more than $300 billion a year.

These numbers make it abundantly clear that while most of us, once or several times, have found a job we thought we could love, our faith in the contention that finding a job we love will lead to achieving happiness is specious at best. My own work tells me this is the case for most people. Many of us have jobs that we enjoy, perhaps even love, yet we are more distressed than we can imagine, and we fear we are descending into a state of burnout.

One cause of this problem, according to Steve, is that even the most rewarding work or career inevitably loses its power to reward us over time. It's not unlike a marriage where the excitement of passionate love begins to wane soon after the honeymoon has ended, in many cases culminating in divorce (the seven-year itch is very real, with the majority of divorces taking place seven years after couples are married). We may have the greatest career, working for the best company, but we will eventually sense that the highs we enjoyed while we grew into that career are no longer there and our happiness has evaporated, only to be replaced by feelings of being burned out.

In his work coaching many of today's top executives, Steve has observed that business leaders often struggle to come to terms with questions of their own shortcomings. Facing them requires vulnerability, which is especially difficult for people who are used to being out front and showing strength. Yet vulnerability and humility are often the difference between a good leader and one who knows true greatness. That's why it is so important that leaders are willing to concede their shortcomings and realize there is always more to learn. They must question themselves, and then question themselves again.

In this remarkably powerful work Steve provides readers with a framework for understanding why they are unhappy in their work and careers and exactly what they can do to find happiness. According to Steve, the ultimate path to happiness in work and career is to adopt a mind-set of *entrepreneurism*—where, in his words, "you wake up in the morning with passion and drive for the day ahead." This, as Steve points out, is the kind of passion and drive that Steve Jobs famously alluded to when he suggested in his 2005 Stanford University commencement address that the graduates should "Stay hungry. Stay foolish."

Again, research indicates that entrepreneurs are, on average, happier than the rest of us. They are happier because they are able to successfully craft careers that enable them to turn their passion into purpose. They don't just *find* careers they love, they *create* careers they love, and they constantly re-create them—over and over again.

The good news, as Steve explains, is that you don't have to start up your own business or be working in the Silicon Valley to benefit from entrepreneurism. Anyone can have the entrepreneurial spirit deep inside them, even a barista at Starbucks, a financial analyst at Citibank, or a salesperson for the Ford car dealership on the other side of town. The key is to find the *why* within you. One of my favorite parts of *Stay Hungry & Kick Burnout in the Butt* is Steve's contention that German philosopher Friedrich Nietzsche's observation, "He who has a why to live can bear almost any how," is arguably the key to deriving sustained joy from your career pursuits.

If you find that your career is no longer delivering the rewards and psychic satisfaction that it once did, I encourage you to take the lessons in Steve's book to heart. Read them; experiment with them; see how they act to change your life. Start small but keep the big picture in mind. I am convinced that if you give the wisdom within these pages a try in your own life, you'll find that a truly satisfying career will be yours.

And, believe me, you won't experience true, long-lasting happiness until you find happiness in your work and career. All the tools you need to do that are here. Embrace them. Use them. Make them a part of your life. When you do, you will know the kind of happiness that few of us ever have a chance to experience.

—Marshall Goldsmith

Introduction

Vision without action is a daydream.
Action without vision is a nightmare.[1]

—Japanese proverb

You have a vision.

It's vague because that is the nature of visions, but you see yourself on a Monday morning popping out of bed thirty minutes before your alarm goes off and feeling a sense of anticipation about the day ahead.

And that's where the vision ends.

Visions are tough to hold on to. They're not recollections, things we've done that we see in our mind's eye, but rather a glimpse into the future, most often the type of future we hope to enjoy.

Indulge me for a moment. I'll articulate your vision of the future in terms of *what you do not like about the present*. See if I understand you. What you see lying ahead is an escape from the hell you are in today, a hell born of a career that neither engages nor rewards you as you feel it should. You also see yourself talking to someone—who is unclear—but you see yourself getting indignant, throwing back your shoulders, and saying, "This is how things *should* be. I should awaken each day eager to work, not dreading another descent into purgatory. I don't ask for much; all I want is to be passionate about and fully engaged in a career."

I hope this sounds reasonable to you; it's the lament I've heard from scores of patients and coaching clients over a period of decades. I believe that you, too, would present this as your vision but for the fact that your work life is nothing like being happy, and you haven't felt happy for so long you cannot recall if you've ever truly felt that way as a result of your work or career.

This book is designed to help you concretize your vision and give you an action plan for realizing it that does not leave you suffering a nightmare scenario. The problem is, it's highly likely that you have lost sight of your ideal vision since it was formed long ago and has never been actualized. Most everyone starts a career feeling that they will enjoy self-esteem enhancement on a regular basis. Most folks look forward to interacting with coworkers who care about them, praise them, and criticize them in constructive ways when appropriate. Doing well and getting "good feedback" are the main ingredients for building and sustaining self-esteem.

My fear is that you abandoned that dream long ago. Thus, to realize something akin to your ideal vision today, after long fearing it would never come to fruition (and between us,

I believe you can surprise yourself with how gratifying work can be if it is approached with a thorough understanding of what makes it work and what makes it deleterious to your health), you need an attitude adjustment before embarking upon a new, professional modus operandi.

Now, here's where the sledding gets tough. I'm sorry to be the bearer of bad news, but I'm going to give you the toughest part right up front, no punches pulled: "The right job," "a job you love," or "the unequivocal dream job" is never, ever, ever, going to appear during the course of your life.

Nothing close.

This book is predicated on the notion that approaching career satisfaction based on the most popular job-hunting directive around today—to "Choose a job you love"—is as ludicrous as shopping for shoes, buying a pair that is attractive (if they're for stepping out) or comfortable (if they're for plodding through a daily grind), and not knowing the size of the shoes you selected or, more important, what your own shoe size is.

I would repeat what I just said a hundred different ways if I could, but it won't help you. Just accept that a job—*any* job—is so fraught with problems you will never be able to find the right one. Thus, you have to control what you can: you, and your approach to jobs.

I'm not being facile or disingenuous—let me explain. Let's suppose you dreamed of being a teacher but decided to go into the IT field because (a) the market for teachers is shrinking, (b) teaching today, with rare exceptions, is more babysitting than what Aristotle did at the Lyceum, and you've admired Aristotle since you began reading, and (c) from your perspective, educators get far less respect and have much less positive influence over society than you believe they should. So now you're writing code in Silicon Valley.

Who prevents you from teaching? You can teach within the context of your job (countless coaches earn fortunes from corporations by doing onboarding, a $100 term that enables a coach to charge $500 an hour to show new hires the ropes, something mentors have done for free since Aristotle was around), or you can teach in a limitless number of contexts after work or on weekends. Why would you do that, you ask? Because (a) it's a passion, (b) as you'll be reminded countless times in this book, working for monetary compensation will not yield self-actualization, and (c) if you engage your passions, it's both emotionally and physically energizing. If you think, "Lord, I'm already exhausted after work and this guy suggests doing yet another job," here's a guarantee: You're exhausted at work because it's drudgery. But if you do something after work that is uplifting, it will give you something akin to a runner's high—a shot of endorphins that is uplifting and energizing—leaving you feeling infinitely better than at the end of your workday.

Where We'll Go—Together

What I just described isn't a vision or a dream. It's the life story of countless people you've read about and I've coached or counseled into crafting careers that they were highly engaged in and elated by. But do not take my word for it, or all that follows will have been written for naught. I'll prove it to you—here's how.

To ensure that you actualize your vision of crafting an engaging and gratifying career, in the pages that follow I will escort you through a detailed learning process that will help you see why you feel you are trapped in a living hell, what got you there, and what it will take to get you out of where you are. These are the key elements I will focus on:

• **Preventing you from wrongly blaming yourself for the components of your malaise that are not your fault.** Self-reproach will kill your capacity to change. I will illustrate what is wrong with work, the rewards of work, and the major problems born of work—95 percent of what makes your job feel like hell and doesn't come close to fulfilling your vision. I'm not saying, "Oh, you're perfect; don't change a thing...." That's a load of crap. What I am saying is that it's advantageous to diagnose your professional situation and your role in it with insight, understanding, and precision. Most of what ails you is a function of what's wrong with *work*, not what's wrong with *you*.

• **Introducing you to, explaining, and having you come to an in-depth understanding of anger.** It's taboo; it's politically incorrect; it's mysterious. It's also instinctive, part of "the human condition," and manageable. Think of it as the German shepherd of emotions: dangerous if misused or abused, an invaluable ally if handled properly. I will present an exhaustive justification for changing how you construe anger—from seeing it as a flaw to realizing that it is a fuel—and demonstrating that, despite its horrid reputation there is ample justification for seeing anger as a protective instinctual drive. I will also illustrate the myriad ways in which anger has been used through the ages to achieve laudable, heroic, and life-changing goals, and how you can do that, too.

• **Help you reexamine happiness versus wealth.** I mentioned this with regard to teaching and holding your IT job. I'll tell you much more about why what seems like suggesting you stretch yourself thinner than carpaccio won't do anything of the sort, and (ironically) *will* enable you to thrive.

• **How to craft a career you will feel engaged in and derive gratification from.** The key word here is *craft*. What most people who follow my program do is adapt, modify, retrofit, or realign existing careers so they are tailored to fit their individual needs as described above. I've repeated myself, I know, but it's hard for some people who have been inculcated to believe that choosing a job you love is the answer to their problems to see things differently.

You bought this book seeking relief from a job, or a series of them, that have left your self-esteem bruised or battered. Your spirit is probably drained, and I would imagine that you are less optimistic than pessimistic. Part of the problem stems from the fact that you are not a quitter ("Winners never quit and quitters never win," right?). But since making a major life change is as scary as drifting in the ocean on an air mattress and finding yourself knocked off it by a shark, you're feeling anxious. This is 100 percent normal. So, too, is resisting change owing to a slew of psychological forces.

Don't start changing yet, but do stop entrenching yourself in your job owing to the misguided notion that if you try *just a bit harder* and dig down *just a bit deeper* for that extra ounce of commitment, things will improve. Instead, don't quit your job, but do whatever it takes to maintain the status quo and nothing more. Do not—as most motivated careerists do prior to an emotional collapse—strain, with every fiber of your being, to see if turning up your intensity on the job won't get you past the threshold you've yet to break through so you can land where you will finally be rewarded as you deserve to be. That place doesn't exist save for a select few who've crafted custom-made careers for themselves. The good news is I promise to show you how you can do it, too. For the time being, however, just stop digging.

One Final Point

"The critical first step in every treatment plan is a thorough diagnosis." Those were the first words I heard on day one of my postdoctoral fellowship at Harvard Medical School more than forty years ago. The image in my mind today of the professor who made that statement is as vivid as a peacock's tail feathers. The professor then added, "In psychiatry *we cannot afford a misdiagnosis*—it would ruin a person's life."

You are in no danger of a ruined life, but to extricate yourself from the job-induced malaise you are suffering you need to know much more than "this situation stinks." You need to diagnose what got you into the hellhole you are in and why you have not been able to escape on your own. I will urge you to hold a mirror up to yourself more often than any other "advice book" you can find. This is not done to be critical of you or, heaven forbid, have you be critical of yourself. It is designed to enable you to be *constructive*.

The advice I offer is never one-size-fits-all, and some of it won't fit you. To know what does and what doesn't you have to follow the ancient Greek Delphic maxim inscribed in the wall of the Temple of Apollo at Delphi and used by Socrates as a precursor to gaining knowledge: *Know thyself.*

I worked my way through college as a bartender and heard countless toasts. As you get ready to embark on the journey of finding passion and purpose in your career I want you to take a moment to raise a toast to your own courage and commitment to change. Thus, please view the material presented in this book from the perspective of my all-time favorite toast:

May you have the hindsight to know where you've been, the foresight to know where you are going, and the insight to know when you have gone too far.

CHAPTER 1

Why Sooner or Later Everyone Wants to Scream "Take This Job and Shove It!"

A bad day of fishing is better than a good day of work.
—Author unknown

If I fished only to capture fish, my fishing trips would have ended long ago.
—Zane Grey, American writer

There is a fine line between fishing and just standing on the shore like an idiot.
—Steven Wright, comedian

Nowadays if you tell someone, "You know, I became disengaged recently," there's little chance that person will assume your wedding plans went kaput. Owing to how prevalent actively disliking the jobs most of us have has become, the term *disengagement* now most commonly denotes being emotionally detached from, or "caring less about," the work that we do.

Sure, "disengagement" can still refer to planned nuptials that got called off, but rarely. If you read Gallup's 2017 *State of the American Workplace Executive Summary*, you learn that only 33 percent of workers in the US report feeling "engaged"—i.e., committed to what they are doing professionally. The rest? Either not engaged (51 percent) or actively disengaged (16 percent).[1]

Why is it that so few people show an interest or involvement in their jobs?

The problem is that jobs—the one you have now and ones you have had in the past—rarely, if ever, tap into your passions in ways that evoke a sense of purpose. To prepare you to put an end to that I must begin by helping you understand what working at a job does to any jobholder, psychologically speaking. More important, I must give you an in-depth understanding of the most flawed aspect of any and every job you can hold: its failure, over time, to provide consistently impactful rewards.

By "impactful rewards" I mean rewards that do what they are designed to do. This statement needs a bit of explaining, so what follows is a proper orientation to jobs and work, in general, that I hope will help you comprehend why, if it is psychological gratification and a sense of fulfillment you seek, your career path must follow feelings of purpose and passion, not a compensation package, regardless of what's in it.

Everyone presumes they understand what a reward is, but humor me as I present the scientific definition of a reward: "The motivational property of any stimulus is what induces appetitive or approach behavior." When the famous psychologist B. F. Skinner used the term he noted that the rewarding properties of a stimulus make it more likely that a person who is rewarded will repeat the action(s) the reward was applied to.

The preceding definitions of a reward, while precise, are also too sterile (and possibly confusing) for most. When the lay public discusses rewards they are typically referring to outcomes that boost a person's spirits or enhance his or her self-esteem. But this, too, is understating the significance of rewards. You see, rewards determine how we eat, drink, mate, and above all, evolve as a species. In conjunction with regions of our brains that organize how we acquire rewards—identifying the best available and rejecting the inferior—we keep moving through the world to find better, ever more uplifting rewards, and avoiding those contexts that afford unimpactful ones.

The problem with rewards is that they should come with a sell-by or expiration date, but they do not. Every reward, even the most intense (e.g., the love of another person) is initially uplifting but will, in short order, not work as intended or expected. This is the primary reason people disengage from work over time. Rewards that were uplifting (when you began a new job and you learned new skills, faced novel challenges, etc.) cease to be so when the work you do to receive them becomes the same old, same old.

When a reward feels like the same old, same old, it represents an obligation more than anything resembling an uplifting experience. You are cognizant of *needing rewards* (for example, money to address your basic needs), but once you work because you must, as opposed to working because of *rewarding feelings*, you find yourself sliding down a slippery slope toward feelings of exhaustion, ennui (boredom, tedium, lassitude), and, above all, the sense of accomplishing little or nothing of value, culminating in despondency born of low self-esteem.

Since entering the job market you have doubtless believed the maxim "If you find a job you love, you'll never work a day in your life" that was foisted on careerists by Confucius more than two thousand years ago. But it's the Big Lie. If it were an animate entity, this advice from Confucius would be the Prince of Darkness. Like the Sirens of Greek mythology who lured sailors with their enchanting music and voices to sail near rocky shores and get shipwrecked, Confucius's siren saying has lured countless careerists to the depths of Sisyphean hell[2] by dint of their repeatedly falling in love with a job, feeling nothing but disappointment, dejection, and depression soon after mastering its demands, yet refusing to abandon the belief that "out there, somewhere" exists the ideal job to love, forever after.

I promise you, it doesn't. Sure, you'll be smitten, have a crush on a job, or think, "This one's the one." That's normal. But do not be deluded into believing what Confucius promised: "If you find a job you love, you will never have to work a day in your life." It's baloney.

To prepare you to anticipate, cope with, and, ultimately, prevent the inevitable self-esteem depletion that results when the primary reward from a job (money) loses the capacity to provide you with uplifting feelings, you must understand why all jobs are, ultimately, inherently unrewarding, problematic, and disliked.

After more than thirty years of studying careerists yearning to do good and feel good at work while accumulating clinical expertise in helping clients redress the effects of work devoid of psychological gratifications, I've seen countless surveys documenting the fact that most Americans are miserable on the job. According to a recent article in *Forbes*, a Conference Board survey on job satisfaction reported that 52.3 percent of Americans are "unhappy at work."[3] Not long before this report was issued, a Gallup survey claimed that 87 percent of all workers worldwide were "emotionally disconnected from their workplaces and less likely to be productive."[4]

As a vehicle for looking beneath the surface of survey data just reported I chose to examine the three quotes about fishing that open this chapter. None are from commercial fishermen like those depicted on boxes of Gorton's frozen fish products—hardy, danger-defying men sailing out of the Gloucester, Massachusetts, harbor to bring home cod and other creatures of the deep. I won't use quotes from them because I'm certain they would confirm what the Conference Board and the Gallup agency found about workers' attitudes toward their jobs. Instead, the quotes I want to analyze are from people fishing for sport, for the fun of it. You will begin to see why, ultimately, every job makes you miserable.

Purveyors of bait and tackle shops that support sport fishermen rightly claim that "a bad day of fishing is better than a good day of work." Why is this so? For one, as Mark Twain pointed out in *The Adventures of Tom Sawyer*, "Work consists of whatever a body is obliged to do. Play consists of whatever a body is not obliged to do." Since you're not obliged to do it, sport fishing is, per Twain's definition, play.

But Twain gave us more than this insight about play versus work. He observed that what is play on one occasion can devolve into work on another, under certain specific circumstances, circumstances that impact anyone who holds a job:

> There are wealthy gentlemen in England who drive four-horse passenger-coaches twenty or thirty miles on a daily line, in the summer, because the privilege costs them considerable money; but if they were offered wages for the service, that would turn it into work and then they would resign.[5]

This observation resonates, in psychological terms, with what Zane Grey asserts at the beginning of this chapter about the goal of fishing trips: If your (sport) fishing trips are designed to catch what you intend to eat for dinner, then by dint of their goal orientation they are work. In contrast to the hungry fisherman whose goal it is to catch dinner, or the professional fleet fishermen working out of Gloucester Harbor, sport fishermen are out for the thrill of the catch and the fight with the fish, not the fish itself. Proof of this lies in the fact that most sport fishermen (myself, as a passionate one, included) engage in a practice known as catch and release: After they bring the fish to the boat and photograph it, they set it free. If those Gloucester fishermen who were hired by Gorton's to do the job of catching fish practiced catch and release, they would soon be out of a job. If I *didn't* practice catch and release, sport fishing would *feel like work* to me.

Finally, I included the quote from comedian Steven Wright because, in a sense, it is most informative in terms of demonstrating the devolution of work from an initially uplifting experience (when, as a new careerist, you climb the experiential ladder on the job) into a mind-numbing obligation that makes you vulnerable to psychological distress that can be devastating. What Wright's quip illustrates is that even play, something we do not do because we're obliged to, can, under certain circumstances, leave us feeling bereft of positive feelings—standing on the shoreline like an idiot.

If a person were to go fishing in the Dead Sea or cast his bait into a polluted lake that hadn't had life in it for decades, it would not take long to feel like an idiot. The simple reason this is so—and speaks volumes about why most Americans are unhappy doing their jobs—is that everything we do must, ultimately, afford us some modicum of reward, uplift, or pleasure.

Freud was the first to codify this notion in his *pleasure principle*—humans are instinctively hardwired to seek pleasure and avoid pain—and since he did so there have been thousands of studies documenting the simple fact that if you don't *get* something by way of psychological rewards for *doing* something, you'll stop doing that thing.

This principle also applies in the workplace. Many of us work not because we love our jobs but because we need the income and health care and other benefits these jobs provide. So, when we find ourselves stuck in a job we dislike, instead of resigning in a cordial manner and seeking rewarding endeavors in a different venue, we disengage from the jobs we loathe (but desperately need) in a variety of different ways. Included among these are chronic absenteeism, self-inflicted illness or injury, and acting out (misbehaving) in order to get fired, thereby becoming entitled (in most states) to collect unemployment insurance.

Why Would a King Fall Out of Love with His Job?

Long before Gallup reported job satisfaction statistics, King Solomon wrote an autobiographical account of the suffering and misery he experienced during a lifetime of seeking meaningless materialistic rewards that left him feeling emotionally empty. Using the nom de plume Ecclesiastes, Solomon wanted to offer his wisdom to future generations of Israelites by guiding them to discover the gratification that is only available by becoming involved with the words of the Lord.

Solomon was unambiguous regarding his feeling that work engaged in simply for wages or money could not possibly provide spiritual and psychological fulfillment: "I have seen all the things that are done under the sun; all of them are meaningless, *a chasing after the wind*" (Ecclesiastes 1:14). In a later chapter Solomon notes, "Everyone's toil is for their mouth, yet their appetite is never satisfied" (Ecclesiastes 6:7). Given that Ecclesiastes was written when Solomon was old and he was reflecting on his life—the good and bad, the successes and failures—it is important to realize that he made note of the fact that among the most important things he learned during his lifetime was that neither engaging in a job per se nor obtaining the rewards most jobs afford can be sufficiently satisfying to justify the energy men and women invest in them.

Hundreds of years after Solomon penned Ecclesiastes, psychologist A. H. Maslow published a seminal research report on what he called a *hierarchy of needs*,[6] the classic five-tier model of human needs people are innately motivated to master. After I read Ecclesiastes I thought Maslow should have credited Solomon in his references section.[7] Maslow's fundamental thesis is that a person goes through life traversing a series of needs that, until satisfied, hold that person back from the ultimate goal of humanity, *self-actualization*—a term that means being all you can be. When pushed to provide a formal definition for self-actualization Maslow said,

> It refers to the person's desire for self-fulfillment, namely, to the tendency for him to become actualized in what he is potentially. The specific form that these needs will take will of course vary greatly from person to person. In one it may be an ideal mother, in another it may be expressed athletically, and in still another it may be expressed in painting pictures or in inventions.[8]

Maslow maintained that a person must initially gratify the so-called deficiency or d-needs that include all of what the rewards of a job are used for: physiological needs (the physical requirements that must be addressed to ensure survival) and safety and security needs (including shelter from harm, financial security, and protection against accidents). When d-needs are met, a person can be open to love and belonging, then self-esteem needs, and ultimately go on to become self-actualized.

Reading Maslow in the original, particularly what he says about the processes one needs to engage in to become self-actualized, is an aid in understanding him and how closely his work overlaps with what Ecclesiastes says about work. In the following quote Maslow intentionally distorts Matthew 4:4—"It is written: 'Man shall not live on bread alone'"—albeit in a clever and instructive manner:

It is quite true that man lives by bread alone—when there is no bread. But what happens to man's desires when there is plenty of bread and when his belly is chronically filled?

At once other (and "higher") needs emerge and these, rather than physiological hungers, dominate the organism. And when these in turn are satisfied, again new (and still "higher") needs emerge and so on. This is what we mean by saying that the basic human needs are organized into a hierarchy of relative prepotency.[9]

Speaking of Hunger—and Thirst

Taken together, Ecclesiastes and Maslow make clear why being hungry even after a job has enabled you to satisfy your nutritional cravings or d-needs is a blessing and not a burden. If you view hunger according to its secondary definition or denotation—as a drive to achieve psychological fulfillment, not satisfy nutritional needs—you will grasp why scholars have for millennia urged those with the opportunity to do so to *stay hungry* or *stay thirsty*. Obviously, you will still need to address your d-needs, when those drives dominate your attention, to kindle a burning dissatisfaction with the status quo that leaves you craving challenge and career satisfaction.

Your ability to understand the deep link between hunger and happiness receives support from a number of different sources. Anyone who watched TV from 2006 on is aware of a wildly popular advertising campaign for Dos Equis beer (Havas Worldwide): the most interesting man in the world. When a commercial becomes an internet meme you know it's popular, and the one for Dos Equis did. Why? It's brilliant: Starring Jonathan Goldsmith, a bearded, debonair gentleman who looks to be in his mid- to late sixties, the TV ads feature a montage of daring exploits with commentary that tells precisely why this guy is so astounding. My personal favorite: "He found the Fountain of Youth but didn't drink from it because he wasn't thirsty."

I recall that particular segment of this ad campaign because it was tied to the aspect of the commercials that resonated with me most. In each most interesting man in the world promotion, after the star's heroics were presented he was shown sitting at a bar with several stunning young women hanging all over him. He would look away from his admirers and address the camera: "I don't always drink beer. But when I do, I prefer Dos Equis." Next, in a voice-over, he delivers his signature sign-off: "Stay thirsty, my friends."

The wisdom inherent in the concept "stay thirsty"—a version of "stay hungry"—has been a cornerstone of most religions and intellectual schools of thought since great thoughts were recorded. The earliest iteration I am aware of is from the Buddha, who taught that since all physical and mental objects are inherently impermanent, being desirous of securing a permanent attachment to them will cause suffering. Hence, it is better to chronically seek enlightenment if you want your life to move in the right direction. In other words, stay thirsty for enlightenment.

In 2005, Steve Jobs, the late CEO of Apple Computer and Pixar Animation Studios, delivered the commencement address to Stanford University's graduating class. He told of his fascination with the *Whole Earth Catalog*, one of the bibles of his generation, and how when the final edition of it was published the farewell message on its back cover bore the words, "Stay Hungry. Stay Foolish." That catchphrase stuck with Jobs, and they are the words he used when he closed his address to Stanford's students. He told the assembled students, "I have always wished that for myself. And now, as you graduate to begin anew, I wish that for you. Stay Hungry. Stay Foolish."

You know, at a gut level, what Jobs was referring to. You know what the most interesting man in the world was referring to. They (and I) urge you to find the drive within. If you fail to do so, screaming "Take this job and shove it!" may prove to be the mildest reaction you can have to finding yourself in a horrific circumstance.

The Upside of Work: It's Not Sloth

Since virtually the dawn of time, scholars have recognized that it is as impossible to live without nourishing work as it is to live without physiological nourishment. The concern isn't approached by asking "What's so good about work?" but by examining what happens to people when they don't work in an appropriate manner or are conscripted to engaging in malnourishing work. Every analysis I am aware of concludes that if people do not work in what theologians, philosophers, and mental health professionals deem a healthful manner, they will not only suffer acute distress and psychological pain but will find that however bad their problem is when they initially become involved in unhealthful work, it is guaranteed to keep compounding in negativity throughout their lives.

In 590 CE, Pope Gregory I revised the work of the Christian monk Evagrius Ponticus, also called Evagrius the Solitary, one of most influential theologians in the late fourth century. In 375 CE, Evagrius Ponticus generated a list of eight terrible temptations from which all sinful behavior springs. His purpose for generating this list was prescriptive: He intended it to serve as a diagnostic tool to help readers of scripture identify the process of temptation and their own strengths and weaknesses and, ultimately, to be able to identify whatever remedies existed to help them overcome temptation. For reasons that are unclear, Pope Gregory condensed this list from the original eight into what are now commonly known as the Seven Deadly Sins.

When Pope Gregory edited the work of Evagrius Ponticus he used his red pencil on two "sins" that have a direct bearing upon work (and, ultimately, vulnerability to having your self-esteem starved by your job), combining them into one. In the original list of Eight Terrible Temptations, one of the eight was acedia (aversion to work) and another one was *tristitita* (sorrow). When the list of Seven Cardinal Sins was published, those two components of Evagrius's list were amalgamated into one: sloth, a habitual disinclination to exertion; laziness.

Many people have trouble with the term *sloth* because it has a blurred meaning. In addition, those who study the history of religion find it hard to understand precisely how sorrow was subsumed within sloth. Granted, the slothful generally suffer from ill humor, but sorrow seems more applicable to traumatic loss. Nevertheless, since Pope Gregory won't be contradicted anytime soon, we must live with the understanding that the cardinal sin of sloth along with feelings of sorrow is manifested by an avowed aversion to work.

However you construe what sloth means is of little or no concern to Christian theologians. They are unanimous and unambiguous about asserting that in the absence of spiritual commitment and appropriate vocational pursuits a person will not be granted access to the Kingdom of Heaven. As noted in Genesis 2:15, "The LORD God took the man and put him in the Garden of Eden to work it and take care of it." The only way to understand this statement is that work is a divine institution because Adam was *commanded*, before the fall, *to work*. From a theological perspective, if you are directed by the Bible to "work it and keep it," a person cannot possibly be seen as doing His will if he is slothful. Parenthetically, as you will see below, even if you happen to discount Christian theology the biblical condemnation of sloth is supported by both psychological and medical research.

Like all other deadly sins, sloth is considered to be a breeding ground for related immoralities. Some would argue that sloth is a particularly fertile breeding ground for associated disorders. Who hasn't been warned, "An idle mind is the devil's playground?" This timeless wisdom has more literary and psychological supporters than you can possibly imagine, from the ancient Roman poet Ovid, who observed, "Thou seest how sloth wastes the sluggish body, as water is corrupted unless it moves," to a more modern philosopher, Benjamin Franklin, who claimed, "Sloth makes all things difficult, but industry all easy; and he that riseth late must trot all day, and shall scarce overtake his business at night; while laziness travels so slowly, that poverty soon overtakes him."

But those are just insightful commentaries; you doubtless want proof of the damage done by sloth. How about a report from the animal kingdom, an analysis of how a former star attraction of New York City's Central Park Zoo, Gus the Polar Bear, became depressed because his keepers turned him into a pampered pet rather than allowing him to be a hunter, a creature who provided for his own needs? What happened was that four or five years after moving to the Central Park Zoo Gus started to behave oddly: He would swim back and forth in his pool for hours on end or lie passively on a rock. He lost weight. He was invariably lethargic. Physiological tests revealed nothing amiss, so a behavioral psychologist was called in to assess Gus. The diagnosis? Gus was suffering from a dearth of challenges or, more fundamentally, not living a lifestyle that forced him to work for what he got. After an "enrichment" program was designed for Gus—he was forced to "hunt" for food within his encampment—his symptoms abated. Bottom line: If you fail to engage in work constructively as Adam was told to do by the Lord ("work and keep it"), you are doomed to suffer in a manner equivalent to what a person endures in the inner circle of Dante's Inferno.

Tales like this remind me of Fyodor Dostoevsky, the Russian author who wrote about the lives of convicts in a Siberian prison camp. That work, *The House of the Dead* (1861), was authoritative because Dostoevsky himself spent four years in one of Siberia's *katorga* labor camps and was traumatized by his experiences there. *The House of the Dead* incorporates several of the horrifying experiences he witnessed while a prisoner, among them how guards would brutally perform unspeakable acts of cruelty against the prisoners. Dostoyevsky's imprisonment was so traumatic he began experiencing epileptic seizures while there, and he suffered from them for the rest of his life.

Yet among the atrocities he documented in his semiautobiographical *House of the Dead*, one of the worst, according to Dostoyevsky, involved the nature of the work prisoners performed:

> To crush, to annihilate a man utterly, to inflict on him the most terrible punishment so that the most ferocious murderer would shudder at it beforehand, one need only give him work of an absolutely, completely useless and irrational character.

Given the accumulated wisdom pertaining to the consequences of sloth it seems that if your job is feeding you a diet devoid of nutrients for your self-esteem, the result can be as detrimental to your health as a diet consisting solely of artificial ingredients.

Must All That We Love Eventually Lose Its Power to Reward Us?

If honeymooners were, for some strange reason, reading this book while lying barely inches away from their soul mate, their wedding bands still glittering as brightly as can be, they would surely say to themselves at this juncture, "I can understand that Confucius may have overstated the case. I can see falling out of love for a job since the boss who pays me calls the tune I dance to. But my love for my spouse will last forever. She/he elates me every moment we are together."

If this is something you would say about your spouse, I have a warning for you: Check the fine print in your prenuptial agreement. It's more likely than not that although you and your betrothed will last together for a while, statistics predict that you will eventually fall victim to the phenomenon known as the seven-year itch.

The seven-year itch is a development in the life of a marriage wherein a couple once in the throes of passionate love becomes likely to divorce. Famed anthropologists Margaret Mead, Gregory Bateson, and Ruth Benedict are generally credited with being the first scholars to make this observation regarding the fragility of monogamous marriages. What is less well known is that they also claimed the seven-year itch applied to careers. Granted, "the couple that tills the field together, stays together," but for how long? Couples and careerists cannot help but seek greener pastures, since "variety is the spice of life." This is why monogamy breeds a sense of monotony, both on the job and in marriage. Without the highs experienced on honeymoons, people feel ennui rather than a sense of psychological engagement toward "the same old, same old."

Data collected by the US Census Bureau establishes that marriages are vulnerable to dissolution during years two through seven, although these same statistics show that the seventh year is empirically demonstrated to be when most married couples untie the knot. You may be asking yourself if there is something special about becoming disengaged (vis-à-vis something you loved) after going at it for seven years. I don't know the answer to that. I do know that during Major League Baseball games there has been a long-standing informal ritual, formalized in the wake of the 9/11 tragedy, that involves fans, fatigued as a result of not moving around for six and a half innings, standing up from their seats and stretching prior to the start of the seventh inning. And since we are looking at "growing fatigued and disengaged after seven," has it occurred to you that the Lord proclaimed the seventh day the Sabbath day? "And on the seventh day God ended his work which he had made; and he rested on the seventh day" (Genesis 2:2, KJV).

I am not a numerologist so I won't even consider

examining seven beyond these coincidences. What I will do, instead, is present you with a number of theories that have been advanced to account for why seven years is typically the longest period of time marriages last without falling victim to some form of fatigue, ennui, or worse. I do this to reveal the factors that impact all careerists who have held one job for seven years (more or less) and feel overwhelmed with ennui.

I previously noted that a job should come with a sell-by date stamped on it; the factors that account for the seven-year itch tell us why this should be the case. A person new to the job market may love the job a person who has toiled at it for seven years looks at askance, just as someone who leaves a spouse for a paramour should not be surprised to find their dumped lover in the arms of another. The issue isn't the partner in the marriage or the nature of a job that causes seven-year itches. What is at issue are *the rewarding aspects of the marriage or job, and/or how the jobholder or "itchy" spouse developed a changed perspective toward what was once an exhilarating entity or experience.*

What Accounts for the Seven-Year Itch? (It's All in Your Head.)

Clinical psychologists have proposed a number of explanations for why couples fall victim to the seven-year itch. A simple one is that differences overlooked in the initial, wildly erotic phases of a marriage become salient when once-exhilarating lovemaking becomes ho-hum. This theory spawned the so-called penny in the jar law, which asserts that if a husband and wife place a penny in a jar each time they make love during year one of a marriage, they can extract a penny each time they make love from year two until forever after and still have enough left in the jar to buy two (Un)Happy Meals at McDonald's.

Although the penny in the jar law doesn't include a causal analysis of why couples amass all of those unused pennies, it suggests that the sexual thrills derived from being unfaithful to one's spouse with a new, exciting, unpredictable lover might be a significant cause.

Given the near universality of bouts of the seven-year itch it is not surprising that a play by George Axelrod titled *The Seven Year Itch* was written and later made into a movie starring Marilyn Monroe. Both works explored the inclination to become unfaithful to one's spouse after seven years of marriage. Specifically, a husband and father gets his head turned by a beautiful woman who threatens to drag the smitten sap away from his loving family.

The problem that arose regarding the concept of the seven-year itch after it was made into a popular movie is that the broad strokes used to make its theme entertaining created a number of inaccurate generalizations. First, and most important, it must be said that *both* men and women are vulnerable to, and act upon, seven-year itches. Since the movie about this phenomenon came out in 1955, the itch was presumed to be an exclusively male problem. Today we know better.

You see, all humans become unfaithful to anything they

have made a commitment to—a job they love, a once favorite restaurant, a to-die-for car—soon after the honeymoon
(phase of intense euphoria with the object) is over. People suffer ennui with something they were passionately wedded to
not because they are lured away by something better; a better
alternative is not responsible for a person becoming dissatisfied with something he once loved. Instead, the seven-year
itch is felt when *the rewards afforded by a relationship don't feel
"as good" as they did at the start.*

A deeper understanding of the seven-year itch involves
understanding the pain of predictability and boredom. If the
stimulation derived from interacting with any spouse (job,
restaurant, car) becomes *too* predictable, *too* repetitive, *too*
"been there, done that," the net effect of this absence of stimulation is sickening. I've often heard married couples say, with
pride, "Oh, we finish each other's sentences." When I hear
that I hear a warning siren. If someone you are connected
to is so scripted that after raising a subject you know exactly
what he will say, you need to tell him that it's time to update
his playlist.

The most cogent explanation for why feelings of ennui,
or worse, occur from predictability was advanced by social
psychologist Elliot Aronson.[10] Given that social psychology
is the branch of psychological sciences focused on how relationships in the real world impact an individual's life, it is
no wonder that Aronson attributed the process that accounts
for couples failing to reward each other to characteristics of

rewarding agents, not the rewards they dispense (for example, sexual favors), per se.

Aronson contended that the impact of a reward—any reward, be it a compliment, praise, pat on the back, or even a glowing performance review at work—*depends more on who says it than what precisely is said.* He calls this theory the gain-loss theory of attraction. Here's how it works.

You are a man who is head over heels in love with your wife. Prior to leaving home for a party she asks, "Do you like this outfit, honey?" As always—*literally always,* for as long as you can remember—you reply, "You're the most beautiful woman alive, Angel." After years of the same apparently scripted bon mot, your spouse hardly hears you, let alone gets goose bumps from your compliments. At the nadir of a relationship a woman who has a doting husband may actually grimace in anticipation of her spouse's routinized praise: "Here it comes again...'You're the most beautiful...'" This is the loss element of Aronson's equation.

Here is the gain: The following evening two business dinners are being held and the couple described above—C-level executives with different companies—each go to the one held by their company without their partner in tow. He has an okay time doing what's expected of him with other executives, but she gets bowled over by a compliment she receives. The EVP this woman reports to—a guy who is notoriously critical—greets her as she enters the party and says, "Jennifer, you look *marvelous* tonight."

According to Aronson, the unexpected, out-of-role praise of the sort Jennifer receives as she enters her business dinner is the stuff that ends marriages. The praise from Jennifer's EVP was six sigma more impactful (the gain) than the praise she received (for years) from her husband because it was novel, out of role (i.e., spontaneous and unscripted), and indicative of the fact that Jennifer "won over" her boss, a man who has a history of being negative in terms of the feedback he gives to others (more of the gain). When a habitual critic tells you, "You look marvelous tonight," the knowledge that you took a "tiger" and rendered him toothless is as powerful as an adrenaline rush.

This last point is key to Aronson's theory: Humans are more favorably impacted by praise if it comes from someone who was once negatively disposed toward us than if it comes from someone who has loved us from day one. If a father tells his son, "Jack, you're the greatest," Jack assumes, "Sure. You cut my umbilical cord, loved me since then, of course you think I'm the greatest." If, on the other hand, Jack joins a baseball team and a coach he's never met says, "Jack, you've got a swing like Ted Williams," Jack will float out of his cleats and have a hard time touching the ground.

In sum, when praise appears routinized it loses its potency. The recipient feels, "He says that because he's my (husband, father, etc.)." Only praise that is unexpected and independent of rule-governed behavior can lead a person to conclude, "I must have really wowed him/her."

It's Also a Product of Our Brain Chemistry

Although the notion of a seven-year itch is now an accepted explanation for why people lose feelings of connectedness with things they once loved, my claim that Confucius's comments were inaccurate and misleading would gain an added dose of support if I were able to demonstrate that the rewards from a job lose potency owing to biochemical factors that are hardwired into our brains. I can.

Psychologist Dorothy Tennov's work on romantic attraction demonstrates that even on a molecular level there is ample proof of the seven-year itch.[11] More than a decade ago Tennov altered the study of romantic relationships by coining the term *limerance*, referring to a state of mind resulting from a romantic attraction to another person. In most instances, a person experiencing limerance has compulsive thoughts and fantasies about a love object, coupled with an intense desire to form or maintain a relationship with the love object. Limerance is a hormonally induced period of excitation that produces feelings of exuberance but also exhaustion owing to how our obsession with our love object prevents us from doing anything but contemplating him or her.

Tennov's theory of limerance is derived from biochemical analyses of people who claimed to be in love. What she found was that a love-related chemical named phenylethylamine (PEA), a naturally occurring trace amine in the brain, causes amphetamine-like stimulation in the brain when, at the start of romantic relationships, it is secreted in excessive amounts. Tennov found that abnormally high PEA secretions in newly bonded couples explain why, "in the throes of love," we experience the "on cloud nine" heart-pounding, obsessed feeling that new love typically brings. High-intensity activities like skydiving have also been found to heighten levels of PEA found in the brain.

Unfortunately, as uplifting as the effects of PEA are at the outset of relationships they diminish over time. Scientists believe that after roughly two to four years a person's body develops a tolerance for PEA, and all psychoactive chemicals, for that matter: You need more of a high-inducing substance to obtain the psychological effect you did from prior, lower, dosages. Unless a person were to receive steadily increasing doses of PEA year after year in a relationship, he or she would be expected to find that feelings of romantic attraction have waned from their initial peaks.

Worse yet, some research indicates that after you become tolerant of PEA's stimulating effects your brain produces more endorphins (naturally occurring opiates) than usual. Why this is so has yet to be proved, but whether it is a natural calming reaction by the body to extended periods of amphetamine-like highs or a means of sedating the mind as it goes through PEA withdrawal, the ultimate outcome is the same: The person notices a dramatic shift from heart-pounding highs to tranquilizing, painkilling lows attributed to their lover.

The fact that the honeymoon period of a relationship is literally fueled by different brain chemistry than that which is present during later years (recall the penny in a jar theory) can explain why most couples uncouple. They long for the hyperstimulating highs of new love born of endorphins, and they feel negatively about the soporific effects that occur when increased levels of endorphins enter the brain. There is grave danger to relationships owing to these effects because people are unaware of the chemical reactions that occur in the brain. When they start feeling ennui they do not say, "Hmm. My PEA levels are down. I think I'll grab the dirt bike, take on the steepest mountain I can find, and jack up my stimulant level." What they say is, "Justin is just not doing it for me anymore. He's become a bore. Now what do I do?"

The answer to that question is to admit that monogamy— in marriage or on the job—is a fragile orientation unless one is driven by higher goals (for example, family or spiritual priorities). Otherwise, when chemical highs experienced at the outset of a relationship dissipate—and can, on occasion, be replaced by sedative-like chemical reactions—the search for and pursuit of stimulating experiences, challenges, and highs is a natural and appropriate reaction.

Boredom: Responsible for More Deaths than Cancer

> My mind rebels at stagnation. Give me problems, give
>   me work,
> give me the most abstruse cryptogram, or the most
>   intricate analysis,

and I am in my own proper atmosphere. I can dispense then with
artificial stimulants. But I abhor the dull routine of
existence.

—Sherlock Holmes, *The Sign of Four*

When a guy like Sherlock Holmes claims that if you give him complex problems to solve, "I can dispense then with artificial stimulants," that is truly saying something. This supersleuth was far more committed to drugs than the typical recreational user; he was a certifiable junkie! Books have been written and movies have been made about his recipe for injection-quality cocaine—*The Seven-Per-Cent Solution*—and in addition to that habit, Holmes regularly used morphine. When he had to be in public he got juiced up by inhaling any one of a number of smokes, from a pipe to various forms of cigarettes. So, I ask you: Do you think that job-derived highs could get Holmes to shelve his drug habits?

It actually can. Modern theories of addiction demonstrate that there are profound similarities between physical addiction to various chemicals such as alcohol, cocaine, and heroin and psychological addiction to activities such as gambling, sexual activity, and working on challenging tasks. The common denominator in both forms of rewarding behavior is that they produce increased levels of dopamine in the brain, which make a person feel high.

Over time, a psychological addiction can, and often does, overpower the individual just as much as does addiction to alcohol or cocaine. In fact, studies show that being rewarded for working on challenging tasks and using cocaine stimulate the same sections in the human brain. You can say that Holmes's craving for complex problems to solve is virtually identical to a junkie's craving for a fix. Moreover, when Holmes indulged in attempting to solve the most abstruse cryptogram, or set about producing the most intricate analysis, he was manipulating his own brain chemistry by engaging in these activities.

If you're not familiar with dopamine, here's all you need to know: In the brain, dopamine's function is to serve as a neurotransmitter—a chemical released by nerve cells that facilitates their sending signals to other nerve cells. Inside the brain there are countless distinct dopamine pathways or channels for transmitting messages, and one of them is devoted to recognizing and responding to reward-motivated behavior.

Most rewards—like Holmes's puzzle solving—increase the level of dopamine in the brain. As it turns out, cocaine use and falling in love increase dopamine neuronal activity in precisely the same way. Actually, if you measured the dopamine coursing through the pathways that signal rewarding behavior, snorting cocaine, cavorting with a new love, and working on a complex, challenging task, you could not distinguish one of these activities from the other in terms of neurotransmitter activity.

The problematic aspect of the dopamine rush a person can obtain from working on and solving complex problems is that it is only exceeded by the anguish of the crash that comes when either the work ceases to be challenging or is no longer available. Consider, for example, Sherlock Holmes doing a whodunit analysis and beginning to zero in on the offender. As he eliminates uninformative clues, red herrings, and blind alleys, his dopamine levels surge, his brain records pleasure, and Holmes is motivated to continue his analysis, regardless of how much he has slept, eaten, or drunk.

However, once Holmes shouts "Eureka!" upon identifying the malefactor he's been searching for, he literally goes through dopamine withdrawal. This is why mastery of all forms of challenging behavior—particularly for someone who falls in love with a challenging job and believes she will never again work a day in her life—is a double-edged sword. Initially, on the job, mastery gets you ever-increasing levels of rewards. However, when the mastery is complete and no on-the-job challenges remain, a crash sets in.

On his ninetieth birthday, the late Supreme Court Justice Oliver Wendell Holmes Jr. gave a radio address in which he shared his thoughts about avoiding the malaise born when a challenging task ends:

> The riders in a race do not stop short when they reach the goal. There is a little finishing canter before coming to a standstill. There is time to hear the kind voice of friends and to say to one's self: "The work is done." But just as one says that, the answer comes: "The race is over, but the work remains." The canter that brings you to a standstill need not be only coming to rest. It

cannot be while you still live. For to live is to function. That is all there is in living.[12]

It is important to note, parenthetically, that evolutionary psychologists claim that the crash following mastery and the ennui born of boredom are adaptive in that they keep us from failing to be vigilant to potential danger in the environment. According to some, if boredom weren't a noxious feeling, primitive man might not have discovered fire. This is the basis for my advice, Stay Hungry: Unless you are, you cannot encounter the means by which passions will flourish.

But the ultimate value of the aversive feelings born of mastery and boredom is that they have a direct, salutary effect on our brain function. Research shows that our brains actually *need* ongoing stimulation to work as they should, particularly the sort that is deemed *novelty*. Holmes was on to something when he said how much he valued mental exaltation, since it is what allows our brains to maintain plasticity and flexibility. In addition, it initiates neurogenesis, the birth of new brain cells. Without the search for novelty our brains will atrophy, ending any and all growth and development.

Since a job has the power to profoundly affect our lives, I want to close this chapter by examining the consequences of mastery at work. I can still recall how elated I felt when I got my first paycheck. I held it, stared at it, and showed it to my father as though it could, on its own, do something. I don't remember subsequent paychecks from that job, but I do remember that when I was preparing to return to school from summer break I looked forward to not working for money and to learning for a change.

When you start any job it presents you with a number of intriguing options to explore: learning new skills, getting up to speed with technology you haven't seen, novel social interactions, etc.—tasks that are truly stimulating. Moreover, during the initial phases of a job you are rewarded for mastering novel challenges. All the while you have megadoses of dopamine coursing through the neuronal network of your brain. During your probationary period on a new job it is not an exaggeration to say that you can easily enjoy a job-induced high.

The problem, as noted, is that the novelty of your new job soon wears off and you suffer what some call a *Loss of Novelty Effect*. As noted above, you develop a tolerance to the rewarding aspects of your job, and your satisfaction with the job drops as you are unable to infuse your brain with the dopamine you were flying high on when your job was new and intriguing.

I want to underscore one finding from research studies that have explored the long-term consequences of a Loss of Novelty Effect: People continually grow more irritable and, ultimately, become angry. If people do not extricate themselves from circumstances that spawn a Loss of Novelty Effect, they will transition from being angry to suffering despondency, fall into a protracted state of ennui, and ultimately suffer what most people call psychological burnout, a condition that this book is specifically designed to help you defeat. Some highly successful people suffering a Loss of Novelty Effect in the extreme—most notably white-collar criminals, who never break the law in response to a need for material gain—engage in thrill-seeking or daredevil behaviors because even white-collar jobs with eight-figure compensation packages can bore the daylights out of them.[13]

There is no getting around it: If you find a job you love, you *will* work again in your life. You'll work to secure rewards that function as they should (but ultimately will fail to do so), to avoid ennui, to attain mastery, and most fundamentally of all, to maintain dopamine levels in your brain that make you feel good, if not high.

In the pages that follow, I detail how you can address these facts of life, how you can inoculate yourself against falling victim to the self-esteem-starving aspects of all jobs, and how by letting your sense of purpose in life lead to the establishment of your goals you can design career pursuits that will afford you the rewards you need (from interpersonal connections) and that enable you to lead a flourishing life. In other words, to learn how you can stay hungry and enjoy what your hunger brings.

CHAPTER 2

Is There a Useful Definition of *Burnout*?

The beginning of wisdom is the definition of terms.

—Socrates

If you have ever watched an episode of the *Law & Order* TV series, odds are you've seen a defendant, on trial for one heinous crime or another, reject a legal aid attorney and opt, instead, to represent himself in court. Once that decision is made a cast member on the show will invariably tell the defendant, "You know, 'he who represents himself has a fool for a client,'" an observation made famous by Abraham Lincoln, who was a practicing attorney before he became president. Sound advice, since navigating legal waters is incredibly complex.

What few people are aware of is that Sir William Osler, a Canadian physician who helped found Johns Hopkins Hospital and revolutionized the training of medical residents, held a similar view of self-care. Dr. Osler believed that a physician who treats himself has a fool for a patient.

In this chapter I make an educated and amply supported argument against succumbing to the tendency to self-diagnose what has you miserable at work, clock-watching to escape work, and fantasizing about working somewhere over the rainbow as psychological burnout. I will then appeal to your good judgment to let me guide you out of the seemingly inextricable entanglement you are in, rather than trying to escape from it on your own.

Your reaction to the preceding appeal may be, "Why else would I have purchased this book? The title promises to tell me how to *kick burnout in the butt*!" That's a valid reaction, but only up to a point.

Here's my concern in a nutshell: If you've done some reading on what you believe is responsible for your work-induced malaise, you cannot help but assume, "This guy's talking about 'burnout' and how to prevent it. I know what burnout is.... It's what I don't want to suffer." Here's the big problem with that supposition: This book has little if anything to do with burnout as virtually every self-help book and well-meaning work-related website defines it. If and only if you understand burnout as I do as a psychotherapist will you benefit from my years of studying burnout, treating it, and preventing it. That may sound arrogant but it's really not. Let me show you that I know what I'm talking about.

First, however, let me address why the exact manner in which burnout gets defined is not only relevant to you, it's a determining factor in whether you'll be able to kick it in the butt. If you have preconceived notions about why your career is starving your self-esteem or, worse yet, if you've concluded that you are suffering from a well-documented syndrome (burnout), these beliefs may pose impediments to your ability to change as you want to.

I'm dedicated to doing all I can to eliminate impediments to your ability to change. In furtherance of that goal, with special attention to the diagnosis of burnout, this chapter will address two issues: (1) how any and all self-diagnoses are fraught with danger, and (2) how the self-diagnosis "I'm suffering from psychological burnout," in particular, compounds whatever damage your self-esteem may have suffered to date.

Self-Diagnosis

In psychiatry, a misdiagnosis can lead to a ruined life. In other words, if a psychiatrist is off in her assessment of what plagues a patient, nothing will improve, and that patient's circumstances may, in fact, deteriorate.

Self-diagnosis is more dangerous. If a professional misdiagnoses you, she can catch her error, self-correct, and get back on the right track. If you misdiagnose yourself, however, self-correction is highly unlikely. What is there (since you are not a trained professional) to alert you to the fact that you're heading down the wrong track? In addition, self-diagnosis of anything remotely resembling a psychological problem is fraught with danger because the popular press and talk TV love stories about psychological problems. Worst of all, the overwhelming majority of what you learn from the popular press and talk TV about psychological problems is wrong, very wrong, or dangerously wrong.

Even people who wouldn't watch Dr. Phil if coerced to do so by a dognapper holding their beloved Fluffy hostage may form self-diagnoses from friends' experiences or self-help books. Yes, this book would be considered to be within that category, but I footnote most of my claims, have taught psychology and psychiatry, published scores of research papers, and received grants and awards for my psychological research. Is that a guarantee of accuracy? No. Does it make accuracy more likely? Yes.

But I'm not attacking anyone else's work here. What I'm doing, in black-and-white terms, is asking you to suspend judgment regarding what ails you so you can receive what I'm presenting with an open mind. When I've concluded my presentation, you can compare and contrast it with whatever you want. Just please understand that there is so much conflicting and contradictory information about burnout floating around out there, you cannot help but be confused. That is, unless you say to yourself, "Okay—let me erase the blackboard, get a clean sheet of paper, open a new document..."— whatever metaphor you like, and give me a chance.

There is another reason why I am concerned about your use of diagnosis, one that is particularly prevalent among intelligent, highly motivated people who do not keep a tight rein on self-guided deliberations regarding their problems.

This problem, one that can reach epidemic proportions in medical schools and teaching hospitals, is called medical students' disease, or more technically, *medicalstudentitis*. It is a well-documented fact that second-year medical students, as well as interns, often come to perceive themselves to be suffering the symptoms of the diseases they are studying. Why this occurs is the subject of much debate, but that it occurs is accepted as hard, cold truth.

This condition is marked by a medical student's preoccupation with the symptoms of the disorder she is studying in conjunction with an acute sensitivity to experiencing signs and symptoms of a disorder she is not suffering. Actually, this disorder is incredibly widespread among psychiatric interns and residents given the ease with which a psychological symptom (e.g., anxiety) can be inferred from myriad normal sensations—e.g., a hypersensitivity born of the eagerness to perform well.

Thus, I hope you see my concern: The more you come to know about an ill-defined syndrome—*burnout*—from poorly vetted sources, the more likely it is that you will come to the conclusion that you are suffering something I am not discussing. Not only that, but you may come to believe that the protocol I detail in chapter 8 of this book is irrelevant to, and cannot help ameliorate, your concerns and do what it promises to do: inoculate you against burnout.

Here's another very relevant point for you to consider: I am quite familiar with burnout, having written a book on treating the syndrome more than fifteen years ago.[1] Since

38

publishing that book I have studied the burnout literature exhaustively and treated scores of people who suffered self-esteem damage, emotional problems, and other difficulties born of what their careers did to them. As a result, I have concluded that no term in the psychiatric literature suffers from definitional inexactness and ambiguity more than "burnout."

Toward a Useful Understanding of Burnout

Burnout has become a catchall for any work-related problem that leaves people yearning to be employed anywhere other than where they are. Actually, were burnout to be defined simply as "the syndrome responsible for a worker seeking to be employed anywhere other than where he or she is," this would be a major improvement over what you find when you study burnout literature.

Dr. Harry Levinson, a pioneer in the application of psychoanalytic theory to management and leadership and a recipient of the American Psychological Foundation's Gold Medal for Life Achievement in the Application of Psychology, was, arguably, the man who created the field of organizational consulting. Among the myriad firsts Levinson achieved was being one of the first psychologists to offer a definition of burnout. As he put it, "The major defining characteristic of burnout is that people can't or won't do again what they have been doing."[2] Would that all those who have studied burnout had been satisfied with Levinson's definition and stopped there!

But let's say you wanted to embellish Levinson's incredibly

useful, succinct, and precise definition of burnout (the "get me outta here" syndrome) by describing two subtypes, since you notice that some people are suffering it worse more intensively than others. You could identify one subtype as an acute form marked by the fact that a person experiences a compulsion to flee work only on certain days ("clock-watching burnout"). The other subtype could address those with burnout that is chronic and more severe: a yearning to "get me outta here" that plagues a person whenever he is working. You could dub this the "disengagement craving" syndrome, a subtype of burnout.

Refining Levinson's definition of burnout with these subtypes wouldn't take away from understanding the essence of this syndrome—an aversion to work and, implicitly (from the article this definition is taken from), emotional exhaustion with probable self-critical or self-disparaging tendencies. But what does diminish the utility of what Levinson said is how the syndrome has functioned like a massive electromagnet, indiscriminately picking up any and all workplace-generated maladies it comes across.

To name but a few, the burnout syndrome is said to include among its symptoms intense negative feelings toward work and, consequently, oneself, along with exhaustion, apathy, cynicism, despair, helplessness, ennui, anxiety, loss of appetite, and a heightened vulnerability to a limitless range of physical disorders, ranging from respiratory problems to coronary heart disease.

Historically, burnout has been informally dubbed a

"romantic disorder" owing to the fact that it is thought to afflict those whose work ethic is admired in our culture. You gotta love the guy who gives his all and then some for the good of the company, right? A related moniker for burnout is "compassion fatigue," a concept derived from the observation that people whose careers demand that they care more for others than for themselves are uniquely vulnerable to suffering burnout. From this perspective, a person suffers burnout if she has her good/altruistic intentions thwarted when trying to reach unrealistically lofty goals. When this occurs, unmet expectations prompt people to work too hard, assume excessive burdens, and suffer cynicism, depleted energy, and, ultimately, exhaustion.

Support for the compassion fatigue moniker comes from studies that assessed the moods of doctors and nurses. These people who sacrifice themselves for others were shown to be among those most likely to suffer burnout. Others, like police officers and firefighters who exhibit a tireless and selfless devotion to working for the benefit of others—too often without commensurate appreciation—are also deemed likely to fall victim to burnout. As Christina Maslach, a pioneering researcher on the subject, maintains,[3] burnout "refers to a syndrome of emotional exhaustion and cynicism that frequently occurs among people who do 'people work.'"

Finally, one symptom of the burnout syndrome that is almost universally recognized is absence from work not caused by physical illness. This makes sense: Folks not wanting to be working where they are employed evince so-called withdrawal behaviors. According to one thorough research study, chief among the symptoms displayed by people diagnosed as suffering burnout were chronic lateness and chronic absenteeism.[4]

But believe it or not, burnout is such an ill-defined term that other groups of researchers claim that a telltale sign of suffering burnout is *overexertion and overworking on the job*; a syndrome called *presenteeism* in one review.[5] As formally defined, presenteeism is a syndrome where a person who is physically sick and should remain home goes to work because he is suffering burnout and believes he must try extra hard to prevail.

From my perspective, to claim that presenteeisim is a disorder is an insult to and misdiagnosis of those whose careers are in Silicon Valley or any of the AmLaw 100 law firms. In these places, a 100-hour workweek is a boon to employers and not necessarily a bust to workers. To push this point, how do you diagnose an entrepreneur who works at his startup weeks on end, surviving on coffee and donuts alone, eschewing showers, and talking of nothing but "the company"? That's not sickness in any medical textbook I know of, which gives further support to my concern that excessively broad definitions of burnout employing a hodgepodge of carelessly combined symptoms will lead to misdiagnosis.

My Perspective

To explain why I define burnout as I do I want to take you through the sequence of events that led to my ultimate understanding of this syndrome. Actually, it's quite simple: I concluded that of all the scholars who studied burnout, no one understood it better than Harry Levinson did.

The man who coined the term *burn-out*—today the word is not hyphenated—introduced this disorder to the world with a gripping metaphor. According to psychoanalyst Herbert J. Freudenberger, burnout leaves its victims feeling this way:

> If you have ever seen a building that has been burned out, you know it's a devastating sight. What had once been a throbbing, vital structure is now deserted. Where there had once been activity, there are now only crumbling reminders of energy and life. Some bricks or concrete may be left; some outline of windows. Indeed, the outer shell may seem almost intact. Only if you venture inside will you be struck by the full force of the desolation.[6]

There is no question that Freudenberger came up with a truly impactful metaphor for psychological burnout, but in my opinion it fails to convey what burnout *feels like* by those who suffer it. Worse yet, I believe that the metaphor cannot help you understand if you are a victim of burnout, job-induced stress, or malaise that has nothing to do with your job but, for various reasons, is being felt in that context.

Although someone who experiences job-related burnout can be said to feel like a shell of his former self, a wreck who was once energized but no longer is, or is in a state of ruins, these descriptors are insufficient to capture the experience of the disorder. A person suffering burnout experiences these two feelings: (1) I hate this job, and (2) hating this job has begun to affect how I feel about myself: specifically, more negatively than I did when I started working this job.

In my role as their psychotherapist or coach, I have worked with scores of people who have suffered a depletion of self-esteem and a "get me outta here" yearning, and I can assure you that their reports are not nearly as sterile as Freudenberger's structural metaphor. They hurt, emotionally, and are angry—the "take this job and shove it" component of burnout. Freudenberger's empty-shell metaphor is valid, albeit insufficient to identify the pain that a job you hate but must work at for money to pay bills and that you began believing it promised to be a rewarding venture (remember, you followed Confucius's advice to take this job in the first place), yet delivers absolutely no self-esteem-enhancing experiences. Those psychological insults to your ego create feelings that are 180 degrees away from self-esteem enhancing.

When he coined the term *burn-out* Freudenberger must have been thinking that a person suffering it was once on fire, ablaze with passion, or had a burning desire to achieve, but for some reason(s) the flame within him was snuffed out. So far, so good—that's just what I saw in my own patients. The problem is that Freudenberger's burned building metaphor is just crumbling, more or less passively, owing to the damage done to it.

That's not what people I worked with looked like. Having sung or shouted "Take this job and shove it" as an actual farewell address or in their fantasies about fulfilling "get me outta here" yearnings, the people in my care who claimed to be suffering burnout had an active "I'm putting a stop to this garbage" attitude that was too intense to ignore.

Even when self-esteem-starved people told me of their contempt for their unchallenging and ennui-inducing work—a circumstance that you might expect to trigger lethargy—the discussions of their fantasies about how they would leave their job or what they would do if they did not were angry and aggressive. I didn't hear "Oh, Lord, I cannot drag myself out of bed anymore" but, rather, comments on the order of avenging what was done to them. Given many of the vivid fantasies of revenge I heard back then, I would not have been shocked if a client told me, "I feel like Sisyphus pushing a rock up a hill and watching it roll down. Since the guys who sold me on this job were really duplicitous, I'm turning the tables on them. The next time my rock rolls down that hill I'm going to deflect it off its path so it rolls over their cubicles and crushes them beyond recognition!"

Let me stop here for a moment and return to the issue of reading about a panoply of burnout-related symptoms that are not focused on in this book. In many discussions of burnout that ultimately aim to define it, the term *emotionally overwrought* is used extensively. This suggests that a person suffering burnout is weak owing to the experience of rewards not functioning as expected or from having their self-actualization needs beaten down.

Just the opposite is the norm. As noted above, the burn-out sufferers I've worked with were anything but "too weak to move." They would have leapt at the chance to strike out at the person(s) responsible for the Sisyphean hell they were in, but no such person could be found. Not that this would be advisable or something I would sanction, but the will was there: The clients I treated were not exhausted but, rather, mad as hell.

Now, in all fairness, and to be 100 percent candid, I did meet many patients whose presenting symptoms included emotional exhaustion and its sister symptom, depression. But when they came in for psychotherapy they didn't say, "I'm suffering from burnout," and I had no way of knowing that long before they experienced emotional exhaustion they were having their self-esteem battered like a punching bag at a boxing gym and for a long while were feeling like they would give anything for the chance to tear into the SOB responsi-ble for their malaise. For a number of reasons, however, they wouldn't or couldn't—actually, they were unable to express anger constructively—which is why, as a result of swallow-ing, bottling up, and generally squelching their anger, they ended up in my office depleted and emotionally exhausted.

When the myriad self-esteem-depleting experiences that have been called burnout lead to anger, and if this anger is not dealt with in a constructive manner, then and only then will job-induced malaise yield emotional exhaustion. The real problem—the one responsible for why most definitions of burnout erroneously focus on emotional exhaustion—is *anger*. And since this is the root cause of all that evolves, over time, to hurt those suffering misdiagnosed burnout, what you will learn is that the best inoculation against suffering burnout is the one that directly targets the root cause.

And what is that inoculation? Preempt acting-out anger ("take this job and shove it"), preempt swallowing and squelching anger (leading to emotional exhaustion), and learn to channel anger into a healthy energy that will enable you to turn passion into purpose and career satisfaction.

Dr. Christina Maslach,[7] mentioned above, is arguably the most prolific researcher in the burnout field. Maslach describes burnout as a syndrome of emotional exhaustion, depersonalization, and reduced personal accomplishment. Specifically, in one of Maslach's many reports she claims that burnout is "a state of exhaustion in which one is cynical about the value of one's occupation and doubtful of one's capacity to perform."[8] In addition to these emotional symptoms, her research has shown that people diagnosed as suffering burnout report a range of psychological and physical health problems including anxiety, depression, sleep disturbances, memory impairment, and neck pain.

I found what Maslach describes to be intriguing but, like Freudenberger's descriptions, far more inactive than the emotionally troubled, always angry (as opposed to exhausted) people I worked with. Where Maslach saw those who suffered burnout as being "exhausted and cynical about the value of one's occupation and doubtful of one's capacity to perform," I saw contempt and fury born of the feeling "Those jackasses are denying me a chance to be all that I can be." The people I worked with who reported that their careers "starved their self-esteem" didn't doubt their capacity to perform. They doubted themselves because, as they told me, "I've put up with so much crap because I need to earn a living. I hate myself for being a wage slave. I want to thrive."

Burnout Is Not Stress (The Yin and Yang of Stress)

Before proceeding further toward telling you all you need to know about burnout, it is important that I provide you with my personal view of stress and how stress and burnout relate to each other. Here's the problem: If you are a devotee of reports in the popular press that discuss problems derived from your job, the terms *stress* and *burnout* are used interchangeably and indiscriminately. Many of those reports also equate *stressed-out* with *burned-out*. Forgive me, but that is as grossly inappropriate as equating a broken bone with a broken heart. Both hurt, but the hurts are so different they don't overlap at all in terms of causes or consequences.

There's another reason I want to address stress and explain what it is and why it is not equal to, or a form of, burnout. You see, even the American Institute of Stress claims, in one of its web postings, "Most people consider the definition of 'stress' to be something that causes *distress*." Huh?

This is how bad things are when it comes to defining stress. It's not simply that making sense of stress is more difficult than disentangling a Gordian knot; it's the fact that stress is impossible to define owing to how the general population and (although I hate to point fingers) the popular press have mangled the term.

Here's what I mean: If you're feeling put-upon at work or feel you may crack under the pressure of performance demands, you may say, "Getting my report rejected was the straw that broke the camel's back." This view of stress as "cracking under the weight of accumulated burdens," originally co-opted from engineering science, is the most common way the term *stress* is used today. In this engineering usage, stress is understood to be identical to a force applied to a structure—for example, a bridge or a material such as concrete or bone that causes change (strain, cracking, or failure) in the integrity of the material. What this notion led to is the widely held erroneous belief that—as you should know—psychological stress is a force lurking outside us, like fire; something that would have a uniformly adverse effect upon anyone who came in contact with it.

Not true.

Stress does not lurk outside. In fact, psychological stress exists only in the eye of the beholder. The reason this critical component of stress research was ignored for so long is because old-school stress researchers didn't worry about *potential stressors* that did not reach threshold levels capable of tripping an instinctive reaction pattern called the general adaptation syndrome, or GAS. GAS occurs in the organ systems (adrenocortical and others) that control and regulate the release of adrenaline. When activated, GAS consists of four stages: (1) alarm, which signals the body to mobilize against threatened harm; (2) resistance, in which the body engages in adaptations to the stressors; (3) exhaustion, in which the body can no longer engage in fight-or-flight responses; and (4) recovery, the phase in which the body does what is needed to reestablish homeostasis.

The researchers were interested in how stress caused disease and cared only about those events that were perceived as threats, "got to us," disrupted our homeostatic balance, and potentially compromised our health. As a result—with no malice intended—the original theories of stress, while making note of the fact that there is a stress that is positive, downplayed that fact or, at times, just ignored it.

In response to this lack of definitional rigor, I created my own definition of stress. It completely overlooks the physical aspects of stress (save for the adrenaline-releasing action that helps create the experience of anger) and would never get accepted by textbook authors. No big deal. My definition is ideal for our purposes.

I define stress as *the yin and yang of emotional arousal.* Yin and yang themselves come from Chinese philosophy and religion (primarily Taoism), where they are always used concurrently to describe complimentary forces of nature that coexist and interact to maintain harmony in the universe. Yin and yang is a plural noun—neither component is used alone—since the meaning of one term usually derives from the negative of the other. According to tradition, yin stands for negative, dark, and feminine, while yang stands for positive, bright, and masculine. This distinction matters not one whit in my definition of stress, but I thought you might like to know it as long as I was piggybacking my definition of stress upon yin and yang.

The key component of my yin and yang definition of stress is that, like yin and yang, *stress is both positive and negative*. The positive component or the yang is called *eustress*, for good stress—the kind that people derive from confronting and overcoming challenges. The yin of stress is *distress*, which refers to acute physical or mental suffering or pain born of failing to attain a goal, solve a problem, or put an end to a negative experience.

What I like most about my yin and yang definition of stress is that, like the Chinese theory, although one force (yin) is negative and the other force (yang) is positive, *you must have both forces in your life to achieve optimal functioning*, just as you need yin feminine aspects and yang masculine aspects to survive.

Whenever I give lectures on stress I introduce the yin and yang concept to audiences by presenting a completely fictional account of a visit to Steve's Spa. This instructional story is designed to help audiences begin the process of deriving a number of new insights about stress, chief among them that you do not know if an event will generate distress or eustress until you experience it.

Here's my story.

Welcome to Steve's Spa. You're in for a truly special time. Since you've checked in already, let me take you to a special chamber where one of our associates will prepare you for our special treatment: the "You want freedom from noise, hassles, and the like? You can't handle freedom from noise, hassles, and the like" session.

Okay. Rachel will be your guide. What she'll do to prep you for this session is first wrap your body, head to toe, in cotton swaddling. She'll then place earplugs where appropriate and cover your eyes with a blindfold. Next, Rachel will place you on a flotation platform—she's quite strong and has, in the past, been able to lift men weighing more than 250 pounds—and once you're situated comfortably on the platform she'll lower you into a tank that, when sealed, clamshell-like, blocks out all light and sound that would otherwise impinge upon you. You are now ready to float for as long as you wish until all of the accumulated stress that you brought to Steve's Spa has been lifted away.

The fob that Rachel placed in your dominant hand before wrapping you in cotton swaddling, which is just like the call button used in hospitals to summon a nurse, is for signaling Rachel when you are ready to end the session.

I know you are not now at Steve's Spa, but please imagine that you are. Okay, good imagery on your part. Now concentrate on what's ahead of you. Great. Since Rachel is on her lunch break and you will have to wait to enter the flotation chamber, I would like you to please give me your best guess as to how long you will stay in the tank. This will let Rachel decide if she'll stream a TV show or read a magazine article or two. She hates getting interrupted midtask.

Unless you are familiar with the process and consequences of sensory deprivation—which is the experience that Steve's Spa creates—I'm certain you've *over*estimated how long you could tolerate, not enjoy, floating stimulus free in a sealed chamber. You see, what happens to everyone who is subjected to sensory deprivation is that at some point—in as little as fifteen seconds but no longer than fifteen minutes, give or take—the spa treatment described above creates a psychotomimetic (mimicking a psychosis) experience: Most people start suffering auditory and visual hallucinations immediately, long before Rachel can settle into her easy chair to read or watch TV. Next comes one or more wild thoughts that people struggle to fend off until they terminate the session. Bottom line: Nothing about zero stress induces euphoria.

More to the point, we need a modicum of eustress to live. Luckily, we are bombarded by eustress-generating stimuli that create baseline arousal in us in countless ways we are not aware of—background noise, tactile stimulation from coming in contact with everything from keyboards to our clothing, etc.—which is great. As you saw from what happens at my spa, those who don't get baseline arousals go mad.

If you doubt the value of arousal for calming you and relaxing you—"de-stressing" if you will—consider this: Most folks who live in urban areas go batty when they take a vacation on an island resort that has no nightlife (restaurants, bars, gambling, and so forth) and gives guests nothing but the natural habitat they are in during the nighttime hours. When my wife and I honeymooned, we went to a resort in the US Virgin Islands. We had a beachfront villa, and all night long we could hear the waves lapping at the shore. My wife was in heaven; I couldn't sleep. She came from a beach town adjacent to Los Angeles and lived steps from the Pacific Ocean. I came from Boston and lived steps from a major thoroughfare. She found the lack of excitatory stimuli in the Virgin Islands as calming as mother's milk. I, in contrast, was stimulus-deprived in our villa and distressed.[9]

I fear I still haven't given you a sufficient explanation of eustress for you to know it when you see it as it has been presented to you only in contrast with distress. So, in a nutshell, *eustress feels exciting; it's motivating, it focuses our attention, and above all else, when no longer engaging us, it leaves us with an enhanced sense of self-esteem.*

Having read this, please do not make the mistake of labeling events in your world as either eustress provoking or distress provoking, because any and every event can cause eustress (if we stretch our interpretive boundaries) and, likewise, any and every event can cause distress.

Let me summarize the preceding discussion:

Stress is any change in your emotional equilibrium. If you are golfing with friends, no money on the line, and you've known the members of your foursome since you were shorter than a putter (so there are no salient competitive pressures at play), you can still experience eustress or distress in an instant. Any stimulus that moves you from neutral can be considered a stressor. So, let's play golf and see how we feel:

- *Eustress* would be the reaction you have to any hole you play where you either shoot for an eagle or make a hole in one (you should be so lucky). You're startled, but with a host of euphoric feelings attached.
- *Distress* would be the reaction you have if, for example, you're putting and a kid who lives in one of the homes adjacent to the golf course sets off a firecracker. Here, too, you'd be more than startled; you'd probably four-putt and get the yips the remainder of the round. You'd also probably have intrusive thoughts about retribution targeted at the kid. Those negative feelings about a delinquent kid are sufficient to cause distress.

One last point to show you how your mind determines which sort of stress—eustress or distress—you feel. Imagine that you come to one of my book-signing parties wanting me to autograph your copy this book. The event is in a hotel conference room. As you enter the room you see me with my fist raised in the air. The only thing you can conclude with certainty at this moment is that a GAS response will be evoked within me because raising a fist shifts me out of "neutral." If you discover that I'm raising my fist and shouting "Yes!" because my book just made the *New York Times* bestseller list, I've enjoyed eustress. If you discover that I'm raising my fist and shouting "No!" because the hotel staff is stacking the books that a cookbook author, signing her books in an adjacent room, ordered for her evening's event, you know I'm experiencing distress.

Burnout Sufferers Are NOT All Impotent and Ineffectual

Among the seemingly endless number of definitions of burnout out there in the scientific and self-help literature, you occasionally see it said that one of the symptoms of this syndrome is anger. But when you do, it is found at the end of a symptom checklist headed by exhaustion, despair, and comparably drop-dead-on-the-sofa symptoms. The image one gets of a burnout sufferer from that literature is of a person crawling out of an office sobbing, "I can't take it anymore...."

But whenever I've talked to victims of burnout, I see that they exhibit a profound lack of vitality *on the job*, that is, they are visibly disengaged from the professional context they are in. Internally, however, within the regions of their minds where thoughts about the future reside, there exists a flurry of activity.

The people I've worked with, because they have suffered self-esteem starvation from their careers, are emotionally aroused with thoughts, fantasies, and obsessions *about redressing wrongs done to them.* Dr. Harry Levinson shares my view. More than thirty years ago, when studies of burnout were novelties, Levinson reported that people who were burned out (Levinson, like Freudenberger, used the two-word term) as a result of being thwarted from self-actualizing goal attainment *regularly reported feeling overt hostility toward those seen as standing in their way.*[10]

In addition to feeling anger toward others who are seen as causing their job-induced distress, Levinson claimed that people who were burned out were often crippled by feelings of self-reproach and self-condemnation owing to the belief that they failed to prevail as they believed they should have. My clinical experience confirms both observations, although I have seen more feelings of retaliatory hostility than instances of self-reproach.

Which brings me to my biggest problem with the literature on burnout: *Taken as a whole it fails to recognize or report how central anger is to the disorder.* The patients I have treated for burnout have told me, usually in profanity-laced tirades, that they are "angered," "enraged," "pissed off," or worse. This is why, from my vantage point and Levinson's, *anger is the core component of the syndrome known as burnout.* And for this reason, I define burnout as Levinson did.[11]

Please understand that this definition is provided to aid your understanding of a disorder that is entrenched in the mental health literature. Later in this book I will demonstrate how you can put an end to the influence of those forces that caused your self-esteem to get pounded without the need (or advisability) of your diagnosing yourself as suffering burnout. On the contrary, as noted above, that diagnosis is more likely to impede your achieving your goal of deriving passion from career pursuits than facilitating it.

Back to my definition. According to Levinson, a person suffering burnout experiences:

- A number of negative emotions ranging from despair and helplessness to rage
- A sense of having been victimized
- An inescapable sense of inadequacy
- A feeling that their work is pointless, as though they could no longer find purpose in what they were doing
- Above all, as Levinson defines the burnout syndrome, it is the result of people expending a great deal of effort at work, intense to the point of exhaustion, without visible results. Consequently, these people felt angry, helpless, trapped, and suffered a depletion of their self-esteem.

In addition to defining the syndrome, Levinson emphasized the negative activity I consistently see in my clients but find missing from many definitions of burnout:

Those who suffer burnout may inappropriately vent anger at subordinates and family, or withdraw even from those whose support they need the most. They may try to escape the source of pressure through illness, absenteeism, or drugs or alcohol.... They may display increasingly rigid attitudes or appear cold and detached.[12]

Among the few prescriptive comments Levinson made in his 1981 paper, he claimed, "Physical exercise is helpful [in the treatment of burnout] because it provides a healthy outlet for angry feelings and pent-up energy." I'm less confident than Dr. Levinson was that going to a gym will ameliorate the anger born of being blocked from self-actualization, but it cannot hurt. That said, in the chapters that follow I promise to give you a host of alternatives that should be more effective than working up a sweat.

Blocked from Self-Actualization and Mad as Hell

Some of you may think that Dr. Harry Levinson and I have a folie à deux relationship (a shared psychotic disorder where delusions are transferred from one person to another) born of our conviction that the primary symptoms of burnout are anger and retaliatory impulses. If you feel this way, you are not harboring an irrational concern given that ours is clearly the minority opinion. But before you condemn Dr. Levinson and me to lunatic fringe status, please consider this breakdown of the issue:

• The burnout literature deals with people whose professional goals, growth, and development are ignored, thwarted, or trod upon.

• Some so-called experts studying this cohort of careerists feel that they will suffer profound emotional fatigue and not go apoplectic.

• Given that view, I would have to wonder if those experts ever heard of the frustration-aggression hypothesis.

The so-called *frustration-aggression hypothesis* (more formally, the frustration-aggression-displacement theory) is a principle advanced by two psychologists, Dollard and Miller, more than seventy-five years ago.[13] Today, it is one of the few principles in psychology that has never been qualified or disproven. In a nutshell, it claims that if you are blocked in pursuit of goal attainment, you get angry and evince aggressive behavior(s). Simple. Sage.

If you live in Los Angeles as I do, driving on one of the infamous freeways Angelinos spend one-third of their lives on, you would have all the data you need to know that Dollard and Miller were geniuses. This may not be entirely true, but I've been told that the term *road rage*—"violent anger caused by the frustration derived from driving an automobile in impossibly congested conditions"—became part of our vernacular when an editor of the *Oxford English Dictionary* (OED), after attending a conference at UCLA's Westwood campus, tried to get to Los Angeles International Airport for a flight back to London. The editor never got to his assigned seat on the British Airways flight to Heathrow that afternoon because, in a traffic jam en route to the airport, he leapt from his car (while it was stopped, dead on the highway) and attacked a motorist who cursed and flashed a vulgar hand sign at him, beating the guy into a coma. The editor got two and a half years in jail for assault, and we got a term that describes an event that occurs on LA highways four to five times a day.

Okay, I'm joking, but I ask you: If being the victim of a traffic jam precipitates road-rage symptoms that range from rude gestures and profanity-laced screaming to hostile driving and actual physical assault using fists, bats, tire irons, or guns, what symptoms do you think would be generated by a job that promises self-fulfillment yet completely fails to deliver? This is not an inappropriate question when you consider how devastating and ego-annihilating being thwarted from attaining career goals can be, and how an insignificant event like being thwarted while trying to get from point A to point B precipitates rage.

We will examine this issue from a different perspective when we look at anger in the next chapter. For now, I want you to ask yourself how some scientists can investigate a syndrome (burnout) derived from a job you expected to be reinforcing but that, in the end, results in a *thwarting of your opportunities for self-esteem enhancement and self-actualization* could not have as its primary symptom "intense anger."

A Mind Is a Terrible Thing to Waste

These days there is a science of everything you can imagine, some of it authentic, some of it not so much. Memory has been the subject of authentic scientific study for decades. Beginning with learning theories—from Pavlov to Skinner and beyond—this is the arena where psychology earned its chops.

Learning theory deals with how and why we remember things, which takes us back to memory. Beyond all the neat aspects of learning psychologists have discovered, they have been a boon to society by demonstrating how regularly and automatically memories can be biased. For example, we are not passive sponges while learning. Actually, the so-called *confirmation bias* shows that we actively search the environment for, and recall much more of, information that confirms our preexisting beliefs. Thus, as a native of New York City who loves his hometown, when I visit Manhattan I remember good events from the totality of my time spent there while ignoring the noise, dirt on the streets, and excessive cost of everything you need to purchase to live.

Another memory bias is called the *picture superiority effect*. This refers to the manner in which a concept you want to remember is more easily etched in your mind if it is presented to you in picture form instead of in word form. This is doubtless the scientific underpinning of the bubbie psychology notion, "a picture is worth a thousand words," as well as the song "Every Picture Tells a Story" (Rod Stewart and Ron Wood, 1971). Even the gloomy poet Edgar Allan Poe gave begrudging support to this notion when he advised, "Believe only half of what you see and nothing that you hear."

With an eye toward exploiting the picture superiority effect I want to put a face on the definition of burnout that

Dr. Harry Levinson and I endorse. By using this tiny slice of the vast literature on learning theory I hope to drive home my conviction that you need to understand the role of anger in getting into and out of job-induced malaise, or you'll be forever stuck in a Sisyphean hell.

The face of burnout I would like you to see is described in the quote the United Negro College Fund (UNCF) used as the slogan of a fund-raising campaign created by the advertising agency Young & Rubicam more than forty-five years ago: "A mind is a terrible thing to waste."

The UNCF was incorporated in 1944 in an effort to combat the fact that African Americans were traditionally denied opportunities for advancement. Today, more than fifty years after UNCF was founded, black teenagers would still doubt that they had the same opportunities to achieve self-actualization as whites do.

I mention this because, since its inception, the constituency of the UNCF was African American high school seniors who had little or no hope of attending college owing to a lack of funds, not intellectual acumen. Consequently, these teenagers—many with aspirations of doing great things—were, in the main, thwarted from realizing their dreams. Only a few of these students—some superstar athletes, a few high-IQ kids—broke the barrier to college admission. Scores of black artists, school newspaper editors, creative writers, dancers, and linguistic wizards were denied the opportunity for a college education afforded their wealthier white counterparts.

I've co-opted the UNCF's slogan to help you grasp the essence of burnout. If you were among the vast talent pool that made up the constituency of the UNCF fifty years ago (and, to some extent, even today), you were acutely aware of how it felt to be wasted: longing for a challenge, willing to do anything to have your mind stimulated and not wasted, and aflame with feelings of rage at being denied a chance to "be all that you can be"—*that's* burnout.

If you wonder what the kids targeted by the efforts of the UNCF—kids blocked from actualizing their academic potential—did with their anger, check out the work of groups like the Student Nonviolent Coordinating Committee (SNCC). Granted, SNCC began on a college campus (Shaw University, 1960), but many of its members were not enrolled in universities, and others who were enrolled had friends and relatives who were the target constituency of UNCF.

According to Julian Bond, a SNCC founding member who went on to serve four terms in the Georgia House of Representatives and six terms in the Georgia State Senate as well as serving as chairman of the National Association for the Advancement of Colored People (NAACP):

> One SNCC legacy is the destruction of the psychological shackles, which had kept black Southerners in physical and mental peonage. The Student Nonviolent Coordinating Committee helped break these chains forever. It demonstrated that ordinary women and men, young and old, could perform extraordinary tasks.[14]

In the late 1960s, led by overtly angry leaders such as Stokely Carmichael, SNCC focused on black power. In 1965, when James Forman headed SNCC, he said the group could no longer remain nonviolent. Consequently, in 1969, the group's name was officially changed to the Student National Coordinating Committee to reflect the use of more aggressive strategies to achieve its goals.

Do you think that being more aggressive was an error on the part of the SNCC leadership? If you do, imagine how you would feel if your mind was wasted owing solely to the color of your skin. If you do not feel that Mr. Forman was off base by asserting that unless or until African Americans were allowed access to the intellectual advancement they deserved, please, when you think of "burnout," imagine an African American high school senior opening a rejection letter from a college, crying, and planning to work at a fast-food outlet rather than pursue a career as an engineer.

In sum, while the literature on burnout is confusing and while I believe I have given you an accurate and useful definition of the term, I want to reiterate that you need not worry about what burnout is or is not to benefit from what follows. This chapter was presented to educate you, demonstrate the need to understand a job that deprives you of opportunities to achieve self-actualization as anger-provoking, and to prevent you from a self-diagnosis that is misinformed.

CHAPTER 3

Anger: The Most Misunderstood Emotion

All cruelty springs from weakness.
> —Seneca the Younger, Roman Stoic
> philosopher (4 BCE–65 CE)

An angry man is again angry with himself when he returns to reason.
> —Publilius Syrus, Latin writer
> (85–43 BCE)

The angry man is aiming at what he can attain, and the belief that you will attain your aim is pleasant.
> —Aristotle, Greek philosopher and
> scientist (384–322 BCE)

Anger is vilified and inappropriately blamed for causing problems totally unrelated to feeling it or exhibiting it. On those occasions when anger really does do us harm—for example, when we express anger in outbursts ranging from road rage to shouting racist epithets—anger is, in reality, a smoke screen for feelings that an angry person is usually unaware of and deeply hurt by. In other words, when we act out in anger we are, in less than optimally effective ways, creating a protective shield around our deepest vulnerabilities in an effort to ensure they are not exposed, exploited, or damaged.

Not only is anger misunderstood, the reason this is so is because people do not know how to manage it. Conventional wisdom would have us all manage our anger by developing new and better ways to squelch or suppress it. In this chapter, I show you that the best way to manage anger is to understand and then harness it. As you read the pages that follow, keep in the back of your mind that anger springs from feeling vulnerable and weak; what makes us feel angry isn't what's done to us but rather what that alleged harm exposes within us; and when harnessed, anger can help us reach our aim(s).

Abolish Anger?

The most troubling mutation to develop over the past two thousand years in the conventional wisdom pertaining to anger is the belief that it can be legislated out of existence. Pushing for this sort of emotional regulation is as ludicrous as striving to banish feelings of sexual attraction between students in high schools and on college campuses. If a boy sees a beautiful girl walking across campus, he'll likely feel attracted to her unless (a) he knows something about her character that makes her unattractive to him, or (b) she is his sister or cousin. If the boy does feel attracted to the girl, however, that feeling in no way means that he will strike up a conversation with her or ask her for a date. It's just a feeling. He may be shy; he may have low self-esteem and/or fear of rejection; he may have a steady girlfriend—all reason enough to just have a feeling and do nothing.

What if that same boy sees the school bully walking across campus and the bully shouts out his name and makes an obscene gesture directed at him? The boy would likely feel angry, but that feeling—just like attraction to the beautiful girl—has no direct connection to the initiation of any sort of behavior. The boy who is the target of the obscene gesture might have thoughts such as "What a jerk" or "I hope I see that guy at the beach...I'm not gonna hit him at school. I don't want to get suspended." You see, anger does not automatically lead to a fight, just as attraction doesn't automatically lead to approach.

What high schools and colleges object to and should rightfully legislate out of existence is if a boy or man acts on his feeling(s) in a manner that is harmful to girls, women, and even bullies. What to do with anger when you feel it is an incredibly complex issue that I devote considerable attention to at the close of this chapter. For now, it is important to understand that anger has always been, and will always be, a component of the human condition. Moreover, it serves a very adaptive function.

That said, the reason anger has such a bad name is that

the adaptive function it serves is elicited in a blink of an eye, virtually automatically, when we rightly or wrongly perceive severe threat or harm to our integrity or our self-esteem. Psychologists who understand the adaptive and protective function of anger understand how it benefits mankind because they have conducted retrospective analyses of provocations to anger and angry outbursts. Anger, simply stated, is our first line of defense against an antagonist who places any component of our identity under attack. Like a junkyard dog warding off an intruder, anger springs from within us to counteract any and all threats to our psychological self-system, from self-esteem to our public personae.

Anger, from an Aristotelian (teleological) perspective, fulfills its purpose in our instinctual makeup by affording different types of psychological protection just as an acorn fulfills its telos by becoming an oak tree.[1] That said, both anger and oak trees are subject to environmental influences. As an avid bonsai enthusiast, I have shaped both oak trees and pine trees—typically twenty feet tall in the wild, or bigger—to be less than eighteen inches tall and formed to look as though they live on a windy mountainside. Anger can be shaped as well: As Aristotle notes, "The angry man is aiming at what he can attain, and the belief that you will attain your aim is pleasant." In other words, when you learn to master anger—i.e., channel it rather than allow it to erupt—it helps to sharpen and focus your attention while aiding you to overcome obstacles that stand between you and the attainment of desirable outcomes.

People benefit in myriad ways when they develop an in-depth awareness of how to utilize anger. Then and only then will we be able to prevent the unwanted and inappropriate instances of acting out in anger that are offensive to all.

Starting to Understand Anger

Speaking of how acting out in anger is plainly offensive, in Los Angeles, where I live, rarely a day goes by that my local newscast fails to report incidents of drive-by shootings, road rage, or killing sprees in schools, houses of worship, or fast-food outlets. You cannot deny the pervasiveness of anger-fueled violence in America these days, nor can you ignore how many different ways people give vent to angry feelings in harmful—to self and others—ways.

Dr. Lisa Barrett, a professor of psychology at Northeastern University where she focuses on the study of emotions, observes[2]:

> Anger is a large, diverse population of experiences and behaviors.... You can shout in anger, weep in anger, even smile in anger. You can throw a tantrum in anger with your heart pounding, or calmly plot your revenge. No single state of the face, body or brain defines anger. Variation is the norm.

The Russian language has two distinct concepts within what Americans call "anger"—one that's directed at a person, called *serditsia*, and another that's felt for more abstract reasons, such as the political situation, known as *zlitsia*. The ancient Greeks distinguished quick bursts of temper from long-lasting wrath. German has three distinct angers, Mandarin has five, and biblical Hebrew has seven.

Dr. Barrett makes an excellent point when she notes that "no single state of the body or brain defines anger." Nevertheless, it is known that the physiological consequences of being stimulated to feel anger conform to a predictable pattern. Since there is a strong relationship between anger and fear, anger is understood to be the *fight* component of the fight-or-flight acute stress response pattern identified by Walter Cannon.[3]

Cannon's acute stress response, a physiological reaction in response to a perceived threat or attack, unfolds as follows: When you sense you are about to be or are being harmed, a mass of gray matter in your brain, the amygdalae—two almond-shaped structures composed of brain cells that are responsible for identifying threats to our well-being—send out a warning that essentially alerts us, "Threat ahead!" Scientific studies have shown that the amygdalae fulfill their role as warning siren so well, and so quickly kick into action signaling other parts of the brain to start reacting, that before our cortex—the thinking, judgmental, part of the brain—can assess the nature of the perceived threat, we are already feeling anger and probably behaving in a manner an observer would describe as "angry."

You now know why we often fly into a rage over trivial

perceived wrongs: The circuitry in our brain prompts us to go on the offensive before we can discern whether a full-fledged assault is necessary. If this occurs, that is, if a person becomes angry without just cause, he is said to be "barking up the wrong tree"—rebuking someone (barking at them) who does not deserve to be told off.[4]

Back to the amygdalae, which, after they have sounded the alarm, signal our adrenal gland to secrete a compound (catecholamine) that contains epinephrine (also known as adrenaline) that increases blood flow to muscles and blood sugar—the stuff our bodies need if we are going to lock horns with an adversary who has not fled the scene in response to our barking. It also gets your heart pumping at an increased rate, which is why, when you are angered, your face flushes and your heart pounds. At this point, you are literally "fighting mad."

When humans were uncivilized what got adrenaline surging through our systems were threats to our survival, such as dangers to our ability to secure food, shelter, and physical safety. In response, we attacked in ways that threatened the survival of our adversaries. Today, most of the threats we experience are to our self-esteem or the components of our identity (e.g., principles), and we retaliate with harsh words that, if well crafted, can wound like weapons do. It's not hyperbolic to assert that being demeaned or disgraced causes intense pain. As members of the US Marine Corps proudly proclaim, "Death before dishonor!"

Anger: Retaliatory Attack by a Wounded Ego

Good name in man and woman, dear my lord,
Is the immediate jewel of their souls:
Who steals my purse steals trash; 'tis something,
     nothing;
'Twas mine, 'tis his, and has been slave to thousands;
But he that filches from me my good name
Robs me of that which not enriches him
And makes me poor indeed.
                    —William Shakespeare, *Othello*

To grasp the true, fundamental nature of anger, you have to differentiate it from pain. Physical pain alone rarely, if ever, gives rise to anger. But emotional hurt and pain regularly give rise to anger. Why? Because *anger is an interpersonal phenomenon.* If someone hurts you and you feel that he knew, or should have known, that what he was doing would hurt you, your anger isn't born of pain but rather from the sense that the person who hurt you has demeaned you, disregarded your sense of self, and disparaged your social standing by acting as if how you feel doesn't warrant his concern.

The best example of the distinction I am drawing is available from watching an NFL football game, where extremely well-conditioned athletes hit one another for sixty minutes and rarely get angry at the members of the opposing team. In fact, when an NFL game ends and players stop giving and receiving physical punishment, these gridiron gladiators will cross the playing field to congratulate and hug one another, or to simply seek out old friends to chat with about a contest well fought.

The exception to the observation that NFL football is rarely anger provoking is if, during a game, one player does something demeaning to an opponent—say, mock him for dropping a pass, fumbling the football, and so forth. When a personal put-down of that sort occurs, fists will fly. This is why the NFL imposes the same exact penalty (fifteen yards) for taunting an opponent that it does for an illegal, potentially physically damaging late hit against an opponent (after the whistle has blown to end the play). Each offense poses the same threat to the integrity of the game.

Think about it: During a football game players endure countless *legal* hits that have the force of a shoulder-launched rocket, yet they evince no anger. But a late hit—one possessing the same force as a legal one but not sanctioned by the rules of the game—is dangerous and career threatening, and for that reason likely to elicit anger. Taunts, on the other hand, which do absolutely no physical harm to an opponent, often elicit the most intense displays of anger seen on football fields simply because they are a blow to a player's ego, in contrast to a blow to a player's body.

For those of you who don't enjoy football, let's leave the gridiron for your home so I can give you a final example of the absolutely crucial role that ego plays in eliciting anger—i.e., when a loved one diminishes your value.

Assume, if you will, that your spouse left his or her shoes on the stairway up to your bedroom and you tripped over them one night. If this only happened once, you would hurt, if tripping bruised a part of your body, but you wouldn't conceivably attack your spouse for an inadvertent error as minor as this. If the morning after tripping you mention to your spouse that leaving shoes on the stairs is dangerous, and that evening your spouse once again leaves shoes on the stairs, you would be displeased and would likely discuss the matter again. However, if after the second discussion you found shoes on the stairs that night you would likely get angry. (Note: Everyone has his or her own thresholds for becoming angry. You might give a spouse four or more chances or you might find that three chances was your limit.)

How could something as insignificant as "shoe leaving" provoke anger? I mean, why not just pick the shoes up and carry them to the bedroom, playing the role of good spouse without throwing a fit? Not because you may have tripped and gotten bruised several times, but because your spouse's disregard for your feelings—how he or she metaphorically slapped you in the face by demeaning your significance—would be what provoked you to become enraged.

The bottom line is that anger is aroused by a kick in the ego or a punch to your self-esteem that makes you feel demeaned, belittled, and the like. When this occurs, you feel a passionate yearning to redress the improper actions taken against you. You want to defend your self-esteem, your public persona, or the role you feel you should play in the offending person's life. This is why anger almost always provokes some form of action that is aggressive or confrontational, initiated to right the wrong a person has done to your sense of self.

Anger: Vulnerability and Impotence in Disguise

It is often noted that the emotion of anger is a mask, a feeling provoking aggressive behaviors that serve to keep the deeper feelings that gave rise to it—vulnerability, weakness, insignificance—hidden from the targets of anger as well as from the person who experiences anger. In this regard it is referred to as a "substitute emotion" since, when angered, a person can avoid feeling a deep-seated pain that produces far more suffering than the components of an angry outburst.

When, as Shakespeare noted, the actions of another person refute your sense of self-worth, the pain you feel and your reaction to it are infinitely more intense than what would be aroused by theft. Some psychologists argue that only if you are embarrassed, shamed, or belittled will you feel anger. And since the injuries to your ego that give rise to anger are painful *primary emotions*, the final sobriquet I will give you to describe anger is that it is a *secondary emotion*—that is, one that emerges to cover a primary feeling that is intolerable.

Functioning, as it does, as a secondary emotion is how anger serves its most important defensive function. Here's how it works: When an individual suffers emotional pain he becomes preoccupied by thoughts of it. If that person gets angry at the presumed source of that pain, he thinks about harming whoever caused his hurt, not how he is hurting. In this manner anger is comforting in that it shifts our attention from a self-focus on pain in the ego to an other-focus with an eye toward securing retributive justice.

The first time I became aware of how anger functioned as a secondary emotion or a mask for vulnerability was when, as a fourteen-year-old, I went fishing for striped bass with my neighbor one evening. My buddy (foolishly, I felt) told his mother where we were going: to the train trestle near where we lived. This structure was made of wood pilings that fostered the growth of algae that baitfish, which attracted bass, fed on. I promised my parents I would be home that night by 11:00 p.m. but the fishing was so incredibly good that I didn't stop hauling in bass until well after midnight, which got me home at 1:00 a.m. When my mother greeted me, she was enraged and hit me several times with the largest Le Creuset skillet she owned. Once she stopped swinging the frying pan my mother cried, "I was scared all night! I feared you got hit by a train!" My response was a bile-laced, snarky, "Nice way to show you were worried about me."

The good news derived from this life-altering event was that I learned how to help patients and clients deal with their anger much more artfully than I would have had I not realized that my job was determining what primary feelings provoked their secondary emotions. I wish I could tell you that it was easy for my patients and clients to let go of anger and analyze it after I said words to the effect of, "Yes, I know you're angry, but what *feeling in you*, as opposed to flaw in the SOB you're angry at, do you see as prompting anger?" But it wasn't.

The difficulty that almost everyone without training has in understanding the actual core ego wound that provokes anger is why I am taking you on this journey to comprehend every possible nuance of anger there is. If you do not want to become a prisoner to anger, you must be able to trace its source and address why you felt it, not punish yourself because you did or, worse yet, dwell on punishing whomever you feel is responsible for smacking your self-esteem.

Restraint: The Ticket to a Sisyphean Hell

> "It's freezing up here. What did you use to keep warm?"
> "Indignation," said Michelangelo. "Best fuel I know. Never burns out."
> —Irving Stone, *The Agony and the Ecstasy*

I hope it is clear that anger is an emotion born of an insult to a person's sense of self, where "insult" is used as it is in medicine—the cause of a physical or mental injury. For example, humiliation (the injury) may result from a publication that demeans you (the insult), such as an embarrassing report (e.g., an arrest record) or a false report that damages a person's reputation (e.g., a libelous magazine article).

An event that is not typically seen as an insult to a person's self-system is *restraint* (or restraining that person's freedom to behave as he chooses), because its psychological consequences may not be immediately obvious. Keeping a person tethered to the status quo isn't as clearly damaging as, say, throwing acid on her skin, but consider this: What is the essence of the punishment the gods of Olympus imposed upon Sisyphus? He was forced to roll an immense boulder up a hill and watch, helplessly, as it rolled back down, for eternity. Yes, the gods imposed some physical pain on Sisyphus—pushing that boulder was strenuous, and when it hit him after rolling downhill, he would surely suffer physical trauma—but restraining Sisyphus from engaging in any challenging or stimulating tasks meant that the ultimate punishment he suffered was an eternity of ennui and futility born of being restrained.

For anyone, not just Sisyphus, restraint—in whatever form it occurs—is among the most damaging insults a person can suffer. My goal in the balance of this chapter is to demonstrate to you that a job that restrains an individual from enjoying psychological growth is actually the primary cause of suffering a Sisyphean hell.

From our childhoods on, restraint is something we rage against. Consider: Toddlers cry for many reasons—hunger, fatigue, discomfort caused by dirty diapers—but the child who has her exploratory impulses restrained by a parent who is holding her back from wandering will let loose with an earsplitting howl of anguish audible to anyone within a one-mile radius. The loving parent isn't spanking the child or withholding comfort—he or she may actually be hugging the child while whispering, "Don't run off without Mommy/Daddy . . . it's not safe." But the restrained child couldn't care less. He or she wants out of the parent's grip, wants the freedom to explore, and is enraged at not being able to do so.

So much for our progeny; what about you? I assume you are educated people holding down responsible jobs, but you would not be reading this if your job boosted your self-esteem as you expected it would. What, then, is the work-based insult that causes you the most pain? It's not actual physical restraint, per se, but after reviewing the work of Frederick Herzberg,[5] a management psychologist who did his best work and gained niche fame by advancing a theory that explains what aspects of a job are motivating, I think you'll see that a form of job restraint created by a failure to deliver what you expect out of work captures the essential feature of a job that causes you the most pain.

Herzberg, paralleling the work of Abraham Maslow on the hierarchy of needs, claimed that if a job *simply* satisfies an individual's basic/fundamental needs by providing appropriate monetary compensation in a safe, clean, work environment where bosses/supervisors act appropriately, people would not be angry but would not be particularly engaged in their jobs either. What people presume they will derive from work and expect to be able to pursue on the job are opportunities to gratify higher-order psychological needs such as challenge, achievement, self-esteem enhancement, and recognition from work that is inherently stimulating and gratifying.

Herzberg[6] formalized this notion in a bifurcated theory of workplace motivation he dubbed the two-factor theory or the Motivation-Hygiene Theory of intrinsic vs. extrinsic motivation. This is a complex way of saying that there are certain factors—the motivation, intrinsic factors—in the workplace that yield feelings of job satisfaction, and a separate set of factors—the hygiene, extrinsic factors—that, if not present, can cause dissatisfaction but do not alone lead to positive feelings about a job. Specifically, according to Herzberg:

• *Hygiene factors* in a workplace are those aspects of the work environment that are external to the actual job a person does. These extrinsic factors include salary, job security, administrative policies, supervision/training, etc.

• *Motivation factors* are the actual work a person does. Only when the expected (necessary) motivation factors exist in a job itself—i.e., when it affords opportunities to experience achievement, when a sense of personal responsibility is inherent in the work one does, and when a job is structured in a way that fosters a person's psychological growth and the development of his skills and feelings of mastery within the context of a job—will a person feel satisfied (engaged) at work.

Herzberg's thesis is simple, a tad convoluted, yet extremely insightful. He argues that all the hygiene factors in the world cannot engender positive feelings about, or engagement in, work, but if hygiene factors are poor or absent, they can breed dissatisfaction and disengagement. On the other hand, if and only if a person's job has motivation factors inherent in it will he feel engaged in work and gratified by his job.

The Consequences of Restraining Job Content

Herzberg never addressed what happens to workers whose job content fails to prove motivating. His position was that the intrinsic aspects of a job should reward the needs of the individual in a manner that enables him to achieve his aspirations. He also states that job enrichment—that is, steps that involve restructuring the job content in order to provide opportunities for a worker's psychological growth—is key to organizational health.[7] Would that Herzberg had said, "But if an individual's job-content failed to motivate him to self-actualize..."

He didn't, but Abraham Maslow—the man whose work on a hierarchy of needs was the springboard from which Herzberg launched his two-factor theory—did. In a commentary on what a person needed to do to traverse the route toward achieving self-actualization, Maslow said:

> If work is introjected into the self (I guess it always is, more or less...), then the relationship between self-esteem and work is closer than I had thought. Especially healthy and stable self-esteem (the feeling of worth, pride, influence, importance, etc.) rests on good, worthy work to be introjected, thereby becoming

part of the self. Maybe more of our contemporary malaise is due to introjection of non-prideful, robotized,
broken-down-into-easy-bits-and-pieces kind of work
than I had thought. The more I think about it, the
more difficult I find it to conceive of feeling proud of
myself, self-loving and self-respecting, if I were working, for example, in some chewing gum factory.... I've
written so far of "real achievement" as a basis for solid
self-esteem, but I guess this is too general and needs
more spelling out. Real achievement means inevitably a worthy and virtuous task. To do some idiotic job
very well is certainly not real achievement.[8]

In another commentary Maslow made about "robotized,
broken-down-into-easy-bits-and-pieces kind of work," he
finished his thought on how a normal person would react to
a job that failed to motivate him. I assume Herzberg would
have said the same thing had the question been posed to him:

And now I would ask the question, "How can any
human being help but be insulted by being treated
as an interchangeable part, as simply a cog in a
machine...?" There is no other humane, reasonable,
intelligible way to respond to this kind of profound
cutting off of half of one's growth possibilities than by
getting angry or resentful or struggling to get out of
the situation.[9]

What Happens after You Suffer Job-Induced Anger? Taking the Next Steps

In Maslow's account of what happens to a person in a job that consists of nothing more than "robotized, broken-down-into-easy-bits-and-pieces kind of work," he very uncharacteristically gets mad. There *is* no other humane, reasonable, intelligible way to respond to this kind of profound cutting off of half of one's growth possibilities than by getting angry or resentful or struggling to get out of the situation. Maslow was the founder of Humanistic Psychology, a psychologist whose writings emphasized the need to focus on the positive qualities in humanity and not treat people as a bag of symptoms or pigeonhole them with diagnostic labels. When Maslow spoke of a circumstance that make people angry or resentful and provoke a "struggl[e] to get out of the situation," he was authentically ticked off.

With good reason, as I see it. The myriad ways in which work in general and most jobs in particular insult people striving to do well and feel good about themselves are why you went plummeting into a Sisyphean hell the moment you discovered a job you thought you loved and, therefore, would preclude your need to ever again *work* a day in your life seduced you and betrayed you.

Now what?

As I try to imagine how you are feeling right now, having just read what you read regarding why your job robbed you of your dignity, I suspect that what you want is a strategy for dealing with your anger. You're not unique. Anger mismanagement has been a concern of humankind since the dawn of recorded history. Aristotle, a gifted thinker if there ever was one, devoted a great deal of attention to anger in his *Nicomachean Ethics* where he stated, "Anybody can become angry—that is easy, but to be angry with the right person and to the right degree and at the right time and for the right purpose, and in the right way—that is not within everybody's power and is not easy."

Aristotle concluded the preceding thought by noting that those who were angry "in the right way" would be "praised," which means, since Aristotle didn't dole out praise like vendors who want their products to be carried by Costco pass out free samples, that "doing angry right" is a daunting challenge. What follows is a look at how most people deal with anger of the sort they feel at work *after* they get kicked in the ego by a robotized, broken-down-into-easy-bits-and-pieces kind of job.

Most everyone reacts in a paradoxical manner to getting smacked in the face by insults such as those described by Maslow when he discusses working at a job that has robbed you of your dignity. Believe it or not, they typically keep on working as before, albeit festering and ruminating over hostile and aggressive thoughts. You don't need Aristotle's wisdom to see that this is doing absolutely nothing to improve your situation. Anger is not your problem, and being angry is certainly not a solution for what ails you. Therefore, this is the moment when you would be advised to decide to stop being stuck and follow the First Law of Holes: If you find yourself in a hole, stop digging.[10]

You may believe that if you keep on doing what you have been doing better and with more creativity, things will change. They won't. Albert Einstein is said to have defined insanity as doing the same thing over and over and expecting different results. Please—avoid going insane and commit yourself to doing something other than what you are doing. If you are in a hellhole, stop digging, and work with me to create a plan for getting out of that hole.

To make it easier for you to follow the First Law of Holes consider what most people do with anger: They either give voice to their anger or they suppress it. In adults, there is rarely, if ever, the option to choose between these two natural and alternative approaches to handling anger since a person's reaction to anger is what psychologists call "overlearned"—habitual in that it has been what a person has opted to do when emotionally wounded since childhood. Thus, while you may think you have a choice regarding how to deal with your anger at your job, the truth is that *at this moment* you probably do not.

The following review of alternative modes of responding to anger is designed for you to comprehend the consequences of your habitual manner of dealing with anger.

Catharsis

You're angry, really angry, ten times angrier than "take this job and shove it" angry. So you decide to give voice to your anger. Great. What might you become? Someone—make that some*thing*—akin to the iconic comic book character created by Stan Lee, the Incredible Hulk. As the alter ego of the weak, wimpy, and withdrawn physicist Bruce Banner, the Hulk is a humanoid creature possessing unbelievable physical strength and a really, really nasty temper. The Hulk "emerges from within Banner" whenever Banner experiences distress that gives rise to *his* anger, and the intensity of the destruction wrought by the Hulk is in direct proportion to *his* anger, or as the comic book series notes, "The madder Hulk gets, the stronger Hulk gets."

Believe it or not there are some anger-management experts who would assert that as long as you ensure that a Hulk-like something-or-other emerges from you in private, that would be just fine. Moreover, if you asked the anger-management experts if getting Hulk-like would have negative consequences for you at some later date, say, if you suffered an insult to your self-esteem and could not get angry in private, their answer would be, "Not to worry...purging anger as you did when you let your inner Hulk emerge is cathartic." This *catharsis hypothesis* of anger dissipation that has vast, inexplicable popularity, claims that expressing anger promotes good health and calmness, while suppressing anger is unhealthy, causing physical disease and ultimately leading to a blowup.

This belief is challenged, and often disproven in empirical studies, by researchers who hold that because activities considered to be cathartic are, in the main, aggressive, engaging in these sorts of behaviors can activate related aggressive thoughts and emotions that, in turn, can promote, rather than extinguish, the furtherance of anger and aggression.[11]

Bottom line: Venting anger must be done in line with the wisdom articulated in the previously mentioned ancient Greek maxim, *Know thyself.* Anything other than following that principle would, I believe, fall short of achieving the best type of cleansing anger from our systems. If you're a Freudian, "gaining insight" is how you say "know thyself." If you're anti-Freudian, don't let that stop you from realizing that regardless of how you go about knowing yourself, you must accept that anger is a mask.

To completely purge anger from your system you must ultimately understand why, like a member of the praetorian guard, your anger leaps to defend your soft emotional underbelly like the actual praetorian guard protected the Roman emperor. Getting to an understanding of why anger arose when and as it did should be the goal of all cathartic releases. If you throw in an understanding of what about your self-image got hurt prior to your anger erupting, so much the better. Only if you can achieve these ends will you purge yourself of problematic anger and prevent future recurrences of unhealthy anger.

Suppressing Anger

There are a great number of people who, when threatened with harm to aspects of their self-system, fail to react angrily. Actually, that's not entirely accurate: They do react with anger—anger is as close to an instinctual emotional response as complex behavior patterns get—but these people only react *internally*; they keep *expressions* of anger trapped inside. As undesirable as it may be to go through life fearing that a Hulk-like entity will emerge from within you when you are threatened, it is as detrimental if not more so to your health to *fear that you may express anger or aggressive feelings* and, to ensure that you won't, keep them bottled up!

Thanks to the work of Soviet developmental psychologist Dr. Lev Vygotsky, we know how children accomplish anger control and other complex tasks.[12] Vygotsky pioneered the notion that children's play with others was their "leading activity"—the main source of preschoolers' development in terms of emotional, volitional, and cognitive skill acquisition. What most children do if confronted with a difficult task during play is mentally "talk themselves through the tasks" using the voice(s) of parents, teachers, and, often, peers.

It is important to note that Vygotsky's work demonstrated two invaluable consequences derived from self-talk: (1) self-talk is the most significant aid employed by children in the development of complex skills, and (2) when a child "talks herself through a complex task," feelings of self-efficacy are enhanced. The second point is crucial, since if self-talk is rewarding (self-efficacy gains are elating), self-talk will be repeated as often as possible. On the other hand, if the self-talk a child develops is targeted at suppressing anger—e.g., "Don't be critical of others or you'll be seen as a bad person"—the effectiveness of this process can overrun a child's self-system to the point where the message inherent in the child's self-talk spreads from a restricted focus to the youngster's entire being.

Everyone has a unique "file" or data bank of self-talk (also called "private speech" or "internal dialogue") messages that we play to ourselves, in our minds, over and over through the course of a day. The nature of the self-talk we use frames our reactions to the events of our lives and the circumstances we find ourselves in. Some self-talk is taken from authority figures, modified to fit our mode of speech, and then repeated. Other components of self-talk emerge covertly—when we ask ourselves, "Okay, now what?"—and we draw upon our histories or the pronouncements of others to generate a dialogue that suits our needs.

Once we have a library of self-talk messages we can entrench it in our minds and make it emerge instantaneously by rehearsing our talks to our mirror image. In this manner, when we need self-talk scripts—e.g., whenever we feel pressure to deliver an A+ performance—they pop into our minds without the need to first ask ourselves, "Now what?"

Keep Anger In—Depression Comes Out

In 1917, Sigmund Freud published a paper on depression titled "Mourning and Melancholia" that is responsible for the view, still prominent today among some psychodynamically oriented professionals, that *depression is anger "turned against the self"* (turned inward, or, as some say, "self-hatred").[13] This view arose from Freud's contention that depression occurred in two ways:

• A grief reaction stemming from the loss of a loved one ("love object"), which Freud designated as *mourning*, characterized by sadness and despair over the loss, *but with no self-recrimination*.

• The type of depression a person suffers from a "psychological loss"—of status, a sense of competence, or a favorable self-image, which Freud called *melancholia*. This form of depression, although marked by sadness and despair akin to that brought on by mourning, is characterized and differentiated from mourning by the experience of *self-recrimination*—i.e., shame and self-reproach—as though the person suffering the loss is somehow responsible for the loss or for not preventing the loss. This feature of melancholia is its defining feature.

One additional distinction between mourning and melancholia will help you understand the "depression is anger turned against the self" (or inward) thesis. In mourning, when we lose a loved one to death, we feel hopeless because there is nothing we can do to alter our situation. We are terribly sad but resigned to the fact that our loss is a result of the Lord's will, fate, karma, whatever, and we cannot reverse the outcome.

In melancholia, the form of depression brought on by psychological loss (for example, getting fired from a job), we feel *helpless and worthless* because there are, or were, things we could have done to have prevented or reversed the loss. You feel you could have done better, acted smarter, not done things wrong, etc. What these feelings grow into if melancholia persists for long periods after the loss is growing sadness along with concomitant feelings that we are flawed or inadequate in ways that extend well beyond the loss in question. If you get fired from a job, you will immediately say to yourself, "I should have worked some overtime; everyone does and I looked lazy relative to those workaholics." In time, however, if your melancholia persists, you will likely be saying to yourself, "If I continue being a lazy slacker, I'll never be able to hold a job."

Sixty years after Freud's *Mourning and Melancholia* was published, two research programs turned the psychiatric community's understanding of depression upside down. The first, the *Learned Helplessness Models of Depression*,[14] was the product of more than a decade of rigorous laboratory research into the origins of depressed thinking, and the second was the seminal work of Dr. Aaron Beck,[15] whose theories were born of clinical insights. Both are based on demonstrating that depression emerges from how people think and draw inferences and is not a result of repressed impulses or conflicts. I'll present these theories in reverse chronological order.

The major thesis of Beck's work was that depression is principally a *cognitive disorder* characterized by negative self-relevant beliefs (as well as corresponding negative self-talk) revolving around a negative view of the self. Beck's cognitive view of depression holds that if an external event causes a person to experience distress, that person will become depressed if he has developed (that is, if he is predisposed to view the world according to) what is called the *negative cognitive triad* (of depressive thinking):

- Negative thoughts about the self. When they suffer a psychological loss and feel sad, these people see themselves as inherently flawed or deficient.
- Negative thoughts about the world. If the negative cognitive triad shapes your thoughts, you feel disappointed with your circumstances and see no circumstances in which you will move into favorable circumstances.
- Negative thoughts about the future. Those people whose thoughts are shaped by the negative cognitive triad are pessimistic about getting the outcomes they desire in the future.

A key component of Beck's thinking in this regard is that the negative cognitive triad intrudes on a person's thought processes in an *automatic, reflexive manner* and will ultimately cause the somatic symptoms of depression (e.g., sleeping, lethargy) as well as the ancillary affective components of depression (e.g., intense sadness, hopelessness) that characterize all depressive disorders. Thus, the moment a stressor hits, if you have the negative cognitive triad within you, it will leap into action, shaping how you think and feel.

When he addressed how clinicians might improve their chances of helping depressed patients to redress their disorder,

Beck broadened his discussion of the cognitive biases that cause and sustain depression and identified the fact that depressed individuals suffer from information processing (about the self and world) biased by so-called *negative self-schema*.[16]

According to Beck, the negative self-schemas of people who are depressed lead them to process information that pertains to them in a manner that actively excludes positive interpretations of events and amplifies negatively tinged information or information that can be twisted to fit a negative worldview. Finally, Beck noted that these self-defeating interpretations of events fuel and sustain the negative cognitive triad. Examples of these negative self-schemas include my favorite, *overgeneralization* (after a breakfast meeting you notice a parking ticket on your car and say to yourself, "Well, that's a sign that this is gonna be one piece-of-garbage day"), and my next favorite, *dichotomous* thinking (the propensity to view all potential outcomes in black-and-white or either-or terms).

Psychologist Martin Seligman and his colleagues reached conclusions that fit with Beck's surprisingly well, while adding some very useful insights to the view that depression is a disorder driven by thoughts. Interestingly, Seligman's work grew out of laboratory studies of how dogs reacted to electrical shocks. When first given inescapable shocks, dogs acted "depressed" when they were later exposed to shocks that they could have escaped. Instead, however, their exposure to a situation that "taught" them that they were impotent, insofar as escape from pain was concerned, created a condition in these dogs that, to Seligman and colleagues, looked like depression: The dogs seemed to passively accept their fate (i.e., getting shocked) and took no instrumental actions to escape when escape was made available.

The researchers studying these dogs interpreted what the dogs *didn't do* in cognitive terms, arguing that they learned that there was nothing they could do to alleviate their pain and suffering. Seligman and colleagues dubbed this phenomenon *learned helplessness,* which, over time, grew into a full-fledged theory of depression.[17]

After his work transitioned from dogs to human experimental subjects, Seligman codified his conclusions in a very succinct formulation based on two core arguments:

1. The triggering event that precipitates depression is when people perceive that important life events are beyond their control, and,
2. The reason why those important events are beyond the depressed person's control is because of something inherent in the person, not the context he is in.

If you sense that Seligman's work sounds a lot like Beck's, it does. And the minor ways in which Seligman's and Beck's work on depression differ isn't worth delving into for the purposes of helping you understand why depression was once thought to be a function of "anger turned against the self."

If asked what role self-talk plays in generating episodes of depression, both Beck and Seligman would say that it is central. How else can the core processes in the cognitive models of depression function unless, following a negative event such as a loss, a person will become depressed if and only if he attributes that outcome to a significant component of his self-system (for example, lack of ability; lack of social skills)? Or, as some psychologists who endorse the cognitive view of depression put it, depression results from a form of characterological self-blame for negative outcomes.[18]

Assume I am fired from a job. That event will not result in my becoming depressed if I attribute the firing to the fact that my boss or supervisor was jealous of me. This will be true whether or not my assumption about my boss being jealous is 100 percent accurate or a complete delusion. On the other hand, making an internal, personalized attribution about the cause of being fired could very well result in my becoming depressed. If I tell myself, "Steve, you cannot react to your boss's lying to you by calling him a sociopath and expect to keep your job. Honesty is not *always* the best policy. Your 'candor' perennially gets you in trouble, and it just cost you a job." That is depression-generating self-talk.

Maybe if someone who knew my boss told me, "Hey, Steve! You didn't mess up. John couldn't care less if you call him a sociopath; he knows it's the truth. You got fired because he's jealous of you," a rational person would assume that this clarifying information would stop me from engaging in self-blame for getting fired. Not a chance. Once a self-talk script initiates a self-blame scenario the things you say to yourself about being the cause of a negative outcome roll downhill faster than a luge during the Winter Olympics. Again: *All that matters is how a person accounts for the mess he is in, not what is or is not true.*

Self-talk initially intended to suppress anger can ultimately result in self-blame and terminate with an individual internalizing the negative cognitive triad for depression. You need nothing more than this model to see how attempts at emotional regulation can easily go awry.

I hope you also realize that particularly with anger, as in all things, we should try to achieve what Aristotle referred to as the Golden Mean: The adaptive middle ground between two possible extreme responses. Or, as Grandma would say, all things, anger included, in moderation. If you can achieve this outcome, the good news is that you can turn anger into fuel that can help you craft a career you will feel engaged in and gratified by. In a later chapter, I present several case studies that demonstrate how failing to understand anger and process it properly led to self-destructive ends.

CHAPTER 4

Do Get Mad, Do Strive for Authentic Happiness

Money has never made man happy, nor will it;
there is nothing in its nature to produce happiness.
The more of it one has the more one wants.

—Benjamin Franklin

Although validation of what Franklin asserts in the quotation above comes by way of countless reports of people who chase after money only to discover they are miserable upon amassing it—as well as news reports describing how super-rich Wall Street honchos, CEOs, and heirs to family fortunes routinely self-destruct—people keep chasing after an often elusive pot of gold. You would think that with the weight of more than two thousand years of scholarly wisdom combined with hard data, people would get it: You cannot buy happiness. Alas, for reasons I will present below, there is never a shortage of people who shout, "Show me the money!" thinking that if they get it, they will be on top of the world.

Why is this relevant to you? If you're anything like 100 percent of the people I've met in my clinical and coaching practices, I would bet you harbor, at some level—maybe in the deep recesses of your mind, possibly closer to the front where conscious decisions are made—the notion that Money = Happiness. I would also bet that this delusion has influenced one or more of the decisions you've made during your career regarding a job you have chosen.

Please note: I'm not accusing you of being mercenary, obsessed with wealth, or any such thing. I am, however, being 100 percent honest when I say that you would be truly unique if you have never told yourself, "If I could afford to buy X I would happy forever." Similarly, everyone I know has fantasized that life would be a bed of roses if he bought a penny stock that became the next Amazon.com. That sort of fantasy is virtually universal.

Let me offer a different rationale for claiming that the belief Money = Happiness is truly insane. Remember when I earlier asserted that Confucius's promise about choosing a job you loved and never working a day in your life was the Big Lie? Didn't you pause for a moment after reading that and say to yourself, "Well, it wouldn't be such a big lie if that job was lovable in a manner that enabled me to earn boatloads of money...."

If you've had thoughts like that you are in good company. The American Dream has, historically (as articulated by the writer and lay historian James Truslow Adams in 1931), guaranteed that all Americans would have the opportunity to attain prosperity and success via upward social mobility. The Founding Fathers, including Franklin, said as much in the Declaration of Independence and the Constitution of our nation. Why do you think Emma Lazarus's poem "The New Colossus" was put on the pedestal of the Statue of Liberty? Because it says,

> *Give me your tired, your poor,*
> *Your huddled masses yearning to breathe free,*
> *The wretched refuse of your teeming shore.*
> *Send these, the homeless, tempest-tost to me,*
> *I lift my lamp beside the golden door!*

I am a native New Yorker and have never seen a golden door anywhere on Liberty Island in New York Harbor where the Statue of Liberty stands. So I assume that Lazarus's phrase "I lift my lamp beside *the golden door*" is a metaphor meaning "Let me show you the way [with this lamp] to go from being poor to ending that affliction, since wealth abounds behind this golden door." In case you missed it, the parallel between what Lazarus describes in her poem and how Revelation 21:18 describes Heaven—it has gates, but there is free admission to all who are sanctified, and "*the city [was made of] of pure gold*, as pure as glass" is obvious.

Unfortunately, the fate of the idealistic vision upon which our nation was built, like so many other idealistic visions, got perverted over time. In its youth, our nation celebrated

Horatio Alger's heroes—young, impoverished boys who climbed "from rags to riches." Today we are an "adult nation," too sophisticated and callous to hold the naïve view that anyone can reach for the brass ring and grab it. We know that connections matter, and with the right ones that pot of gold will be waiting. Thus, far too many of us now worship the likes of Gordon Gekko, the fictional antihero (part Michael Milken, the Junk Bond King indicted on ninety-eight counts of racketeering and fraud, and part corporate raider Asher Edelman) from the 1987 film *Wall Street*.

Stated another way, America was once a nation that embraced the teachings of Matthew (6:24): "No one can serve two masters. Either you will hate the one and love the other, or you will be devoted to the one and despise the other. *You cannot serve both God and money*." Today, we embrace the message Gordon Gekko gave to his minions: "The point is, ladies and gentlemen, that greed, for lack of a better word, is good. Greed, in all of its forms... for money, for love... has marked the upward surge of mankind."

One of the many attributes that made Franklin such a stellar individual was that he did not attain millionaire status (he was one of the richest men in the history of America)[1] by concocting a get-rich-quick scheme or hooking up with a Colonial-era Gordon Gekko who let him become part of a scam to counterfeit paper money. Instead, Franklin was driven, almost literally, to become the best printer—as in newspapers, pamphlets, etc.—in Colonial America, and arguably attained that goal. Once he did, then and only then did he actually get contracts to (legitimately) print the money issued by some of the pre–Revolutionary War colonies.[2]

But even that achievement was not what made Franklin so wealthy. What did was that he never stopped inventing, creating, and not giving a hoot about wealth (he eschewed the notion of patenting his designs, preferring to leave them for the public to use and improve), while growing rich without caring about it. What I will show you, and urge you to accept as gospel, is that Franklin's modus vivendi—serial entrepreneurship—is the lifestyle you should craft for yourself to ensure that your professional pursuits will provide you with purpose and passion—the one and only route to authentic career satisfaction.

Why Is It That Wealth ≠ Happiness?

In 1930 when Sigmund Freud wrote, "It is impossible to escape the impression that people commonly use false standards of measurement—that they seek power, success, and wealth for themselves and admire them in others, and they underestimate what is of true value in life,"[3] his remarks used Austrians as a database. Thirty-five years later, using Americans to draw his conclusions, John Steinbeck, the journalist and author who won the Nobel Prize for Literature, saw the same behavioral patterns:

One of the generalities most often noted about Americans is that we are a restless, a dissatisfied, a searching people. We bridle and buck under failure, and we go mad with dissatisfaction in the face of success. We spend our time searching for security, and hate it when we get it....

We scramble and scrabble up the stony path toward the pot of gold we have taken to mean security. We trample friends, relatives, and strangers who get in the way of our achieving it, and once we get it we shower it on psychoanalysts to try to find out why we are unhappy....[4]

Across an ocean, across several decades, the conclusion is the same: "Those who trust in their riches will fall" (Prov. 11:28). The only possible response to this fact, articulated countless times for centuries, is "Why?"

The commonsense answer to this question comes to us elegantly and insightfully articulated by Mark Twain: "Any so-called material thing that you want is merely a symbol: you want it not for itself, but because it will content your spirit for the moment." "Moment" being the operative term, since the salutary impact of any material reward lasts roughly half as long as magnolias stay in bloom.

I recall a client of mine, the managing partner of a hedge fund, who gave himself, years before we met, an incredibly expensive Howard Miller grandfather clock to commemorate the first million-dollar check he received. It dominated his office and he spoke of it with pride several times at the start of our relationship. "That clock talks to me daily; it tells me, 'You done good!' Every time I hear that clock chime it reminds me to reach for the stars."

A year or so into our relationship I was in that man's office and was shocked to notice that he would routinely check his iPhone when he needed to know the time. His Howard Miller clock stood silently, never chiming, in the corner of his office, seemingly forgotten. This man, who hired me to be his coach because, he said, "I'm completely burned out working as a glorified stock picker," was earning in excess of $20 million a year but couldn't name a single thing in his life that made him happy. Of course, he claimed that his son was "my reason for living," but he rarely, if ever, had time to spend with the boy. He had a fund to manage.

As dispiriting as it may be to accept that material rewards lose their positive impact faster than we can imagine, evidence of this occurrence is irrefutable. The reason this is so is simple—it's the same reason that a drug addict needs ever-increasing dosages of the agent that got him high in the past to stay high in the present: adaptation or, more technically, *tolerance*. No matter how much of anything you amass, your hoard will not keep you happy because over time, as you grow tolerant of a reward, you no longer feel the uplifting effect of what once got you high.

Assume you exist comfortably on an income of $50,000 a year when you are offered a job that pays you $100,000 a year. Initially your mood is boosted; you may get that new car you've coveted for years and your mood rises anew. You might even take a vacation you previously could not afford, and you get another spike in good feelings.

Unfortunately, your $100,000-a-year lifestyle soon becomes your baseline expectancy, and soon thereafter becomes the "same old same old." What's worse—much worse—is that humans are hardwired to strive for more and greater *everything* once a baseline has been set. This propensity is called *eustress seeking*, and it is natural and as imbedded in our DNA as breathing in after we exhale. The same principle applies to the enjoyment of wealth: When you can afford a BMW and drive it for a while, you notice yourself eyeing a Bentley and telling yourself, "Someday...." Before too long after that, when the high of the BMW wears off completely, you suffer a hedonic disconnect between the elation your BMW once gave you and a new unavailable level of income you aspire to in order to obtain highs (for example, that Bentley) you now covet. This, for better or worse, is how humans function.

Reams of survey data support this contention. According to an article published by the American Psychological Association, "Compared with their grandparents, today's young adults have grown up with much more affluence, slightly less happiness and much greater risk of depression and assorted social pathology.... Our becoming much better off over the last four decades has not been accompanied by one iota of increased subjective well-being."[5] One book summarizing a number of surveys that sought to determine if there was a relationship between material wealth and emotional health reliably found that people whose lives were devoted to achiev-ing extrinsic goals—amassing wealth and other tangible rewards—reported greater unhappiness in relationships, poorer moods, and more psychological problems relative to individuals who focused their lives on attaining intrinsic goals such as personal growth and community connection—outcomes that are gratifying in and of themselves.[6]

Finally, a prospective follow-up study of college students endeavored to discover if the nature of the goals people aspire to will affect their emotional well-being throughout life.[7] The unique aspect of this research was that it expanded what, to that point, had been bedrock assumptions in the study of self-esteem and well-being. Specifically, reams of earlier research demonstrated that the more committed an individual is to a goal the greater the likelihood of success. But in contrast to the assumptions derived from those studies, the research described below demonstrated that getting what you want will not necessarily boost your spirits.

The authors of this study found that subjects who aspired to and reached "materialistic goals" (e.g., being a wealthy per-son) reported a host of negative outcomes ranging from feeling shame and anger to experiencing distressing physical symp-toms of anxiety such as headaches, stomachaches, and loss of energy. In contrast, study participants whose aspirations were intrinsic (e.g., having deep, enduring relationships and help-ing others improve their lives) reported being more satisfied as a result of achieving what they aspired to, claiming to have a deep sense of well-being and few physical signs of stress.

He Who Dies with the Most Toys Wins...

Most folks who amass wealth do so to engage in the pastime of conspicuous consumption. These folks don't buy one or two luxury items once in a while the way my former client the hedge fund manager did. The folks who indulge in conspicuous consumption embrace the delusion that it will enable them to "win" the "game of life" when all is said and done. Their modus vivendi is the one championed by Malcolm Forbes, the man who coined the phrase "He who dies with the most toys wins."

The Princeton-educated son of B. C. Forbes, who founded the *Forbes* magazine empire, Malcolm got involved with the magazine full-time in 1957 and ran it until his death, at age seventy, in 1990. Although his stewardship of *Forbes* resulted in the magazine's growth and he diversified his earnings into real estate sales and other ventures, Malcolm claimed—only partially tongue-in-cheek it seems—that he acquired his millions of dollars with little effort: "I made my money the old-fashioned way. I was very nice to a wealthy relative right before he died."

An obvious adherent of the view Money = Happiness, Forbes indulged in buying luxury goods with a passion. His acquisitions included a Boeing 727 jet, Highlander yachts, a slew of Harley-Davidson motorcycles, a French chateau, and a multimillion-dollar Fabergé egg collection. In addition, Forbes had a penchant for throwing parties that made the wedding celebration held in honor of the Duke and Duchess of Cambridge look like happy hour at TGI Fridays. For his seventieth birthday bash Forbes spent an estimated $2.5 million for, among other necessities, a Concorde supersonic jetliner to fly his 800 VIP guests to his mansion in Tangier, Morocco, the Palais Mendoub.

Forbes's mode of conspicuous consumption had little resemblance to how the economist Thorstein Veblen, who coined the term *conspicuous consumption,* conceived of it: "Conspicuous consumption of valuable goods is a means of reputability to the gentleman of leisure." First off, Forbes was born into reputability, so he had no need of indulging in a means to it. Second, Forbes didn't simply *consume* valuable goods; he feasted on them (or, less charitably, devoured them). Clearly, when a person has that sort of appetite for worldly possessions, acquiring them serves a function much more psychologically complex than simply affording a "means to reputability."

Research conducted by two psychologists, Niro Sivanathan and Nathan C. Pettit, to uncover the motives that give rise to conspicuous consumptive behavior reveals that people "consume [luxury goods] not only to create some impressive exterior, but also *to alleviate interior psychological pain*—in other words, to make you feel better when you're down in the dumps [emphasis added]."[8] The psychologists who conducted this research maintained that the commonsense explanation of this behavior—that purchasing luxury goods is an attempt to signal wealth or status or power to others—is a facile explanation of the process.[9] In their view,

The economic explanation—that people purchase conspicuous goods because they want to signal positive things about themselves to others—felt incomplete....
We wanted to delve into what causes people to act out their urge to purchase conspicuous goods, and more importantly, what causes that urge in the first place. Our research shows that part of the impetus behind these consumption decisions is the desire to repair self-threat.[10]

If the term *self-threat* seems strange to you, don't worry; it is, but it is also very useful in this context. The definition of self-threat is "when favorable views about oneself are questioned, contradicted, impugned, mocked, challenged, or otherwise put in jeopardy."[11] In other words, a self-threat is precisely the type of stimulus that provokes anger, the instinctive reaction that springs from within us to counteract any and all threats to our psychological self-system—from self-esteem to our public personas.

Massaging the results obtained by Sivanathan and Pettit only slightly, one could say that these researchers found that when people experienced a self-threat they engaged in conspicuous consumption in order to buy themselves into a state of calmness, rather than directing their anger at the perpetrator of the threat to their self-system. I would imagine that the late televangelist Tammy Faye Bakker would have acknowledged that she was one of the folks Sivanathan and Pettit had in mind when they developed their theory. What she said regarding her style of coping with emotional distress was, "I always say shopping is cheaper than a psychiatrist."

But shopping isn't the only activity stemming from anger that is beneficial. A brilliant review article by Joann Ellison Rodgers, published in *Psychology Today* (online edition), points out that evolutionary biologists, psychologists, and brain scientists "have uncovered [anger's] upside, and proposed a psychological model of anger framed as a positive, a force of nature that has likely fueled the ambitions and *creativity* of the famous."[12]

But beyond creativity—Rodgers notes that Beethoven reportedly beat his students but was nevertheless deemed a brilliant teacher, and Mark Rothko's fury at pop art was what drove his creative endeavors—a growing body of evidence demonstrates that anger impels us to positive ends rather than serving simply to repel us from objects with negative valences. Rodgers further explains,

[Anger is] an appetitive force that not only moves us toward what we want but fuels optimism, creative brainstorming, and problem solving by focusing mind and mood in highly refined ways. Brainwise, it is the polar opposite of fear, sadness, disgust, and anxiety— feelings that prompt avoidance and cause us to move away from what we deem unpleasant. When the gall rises, it propels the irate toward challenges they otherwise would flee and actions to get others to do what they, the angry, wish.[13]

The bottom line is that regardless of what self-threat, provocation, insult to your system, or SOB boss has you praying for cathartic relief, please stop. The analysis that follows will demonstrate that by properly channeling the anger you feel into a fuel, you will achieve infinitely more than palliative relief. You will be able to move in the direction of self-actualization, which is exactly the place where each one of us deeply longs to be.

John Walsh Turns Pain into Action

Happiness is not in the mere possession of money; it lies in the joy of achievement, in the thrill of creative effort.

—Franklin D. Roosevelt

In 1979 John Walsh was a partner in a hotel management company that built high-end luxury hotels, with not a care in the world about anything other than a family he adored and being as good a provider for them as he could possibly be. Then tragedy struck. His son Adam was kidnapped and murdered. It is not possible to comprehend the devastating pain John Walsh felt unless you are a parent who has had a child predecease you. Every parent I know would gladly sacrifice themselves to protect their child. That choice is neither unique nor heroic; it's 100 percent normal. So is feeling pain beyond comprehension when you lose a child the way Walsh lost his son.

On the other hand, what makes John Walsh a unique and noteworthy individual is that he coped with his incomprehensible pain in a magnificent manner. Because he was unable to exact revenge on the man who took his son's life— I believe he would have if he could have—Walsh channeled his anger into a passion *to exact revenge on all criminals in an incredibly entrepreneurial way.* Initially, Walsh crusaded for new laws to protect missing and exploited children and their families. After successfully campaigning to enact two federal laws designed to achieve those ends, Walsh became even more entrepreneurial. He created a TV program, *America's Most Wanted,* that helped bring more than a thousand criminals to justice. He also created a line of instructional DVDs to promote child safety as well as a variety of products for personal safety.

After he stopped his initial, all-consuming grieving for his son, Walsh spent every day of the rest of his life channeling his pain into entrepreneurial pursuits, inexorably moving closer to self-actualization. Granted, nothing could completely free Walsh from the pain of losing his son—that sort of emotional scar is permanent—but when Walsh turned his attention from his loss to avenging it, he was able to enjoy feelings of rapture born of his accomplishments.

In essence, Walsh embodied President Franklin Roosevelt's prescription for achieving happiness: He did not seek to amass material wealth, knowing that it would not make him happy, but, rather, he sought to derive happiness the only way possible: *via the joy of achievement; in the thrill of creative effort.*

Walsh's response to the loss of his son was curative; the more entrepreneurial endeavors he created and remained involved in, the more he felt he was avenging Adam's death and the more his achievements bolstered and boosted his self-esteem.

> Revenge may be wicked, but it's natural.
> —William Makepeace Thackeray,
> author of *Vanity Fair*

I mentioned that I believed Walsh would have exacted revenge on the man who kidnapped and murdered his son were he in a position to do so. I base this belief on a thirty-year history of being a psychotherapist, coach, consultant, and trusted adviser to entrepreneurs. This may sound like hyperbole to you, but 100 percent of the authentic entrepreneurs I worked with or now work for—individuals who either turned an idea into a thriving business enterprise or who took a failing enterprise and transformed it into a thriving one—told me, in one form or another, "*I wanted to show him/them....*"

I'm not saying that other careerists don't get bullied, abused, or subjected to the traumas that few, if any of us, escape in life. And I am definitely not saying that as a result of being bumped and bruised in childhood or as adults some people develop incredibly effective coping styles that have nothing to do with entrepreneurial behavior. People regularly adapt to the chaos of growing up and become professionally successful while having nothing in common with entrepreneurs. That said, there is something unique about entrepreneurs that enables them to adapt to a specific sort of chaotic upbringing—say, abusive treatment—or traumas suffered as an adult, take these hurts inflicted upon them, and convert their pain into positive energy. What the entrepreneur does is assess how he was damaged and tell himself, "I'll show him/her/them they were wrong."

The success of the entrepreneurs I have known, identical to the key psychological strengths responsible for Walsh's success, is based on two factors:

- They never let go of the urge to "show him/them."
- They never sought to "show him/them" according to *lex talionis*, the law of retributive justice or retaliation, "an eye for an eye," whereby a punishment matches the nature of the offense in kind and intensity. Instead, entrepreneurs *actively convert* negative, angry energy into enterprise development.

Dr. Carol Tavris, a social psychologist who has studied anger extensively, observes, "Talking out an emotion doesn't reduce it, *it rehearses it*. People who are most prone to give vent to their rage get angrier, not less angry [emphasis added]."[14] You *must* purge anger from your system (purging being the actual definition of catharsis), but if and only if you first understand why your anger leapt to defend your soft emotional underbelly. I would now like to add that in addition to knowing why you are angry—often it's obvious, as in Walsh's case—you must know what sort of purging will be most beneficial to you.

There exists a long-standing history among detectives attempting to solve a crime and jurists attempting to assess if a defendant is guilty of committing a crime. They ask the Latin question *"cui bono?"*—for whose benefit? Usually this is a pure "What's the motive?" inquiry, but since my earliest days as a clinician I've used this question to help clients who are grappling with the motives of individuals they want to trust but can't, for one reason or another. Now I want you to use it in planning—that's correct, planning—your catharsis.

Should you plot revenge if your heart and soul were ripped out of you in the manner that John Walsh had his heart and soul taken from him? More to the point, would revenge enable you to answer the cui bono question with "Me?" A major goal of any post-trauma coping strategy is gaining the ability to move on, so I ask again, does taking revenge enable you to move toward a life that will enable you to become self-actualized?

No.

Walsh's reaction to the trauma he suffered is a textbook example of how it should be done and how engaging in entrepreneurism facilitates moving on in life. Walsh's enterprise development was initially addressed to improving the system that punishes criminals (via the legislative system), but he then moved to the enterprise of tracking down and apprehending criminals, using television to identify criminals and audience input to find them, and finally protecting the public against criminals through educational tools. Walsh answered the cui bono question with "me" as he felt a modicum of "payback" each time he hampered a criminal's activity and paid homage to his son by realizing the goals of his entrepreneurial pursuits.

The British poet George Herbert is credited with coining the maxim "Living well is the best revenge."[15] More often than not this is accurate, and in my experience, it is what entrepreneurs typically try to do . . . with one significant wrinkle: The entrepreneur seeks to live well in a manner that will show those who harmed him that he is living a far better life than theirs, one that puts theirs to shame.

One entrepreneur I would like to examine got even for being beaten and abused by an older brother he was indentured to as an apprentice from the age of twelve. This entrepreneur, considered by many to be the prototype of living well or living the good life, was so successful in showing and paying back his abuser that he was able to retire at age forty-two as one of the wealthiest men alive at the time so as to live a life spent engaging in the process of inventing new products, enjoying all that money could buy (estates, fine food, wine, etc.), all the while providing service to his community and his country.

Benjamin Franklin: Polymath, Entrepreneur, Abuse Victim, and Avenger

Earlier in this chapter I mentioned that Benjamin Franklin was one of the richest men in the history of America. He was also a self-educated genius who set off on the path to success, self-actualization, and, yes, wealth, by being a phenomenally successful printer, a profession he chose to pursue in large measure to get even with his abusive and inadequate half brother James.

Printing was the first trade Franklin learned and mastered, and he always defined himself as a printer. His humility, in large measure, prevented him from declaring that he was so much more than a printer, despite the obvious fact that he was. He was an astoundingly prolific and successful author; he was a civic activist, statesman, and diplomat; he was a scientist and an inventor. Actually, if Franklin had done nothing more than limit himself to inventing—from his work with electricity and the invention of the lightning rod, a godsend when he created it, to the Franklin stove, which employed a hollow baffle to transfer more heat from the fire to a room's air—and had he never seen, let alone operated, a printing press, it would be an understatement to say that his options in life and his accomplishments were limitless.

Yet Franklin chose to be and to call himself a printer even though as a Founding Father of our nation, someone who was instrumental in writing and getting approval of both the Declaration of Independence and the Constitution, he could have been a huge success simply as a representative of the United States to the world.

But what truly made Benjamin Franklin unique was his character. If all people defined "self-help" as he did, we wouldn't have thousands of self-help books that are nothing more than various iterations of "be all that you can be" or "find greatness within you." If self-help were defined as Franklin employed the term, we would have the syllabus from St. John's College made available to all Americans (the college is famous for its curriculum, which has students read and discuss the great books of Western civilization on philosophy, theology, mathematics, science, music, poetry, and literature). I cannot say this with certainty, but I would bet that Franklin, primarily self-taught, read most of those hundred great books.

Franklin had no one cheering him on to become educated. His father, Josiah, could only afford two years of formal schooling for his youngest son (Josiah had ten sons and seven daughters), so Benjamin left school at age ten and became an apprentice candlemaker to his father. There he learned how run the business, including making and selling the candles and procuring the materials necessary for their production. He hated it.

Visits to tradesmen to explore having Benjamin apprentice for one of them were all met by rejection. Given that Franklin was so fond of reading, his father, reasoning that printing was the trade that enabled people, back in pre-Kindle days, to read, decided to apprentice Benjamin to his half brother James, who owned a printing shop. There Ben learned printing and typesetting, but most important of all he honed his love of great literature, writing, and learning by reading.

Self-help for Franklin was self-education: "From my infancy I was passionately fond of reading, and all the little money that came into my hands was laid out in the purchasing of books."[16] Not only did books educate him, they taught him to become a writer. Inspired by the great thinkers he read, Franklin began to practice writing and improve his skills as an author with a self-conceived exercise. He would take poems and convert them into stories and take stories gleaned from books and newspapers and turn them into verse.

Three years after Benjamin Franklin began his apprenticeship, James published the first issue of *The New England Courant*. Benjamin was responsible for the exhausting process of typesetting the newspaper, after which he was charged with selling the paper in the streets of Boston. His apprenticeship was weighing on him—what Franklin was doing was the non-prideful, robotized work Maslow identified as cutting off half of one's growth possibilities. Benjamin decided that he wanted to write for the newspaper. James, jealous of his half brother's abilities, vowed to not print anything that Ben wrote, so the boy began writing under the pseudonym Silence Dogood.

The column was a hit, but, as you might expect, that success was a mixed blessing. James's jealousy was made significantly more virulent by the praise Benjamin garnered from his writing. Once James discovered that Benjamin wrote the Silence Dogood columns, he constantly berated his younger brother and began beating him. In his autobiography—with what seems to be extreme understatement given how biographers describe James Franklin's abusive treatment, Benjamin wrote,

But my brother was passionate and had often beaten me, which I took extremely amiss. I fancy his harsh and tyrannical treatment of me might be a means of impressing me with that aversion to arbitrary power that has stuck to me through my whole life. Thinking of my apprenticeship as very tedious, I was continually wishing for some opportunity of shortening it, which at length offered in a manner unexpected.[17]

Since Benjamin was getting none of what Maslow showed us people want out of work—opportunities to gratify higher-order psychological needs such as challenge, achievement, self-esteem enhancement, and recognition—and was suffering emotional, psychological, and physical punishment 24/7, Franklin broke the law of the colonies and ran away from his apprenticeship. He bribed a ship captain to take him to Philadelphia (he told the captain that "he got a naughty Girl with Child"[18] and had to flee Boston as a result, an apparently more acceptable excuse for traveling as an unaccompanied minor than breaking your indenture), and so escaped Boston undetected. When he arrived in Philadelphia he entered the city in a manner that did not remotely presage a man who would become a Founding Father of America: Franklin had three shillings in his pocket and rags on his back.

In 1723 Benjamin Franklin was hired as a journeyman printer in the shop of Samuel Keimer. After working as a printer in England for a while he returned to Keimer's Philadelphia printing shop in 1727, all the while practicing the frugality he describes in *Poor Richard's Almanac*. In 1728 Franklin established a printing shop of his own, with a partner he bought out in 1730, and by then his career was skyrocketing as his wealth continually grew. As he earned more and more he purchased a number of printing shops across Colonial America, then became an author.

Franklin's income from writing was astounding: *Poor Richard's Almanac* eventually made Franklin a fortune. The publication boasted a readership of ten thousand subscribers a year, a spectacular feat for that era. Franklin was wealthy enough to retire at forty-two, having amassed the equivalent of more than $10 billion in 2017 dollars. Franklin ranks as the 181st richest person of all time according to *Forbes* magazine's historical wealth ranking.

But as noted at the outset of this chapter, Franklin didn't care for money. What mattered was that he "hit" his brother twice: with success as a printer his brother couldn't dream of, and with success as a writer, something his brother James chided him for and beat him for when "Silence Dogood" became the most popular column in James's soon-to-go-bust *New England Courant*.

For your purposes, it is important to see how Franklin benefited by harnessing his anger in a manner that fueled his optimism and propelled him toward overcoming challenges. Franklin embodied the view Machiavelli had of entrepreneurs, namely, that "Entrepreneurs are simply those who understand that there is little difference between obstacle and opportunity and are able to turn both to their advantage." Franklin's start, painful though it was, is prototypical for an entrepreneur.

Above all, it is important to underscore that Franklin never amassed wealth for any purpose other than retiring early so he could give back to America as a Founding Father, framer of the Constitution, ambassador to France, founder of a college, inventor, and more. Franklin began life as the son of a candlemaker, was treated with utter cruelty when he served as an indentured apprentice to his half brother, yet educated himself so extensively and with such stellar results that he was a deemed a cultivated patrician.

In one sense, you could argue that Franklin embraced and was a prototypical adherent to the Greek conception of the good life that enabled him to achieve the form of true happiness articulated in Aristotle's *The Nicomachean Ethics*: the active exercise of the mind in accordance with perfect virtue.[19] Yet Franklin's attainment of self-actualization took him to a higher level of psychological gratification, one called *generativity*, a term coined by psychoanalyst Erik Erikson. According to Erikson, generativity is defined as follows:

> Evolution has made man a teaching as well as a learning animal, for dependency and maturity are reciprocal: mature man needs to be needed, and maturity is guided by the nature of that which must be cared for. Generativity, then, is primarily the concern for establishing and guiding the next generation.[20]

Is it true, as the Bible tells us, "[remember] the words the Lord Jesus himself said: *'It is more blessed to give than to receive*'" (Acts 20:35)? Without question, and I will explain why in the pages that follow. For the time being, I assure you that Franklin's boundless generativity—he eschewed getting patents for his inventions so people would have unencumbered access to them—afforded him boundless psychological pleasures. I doubt that Malcolm Forbes, the man whose publishing enterprise, years after his death, listed Franklin as being the 181st richest person of all time, ever enjoyed the peace of mind, sense of achievement, or joy of self-actualization that Benjamin Franklin did. Forbes lived according to the maxim he coined—He who dies with the most toys wins—and he surely had more toys than Franklin did, but to what end?

While you may never become as wealthy as Malcolm Forbes or Benjamin Franklin, you can, by embracing the entrepreneurial lifestyle Franklin embodied and eschewing the pursuit of material wealth that obsessed Forbes, fully expect to enjoy the good life if you learn how to engage in generativity.

CHAPTER 5

How to Achieve *Summum Bonum*: How to Be Happy

Happiness is the meaning and the purpose of life, the whole aim and end of human existence.

—Aristotle

Aristotle is arguably and deservedly the world's most respected authority on happiness even though he articulated his views on the subject more than 2,300 years ago. Since then, respected scholars who discuss any aspect of happiness—what it is, how can we achieve it, what thwarts us from achieving it—should begin their analyses by symbolically genuflecting to "The Philosopher" (St. Thomas Aquinas's nickname for Aristotle) or by publicly praising him for his contributions to mankind's accumulated body of knowledge.

One scholar who did the right thing by Aristotle is

psychologist Mihaly Csikszentmihalyi, who proudly acknowledges that his work owes a debt to Aristotelian thought:

> Twenty-three hundred years ago Aristotle concluded that, more than anything else, men and women seek happiness. While happiness itself is sought for its own sake, every other goal—health, beauty, money, or power—is valued only because we expect that it will make us happy. Much has changed since Aristotle's time....And yet on this most important issue very little has changed in the intervening centuries. We do not understand what happiness is any better than Aristotle did, and as for learning how to attain that blessed condition, one could argue that we have made no progress at all.[1]

Since I agree completely with what Csikszentmihalyi says about Aristotle's influence on our understanding of happiness, and since it would be impossible to present you with a thorough summary, let alone complete explanation, of the Aristotelian perspective on happiness, I want to help you understand what you need to know in order to find the correct way to turn passion(s) into purpose and career satisfaction. I will limit my review of the Philosopher's contributions to the psychology of happiness to two of the most important aspects of his work:

• Eudaemonia—roughly defined as what we call happiness, but actually a much more complex and useful concept insofar as living the good life is concerned.

- Aristotle's views on virtues, how to behave virtuously, and why virtue plays a central role in the pursuit of eudaemonia, and more directly, summmum bonum—the good life.

Before I begin I want to share some facts about how Aristotle developed his insights on the subject of happiness to demonstrate why I am so enamored with his work (and have been since age eighteen), and to underscore that his insights into the human condition are, to this day, mind-boggling.

Aristotle presents his views on happiness, virtue, and how to lead a good life in his *Nicomachean Ethics*,[2] a ten-volume exposition on what he claimed was the highest purpose of humankind: achieving eudaemonia. What is significant about this work is that its conclusions, as in all of Aristotle's work, are the result of trying to explain the nature of things via observation and reasoning. Thus, when lecturing to his students in the Lyceum, the school he founded, regarding how best to answer the questions of greatest import to humankind—What does it mean to live a good life? and How can one achieve the supreme human good, summmum bonum?—Aristotle claims that the only way to derive those answers is from observing and studying individuals whose lives are prototypes of the summum bonum.[3]

If you know little about psychology this last statement won't set off sirens in your brain, but let me put what Aristotle said in context. Less than twenty years ago most inquiries into psychological functioning proceeded as Freud did from models of human behavior that took, as their point of departure, the study of the state of being that is the polar opposite to eudaemonia: *pathology*. This approach studied, and offered treatment to, people who were not functioning in an ideal manner, psychologically speaking, asked why that was this so, and then retrofitted a model of what such people should do or how they should function under ideal circumstances.

It's a tribute to Freud that after decades of studying Austrian neurotics and hysterics he came to the same conclusion Aristotle did:

> We will therefore turn to the less ambitious question of what men themselves show by their behavior to be the purpose and intention of their lives. What do they demand of life and wish to achieve in it? The answer to this can hardly be in doubt. They strive for happiness; they want to become happy and to remain so.[4]

Finally, to give you an appropriate context for understanding Aristotle's model for achieving happiness and how modern scholars echo his thoughts, I want to go back to what I noted above: how less than twenty years ago pathology was the focus of clinical psychology. In truth, the seed of the revolution that shifted psychology from its focus on pathology to its focus today, a field called *positive psychology*, was planted in 1943 when Abraham Maslow published his magnum opus on self-actualization theory.[5]

That publication started the movement called *humanistic psychology*, which produced today's au courant studies of happiness under the rubric of positive psychology. As you will see below, the kudos Csikszentmihalyi gave Aristotle could be considered an understatement: Not only did Aristotle presage, as precisely as one could speaking ancient Greek as opposed to English, Maslow's work, his notion of eudaemonia has had a direct influence over all supposedly modern theorists who write about happiness, as Csikszentmihalyi humbly claimed should be the case.

Eudaemonia

Eudaemonia consists etymologically of the words *eu* ("good") and *daimōn* ("spirit"). But it means more than good spirit, it means flourishing. Aristotle noted that eudaemonia is not a static experience. It is "well-being produced through a process of growth (maturity) involving virtuous actions."

It is just as important to understand that eudaemonia has little to do with the type of happiness your grandmother wished for you when she said, "Be happy, darling." Grandma wanted you to enjoy a smile-on-your-face positive feeling, which is all well and good, but achieving eudaemonia is work or, more accurately, *good* work, defined as thinking things through, socializing (having family and friends and actively participating in a community), and functioning in a manner that Aristotle called an "active being-at-work" (*energia*):

being someone who renews the components of a virtuous life in perpetuity.

Given Aristotle's teleological bent it's no surprise that another wrinkle of his complex definition of eudaemonia is that it is a process of movement by a person toward a very clearly defined end or goal, namely, *entelechy*. Translated by some as "becoming a complete being," entelechy is often considered to be the original articulation of what Abraham Maslow saw as an individual's ultimate purpose— achieving self-actualization. One thing that Aristotle was clear about was that the goal of eudaemonia should never, ever be considered as attaining pleasure for pleasure's sake, or wanton hedonism. The reason is that a key component of achieving eudaemonia is behaving in a virtuous manner. Pleasure seeking, per se, is not a virtuous endeavor, so it can never be seen as a component of entelechy or a goal of eudaemonia.

In terms of what you need to know about happiness in order to turn passion into purpose and career satisfaction, Aristotle's operational definition of eudaemonia is invaluable. In the *Nicomachean Ethics* he says, "Human flourishing occurs when a person is concurrently doing what he ought to do and doing what he wants to do." Now, if you're hyperattentive to and hypercritical of what I say, you may have just wondered, "Isn't doing what one wants to do narcissistic?" Good question, but the answer is no. That statement is an expression of self-determination theory[6] if you take it out of context, but in context it is an articulation of what can be considered to be a definition of *flow*.

According to Csikszentmihalyi,

"Flow" is the way people describe their state of mind when consciousness is harmoniously ordered, and they want to pursue whatever they are doing for its own sake. Experiences of flow are states of extreme happiness in which one loses the sense of self and becomes absorbed with engaging in an activity of one's choosing that is challenging, does not exceed one's capabilities, and is not chosen because of an outcome that may accrue from doing it well.[7]

If you are a Taoist and embrace the philosophy of Lao Tzu presented in the *Tao Te Ching*, you would notice that Csikszentmihalyi's idea of flow is similar to something called *Wu wei*. According to Lao Tzu, when you are in harmony with the Tao, the guiding principle of the universe, *Wu wei* is an ability to behave in a completely natural, unforced—as in not trying to impose your will on things or exert untoward control over things—manner. When I learned about this concept in a comparative religion class I took as an undergraduate, the professor who described *Wu wei* emphasized how achieving this state enables one to become more invested in human affairs, and that it enhances one's capacity for realizing connections with others.

Contemporary Chinese philosophers might describe *Wu*

wei as functioning differently from how I understood it forty-some years ago, but its essence—"Do not attempt to impose your will on the natural order of things, from relationships to careers, and you will be better off as a result"—is inviolate. Actually, whether you embrace *Wu wei*, Aristotle, the lifestyle of Benjamin Franklin, the teachings of Viktor Frankl, or any one of a dozen modern gurus preaching that message, it doesn't matter as long as you do so. You see, it is undeniably true: pressuring yourself to attain a "tangible" outcome in life or, more specifically, professional pursuits, has failed to yield happiness every time a person has taken that tack.

Passion for some outcome or some *thing*—say, making it into the Forbes 400—has never, in the history of humankind, enabled a person to achieve the good life. Neither has it ever yielded feelings of flow, which is why, logically, Professor Csikzentmihalyi has addressed this issue directly—distinguishing between aiming for success versus being natural and allowing success to come to you.

Here is my synopsis of Aristotle's and Csikszentmihalyi's and Lao Tzu's views on happiness, representing the lion's share of what you need to know about the topic:

A flourishing life is attained when we pursue meaningful goals we enjoy, without regard for ultimate consequences, just the feelings derived from the pursuit itself.

I'll add one caveat to this definition—what Aristotle said about being virtuous in pursuit of eudaemonia—and then we'll look at how modern thinkers have improved, ever so slightly, on this notion.

Virtues

In describing a flourishing life, I stated, "Human flourishing occurs when a person is concurrently doing what he ought to do and doing what he wants to do." As noted earlier "doing what you want to do" is self-determination, not wanton hedonism. I now want to look at the notion "what he ought to do," since Aristotle was quite justifiably preoccupied with what he viewed as the right way and the wrong way of doing anything and everything—that is, the subject of virtue.

To Aristotle, virtue of character (moral virtue) was something a person had to learn, practice, and make habitual by behaving virtuously whenever called upon to do so. The potential to achieve moral virtue is inherent in humans, but whether someone will actualize that potential is a function of how he or she chooses to behave. Since, to Aristotle, virtues are destroyed by deficiency or excess—that is, not "the Middle state between"—we must act in accordance with what he called the *mean* (some call it the Golden Mean) to be virtuous and, ultimately, achieve eudaemonia.

Aristotle claimed that virtue is achieved by maintaining the mean of physical and mental well-being, which means always striving to achieve a balance between two excessive expressions of an attribute. The key to understanding this contention is realizing that being virtuous involves behaving in a manner wherein each virtue is at the mean, or middle point, at which it would arrive if not interfered with by bad habits acquired over a lifetime. In other words, unless a person has a reason to behave in a compensatory manner—for example, in reaction to being told "you won't amount to anything" by a cruel stepparent, avenging that cruel treatment by illicitly amassing wealth that proves the stepparent wrong— he will naturally behave virtuously. Since most of us are traumatized to some degree and develop a number of bad habits, we won't achieve eudaemonia unless we labor to bring all of our behavior in line with the mean.

Aristotle often illustrated this point by referring to the virtue of courage, so let me follow suit, since it applies to what entrepreneurs are noted for: risk taking. If a person acts with excess courage, like a fool rushing in, he ignores all dangers, takes all dares, and doubtless suffers negative consequences sooner or later. On the other hand, the person who is devoid of courage, the guy who snoozes and loses, is a coward who tries nothing, enjoys no *eustress*, and will likely die of boredom.

When Aristotle describes how to achieve eudaemonia he references the person who evinces virtuous traits, the mean between a deficiency and an excess of the trait. Thus, we should be:

• Energetic, not apathetic or overzealous
• Industrious, not slothful or monomaniacal

- Charitable, not avaricious or extravagant
- Friendly, not hostile or fawning
- Conscientious, not irresponsible or obsessed

Obviously, the list goes on, but I hope you get the point: The virtuous trait is one that falls on the exact midpoint between too much and too little.

One final aspect of Aristotle's discussion of virtuous behavior deserves emphasis. In discussing the limitless number of virtues a person can and should exhibit to achieve eudaemonia, Aristotle notes that the virtue integrating them all and facilitating their expression is the virtue he calls *phronesis*, a term from ancient Greek best captured by our notion of practical wisdom, or what many call common sense.

The virtue of *phronesis* fits snuggly within the Aristotelian notion of developing good habits in order to flourish. Since the days when Aristotle taught at the Lyceum it has been assumed that parents teach children good habits based on their own acquired *phronesis*. When those children, well trained, go out in the world, they are more likely than not to develop *phronesis* of their own.

What happens to the person who, for one of any countless number of reasons, does not have parents available to her who can serve as teachers? Life is clearly more difficult (as studies of how foster children develop demonstrate), but with luck or perseverance a child can learn how to live a virtuous life by finding a virtuous person to emulate. Where does one go to find a virtuous person who has attained the good life? They are all around, albeit in short supply, so you have to look diligently. What I can say is that when studies of successful executives seek to discover how they did it, the most common response is, "Wonderful role models or mentors." It is a rare individual who, in isolation, develops into an authentic success. This is why so many cultures have formalized systems of mentorship designed to teach novices the process of doing things right.

Refinements in the Concept of Happiness since Aristotle...

If I had to choose one quote from the vast body of thought that came out of the Lyceum—most of Aristotle's writings (some say all) came from the notes his students took during those lectures and were compiled over time—and that have had the most profound influence on modern views of success, it would be *"pleasure to be got must be forgot,"* which is often called the hedonistic paradox or pleasure paradox. Many economists (e.g., John Stuart Mill, also a philosopher) and psychiatrists (e.g., Viktor Frankl) who were influenced by Aristotelian thought have argued that "aiming to be happy" or making happiness the "direct end" of instrumental behaviors—saying, for example, "I will do that because doing that will make me happy"—preclude a person from actually *being* happy.

Consider what Mill has to say about this:

Those only are happy, I thought, who have their minds fixed on some object other than their own happiness, on the happiness of others, on the improvement of mankind, even on some art or pursuit, followed not as a means, but as itself an ideal end. Aiming thus at something else, they find happiness by the way.[8]

Frankl echoes Mill's perspective:

Don't aim at success—the more you aim at it and make it a target, the more you are going to miss it. For success, like happiness, cannot be pursued; it must ensue, and it only does so as the unintended side effect of one's personal dedication to a cause greater than oneself or as the by-product of one's surrender to a person other than oneself.[9]

If you consider what Frankl and Mill have to say about success and happiness as though they were lecturing in tandem, their "advanced" view of happiness has three salient elements:

1. **Focus on anything but the end of achieving happiness.** Any orientation resembling "If I attain this, that, or the other thing, I'll be happy" sabotages the process.

2. **The only good self-focus is self-focus for the purpose of self-actualization.** If you focus on self-improvement and you happen upon auxiliary outcomes that connect you with others or benefit mankind, you'll be happy. But if you say, "Okay, how can I build an app that teenagers will buy for their iPhones?" the odds are your app will bomb and the IPO you're dreaming about will never materialize.

3. **Devote yourself to improving mankind, or the life of a person who is significant to you.** If you can, you should do this above all else.

From my perspective—that is, trying to prepare you to turn passion into purpose and career satisfaction—both Mill and Frankl made an invaluable observation that, because it was tucked in along with another point, may get lost. I'll underscore it because it is the most significant concept about how to achieve happiness that has been advanced since Aristotle: Apart from not aiming for success and losing yourself in activity, the most important thing you can do to be happy is to "surrender to a person other than oneself" (Frankl) or "have [your] mind fixed on some object other than [your] own happiness... [such as] on the happiness of others, on the improvement of mankind, even on some art or pursuit" (Mill).

Sigmund Freud claims that "the goal of psychotherapy is to allow the patient to love and to work" and also asserts that "love and work are the cornerstones of our humanness."

In either case his meaning is clear: Neither the derivatives of work nor the derivatives of a loving relationship are, alone, enough to enable a person to experience mental health and happiness; we need elements of both life-enhancing endeavors to be complete.

Erik Erikson, a famous psychoanalyst in his own right who did much to advance Freud's work, claims, "The richest and fullest lives attempt to achieve an inner balance between three realms: work, love and play," which supplements Freud's view regarding what is needed to achieve mental health by adding the notion that hobbies and avocations also contribute to our capacity to achieve happiness.

Generativity

Above and beyond adding his voice to the chorus of those who claim only love *and* work yield mental health and happiness, Erikson's most important contribution to addressing the question "How can I address my hunger for 'more' through work?" comes from his theory about the process he called generativity. As Erikson puts it, "generativity is a concern for establishing and guiding the next generation." This does not mean parenting or raising children but rather contributing to the welfare of future generations by promoting a connection to the whole of mankind.

One way of being generative, per Erikson's directive, would be to look at a business, see how it serves the needs of mankind, and then do new things within that paradigm or do things that are already being done in a new and improved way that will benefit mankind. An example of this might be as much fun as Elon Musk's electric Tesla automobiles or as complex as Craig Venter's work on sequencing the human genome. Obviously, the utility of a generative endeavor need not be immediately obvious, but if you are an entrepreneur who builds the proverbial better mousetrap and it is not manufactured immediately, you've still done your job, according to Erikson. From his point of view, you will feel fulfilled by evincing "a concern for establishing and guiding the next generation"; he said nothing about getting your ideas to market in a propitious manner.

The crucial point to focus on regarding generativity is that you need not create a product to accrue happiness. The outcomes of generativity, love and work, or what Frankl called "dedication to a cause greater than oneself or the by-product of one's surrender to a person other than oneself," aren't products you need to put in a shopping bag or carrying case. The key to happiness is the dedication, surrender, and concern or feeling that you are connected to others in the world. The person who aims to achieve generativity utilizes her wisdom in ways that allow her to realize her dreams in conjunction with enabling successive generations to prepare themselves to realize theirs. It involves saying, "I have all that I need. My world has given me enough. Let me give back to ensure that others are able to say the same thing."

Giving

> We make a living by what we get; we make a life by
> what we give.
>
> —Winston Churchill

> Generous people are rarely mentally ill.
> —Carl Menninger, American psychiatrist,
> Menninger Clinic founder

If, as you were just reading about generativity, you thought
to yourself, "I don't know about the value of this 'enabling successive generations to realize their dreams' stuff; that could take
a ton of work. Who's gonna pick up the slack if I go off and
help folks?" do not dare share your concerns with Grandma.
Since the dawn of time grandmothers have been telling grand-
children, "It is better to give than to receive." The more religious members of that prestigious sorority taught this lesson
to their children's children by quoting scriptures, specifically,
Proverbs 11:24–25, written by none other than King Solomon:

> *One person gives freely, yet gains even more; another*
> *withholds unduly, but comes to poverty.*
> *A generous person will prosper; whoever refreshes others will*
> *be refreshed.*

Erikson didn't quote King Solomon in his various expo-
sitions about generativity, but it's clear that the king and the

psychoanalyst are of one mind when it comes to the psychological benefits of investing in the welfare of others. The notion that a person derives an unprecedented level of happiness from giving to or helping others has been endorsed by great minds for millennia. As Saint Francis of Assisi notes, "For it is in giving that we receive." Benjamin Franklin, an entrepreneur who at age forty-two said to himself, "I have more than enough wealth; I will retire," spent his final forty-two years on earth giving back to society—as an inventor, civil servant, diplomat, and statesman. His view on giving was,

> When I am employed in serving others, I do not look upon myself as conferring favors, but as paying debts. I have received much kindness from men to whom I shall never have an opportunity of making the least direct returns; and numberless mercies from God, who is infinitely above being benefited by our services. Those kindnesses from men I can, therefore, only return on their fellow men, and I can only show my gratitude for those mercies from God by a readiness to help His other children...[10]

I wish I could demonstrate the validity of what King Solomon, Erik Erikson, and Benjamin Franklin each saw are the obvious benefits of giving back, but I cannot: There is very little hard data on this subject. I would like to tell you the reason that this is so is because psychology researchers told themselves "No point setting out to prove what is blatantly obvious," but I cannot. Thankfully, some folks did "set out to prove what is blatantly obvious," so let's consider what they found.

One group of researchers conducted a study on giving that would have made King Solomon smile. These scientists attempted to determine how people felt when they used money on themselves as opposed to giving it away to others. The scientists didn't say they were testing the validity of Proverbs 11:24–25, but one could say that was what the research study ended up doing. Lo and behold, the data revealed that people are happiest when they give away the most money to others (versus holding on to it for themselves).[11]

In a related study that could be called "selfish versus giving" but was dubbed "philanthropy versus fun," research subjects were divided into two groups. One group engaged in so-called pleasurable activities or fun (going to the movies, eating yummy ice cream), and the other group engaged in doing philanthropic work (volunteering at a soup kitchen, reading to the blind). As predicted, both groups felt happy after their outings, but those who did altruistic deeds were happy for a longer time after the experimental manipulation was over—they had a *happiness afterglow*.[12]

The researchers responsible for these studies did not offer a solitary interpretation for why they obtained the results, but one theory took precedence over others in both cases. It was concluded that being generous to others made people happy because doing so satisfies one or more of our fundamental needs: most notably, the need to establish intimate connections with others. The most impressive articulation of this view comes not from science but from folklore.

A story I have seen recounted in at least a dozen different ways captures the value of giving better than any demonstration of the activity I am aware of. I've chosen the version of this tale that appears on Paulo Coelho's website because of how he concludes the story he calls "The Stone." What he added to this tale is, "Having lots of money while not having inner peace is like dying of thirst while bathing in a lake."

A wise woman who was traveling in the mountains found a precious stone in a stream. The next day she met another traveler who was hungry, and the wise woman opened her bag to share her food. The hungry traveler saw the precious stone and asked the woman to give it to him. She did so without hesitation. The traveler left, rejoicing in his good fortune. The traveler knew the stone was worth enough to give him security for a lifetime, but, a few days later, he came back to return the stone to the wise woman. "I've been thinking," he said. "I know how valuable this stone is, but I give it back in the hope that you can give me something even more precious. Teach me what you have within you that enabled you to give me this stone."[13]

King Solomon had lots of money. King Solomon had inner peace. His understanding of why the Lord made him the richest man in the world while he was alive, and why he had inner peace despite it, was arrived at because *he never pursued wealth as a goal.* When he was a teenager and on the verge of succeeding his father, David, to become king, Solomon had a dream in which the Lord spoke to him and asked him what he wanted. Solomon didn't present a laundry list of self-centered demands but instead asked for insight.

Because Solomon did not ask for wealth, the Lord gave it to him. Because he did not aim for success, he achieved it. Granted, this is a biblical tale, "The Stone" is an allegory, and the support I have offered for the contention that "it is better to give than to receive" is primarily anecdotal. I cannot do more or better. When you have the wisdom of the ages affirming that what looks to be an insatiable hunger for achievement is self-destructive while connectedness with others (and with future generations) yields happiness, I feel that you would be demonstrating the insight and wisdom of Solomon if you accepted the consensus opinion.

So, the Answer Is...

If you trust authoritative reporting (I hope you do, but it's possible you do not), you have embraced what I presented, above, which asserts:

- Money cannot make you happy.
- Money cannot buy you love.

144

• Amassing achievements neither builds self-esteem nor improves your psychological health and well-being: it is the quality of your accomplishment(s), not quantity, that matters.

• It is better to give (money) than to receive it.

And although you probably told yourself, "Yup, he's right," you failed to realize that you, yourself, are probably ignoring these insights. According to economist Juliet B. Schor[14] and a host of others in her field, despite not being made happy by working to make more money, Americans have, for decades, been working more, playing less, and enjoying life much less than in years past!

According to Schor, statistics collected about the amount of time Americans spend at work or doing their jobs indicate a steady, inexorable rise since the 1970s. We work more now than at any time since World War II. Couple this fact with data reported by the Centers for Disease Control and Prevention showing that one in ten Americans are depressed and one in thirty meet the criteria for major depression (a clinical disorder), and you have to wonder, "What is wrong with this picture?"

What's wrong is that rather than engaging in hobbies, taking vacations, doing constructive volunteer work, or exercising their minds, Americans are precluding their opportunity to be happy by devoting energy toward pursuing promotions, bigger salaries, and conspicuous consumption. I make this claim predicated on Erik Erikson's thesis that in addition to love and work a person needs an involvement in avocations or just plain play to be psychologically healthy and spiritually fulfilled and happy.

The facts that Schor presents—most notably, that over the past twenty years our working hours have increased by the equivalent of one month per year, making the United States the world's number one workaholic nation—are exactly what they appear to be: symptoms of an illness we, as a nation, are suffering. Stated another way, when most members of a society exhibit a proclivity to chronically choose moneymaking activities over free time and going to work over spending time with family (the key component of workaholism), and that nation is not in the midst of an economic depression comparable to the one our nation endured between 1929 and 1939, then something is radically wrong.

Some years ago, an article written by Daniel Goleman appeared in the Sunday *New York Times* business section. After reading my book *The Success Syndrome*, another with a similar theme, and interviewing scores of successful Americans, Goleman had a gloomy vision of a success and wealth-obsessed America that was completely consistent with Schor's:

> Psychotherapists say there are too many young people being coaxed into work habits that throw their lives badly out of balance...to betray their deepest values—a love of family life, perhaps, or simply their basic integrity—as they chase wealth. Many tell their

therapists that they have lost all sense of themselves, that...money has become the main symbol of their human worth.[15]

Goleman's and Schor's perspectives paint a bleak picture. Their views about how American careerists overinvest in their careers to the detriment of their mental health and happiness also point to two problems that you must address if you are to find the wherewithal to turn your passion(s) into purpose and career satisfaction.

Problem #1: As Daniel Goleman of the *New York Times* noted, many Americans claim "they have lost all sense of themselves, that...money has become the main symbol of their human worth." Eighty years prior to Goleman's piece William James said, in a letter to H. G. Wells, "The moral flabbiness born of the exclusive worship of the bitch-goddess success. That—with the squalid cash interpretation put on the word 'success'—is our national disease." If you believe Professor Schor—and you should—the situation described by Goleman and James is growing worse.

Problem #2: If you accept what Goleman, Schor, James, and countless others claim about our national obsession with wealth, you will need to reconsider the goal that I believe prompted you to pick up and read this book. Not only must you break bad personal habits if you are to avoid ending up in a Sisyphean hell, you must also behave in a manner that flies in the face of what you see most people around you doing.

You are aware by now that I am fond of quoting King

Solomon's writings, Proverbs (his second book) and Ecclesiastes (his third and final book). Ecclesiastes, the final recording of Solomonic wisdom, was written after a life begun as a profligate youth, after which he became a fantastically wealthy man. Later in life Solomon became a great man and was motivated to share the following thoughts regarding how he kept moving toward achieving eudaemonia (my word, not his) as he neared death. In Ecclesiastes 2:10–11, King Solomon says,

> *I denied myself nothing my eyes desired; I refused my heart no pleasure. [...]*
> *Yet when I surveyed all that my hands had done and what I had toiled to achieve, everything was meaningless, a chasing after the wind; nothing was gained under the sun.*

In Ecclesiastes the phrase "a chasing after the wind" is repeated several times. Although I am no biblical scholar, I read that phrase as saying, "I wanted all the wrong things (when I was younger)"—that is, behaving in the manner that Professor Schor observed most Americans engaging in, or, more despairingly, not realizing that chasing wealth is no more likely to yield happiness than a rodent on an exercise wheel is likely to get anywhere other than where he was when he began spinning his wheel.

If I am correct and Solomon saw that his subjects didn't care about the warnings they received about chasing after the wind, his cynicism makes perfect sense.

You *should* care about Solomon's admonitions and the host of comparable ones I present in this chapter and elsewhere. Granted, you will have to work hard to change and learn a new career-related modus operandi, but unless you do so and realize that happiness can only be achieved through engaging in what Erikson called generativity or following the prescription for happiness and success offered by Victor Frankl, Aristotle, Mill, and Csikszentmihalyi, you're chasing after the wind.

CHAPTER 6

Entrepreneurism: The Secret to Happiness?

If you want to be happy, set a goal that commands your thoughts, liberates your energy, and inspires your hopes.

—Andrew Carnegie

What is the aspect of Benjamin Franklin's character that enabled him to rise, phoenix-like, from a childhood marked by abuse and privation, to spend his adult years living a life that afforded him access to limitless eustress-generating experiences, wealth, and the adoration of our nation?

Entrepreneurism.

To be clear about how you will benefit from understanding entrepreneurism, the review that follows cannot magically turn you into a modern-day Benjamin Franklin or even a Silicon Valley startup whiz kid. A thorough examination of the entrepreneurial mind-set will deliver an understanding of the psychology of entrepreneurs and will make it infinitely easier for you to emulate, imitate, simulate, or impersonate aspects of their modus operandi when it comes time for you to craft a career that will enable you to find a passion you can turn into purpose, which will position you to enjoy lifelong satisfaction.

It's no coincidence that entrepreneurs are happier than the rest of us. A study of eleven thousand Wharton MBA graduates conducted by two Wharton professors, Ethan Mollick and Matthew Bidwell, revealed that grads who ran their own businesses were happier than those who did not. Surprisingly, the study also revealed that this finding held true regardless of how much money the respondents made.[1]

The good news is that you don't have to be a business founder or owner or work for your own business to benefit from entrepreneurism—you simply have to have an *entrepreneurial spirit*, where you wake up in the morning with passion and drive for the day ahead. This is the kind of hunger that Steve Jobs was talking about in his commencement address to Stanford's 2005 graduating class when he challenged them to "Stay hungry. Stay foolish."

The definition of entrepreneur that I present in this chapter embodies the message in Jobs's directive. The authentic entrepreneur is inherently *hungry*—hungry to achieve, to succeed in ways never before imagined, to revolutionize society for the better. Entrepreneurs are gripped by a passion for achievement that renders any attention paid to nutritional hunger an annoying afterthought. But more about that later.

To orient you to this finding I want to address a couple of misconceptions about being an entrepreneur before getting into the formal start of this chapter.

A person is not entrepreneurial simply because she bristles at the thought of being managed (controlled) by a boss, decides to prevent that dreaded fate by buying a business or franchise that she operates on her own, and thus ensures minimal interaction with corporate suits forever after. Designing that sort of career path is called *soloing*; being an entrepreneur involves much, much more. Yes, being autonomous is one (among several) hallmarks of the entrepreneurial personality, but it is no more a definition of an entrepreneur than *autonomous* is a definition of cat, the animal whose penchant for independence and behaving in an autonomous manner gave us the idiom *herding cats*, the sine qua non of an impossible managerial task.

This chapter will forever disabuse you of a potentially daunting misconception that to be entrepreneurial and enjoy around-the-clock eustress you will need to create the next Facebook or its wealth-generating equal. That is absolutely, unequivocally, not the case. What you will need is an understanding of what stimulates an entrepreneur's hunger; you must appreciate that it takes a *feeling of deep desire; a passion*—an anticipatory excitement akin to "I want to do this with every cell in my body"—to be able to go off on one's own to craft a career.

You see, the key to being entrepreneurial is finding what all entrepreneurs find before they start their journey: what the German philosopher Friedrich Nietzsche called a *why*. As he put it, "He who has a why to live can bear almost any how." I'll help you find the why within you—a problem or wrong (social injustice) you want to right; a reason to show him/them they were wrong for hurting you or wrong about your worth. Once that is done, learning how to bear the "how" is child's play.

> A way of life cannot be successful so long as it is mere intellectual conviction.
> It must be deeply felt, deeply believed, dominant even in dreams.
>
> —Bertrand Russell

> Entrepreneurship is neither a science nor an art. It is a practice.
>
> —Peter Drucker

I am a stickler for definition or diagnostic rigor. So here, once again, I want to remind you that, per Socrates, "The beginning of wisdom is the definition of terms." But now, to my utter chagrin, I will not be able to give you a universally acceptable definition of *entrepreneur* and *entrepreneurism*. An exact definition of these terms is a near impossibility. There are countless definitions of these terms in the academic literature, each purporting to characterize entrepreneurs and what they do in inclusive terms. None achieve that goal.

The good news is that I grappled with my inability to find a comprehensive definition of entrepreneur and entrepreneurism for a long while. In 2000 I moved from Boston to Los Angeles and soon thereafter began teaching a course titled The Psychology of the Entrepreneurial Spirit at USC's Marshall School of Business. My first hurdle was asking myself how I could help my students gain wisdom if I could not give them a definition of terms.

What follows is a distillation of what I did to overcome that hurdle, beginning with a heartfelt thank-you to Dr. Peter Kilby of Wesleyan University for the brilliant manner in which he dealt with the chaos and confusion surrounding defining entrepreneur and entrepreneurism. With his tongue deeply embedded in his cheek, Kilby compared attempts to capture (define) these constructs to hunting for the imaginary animal, the Heffalump, a fictional elephant created by A. A. Milne for the Winnie-the-Pooh stories. As Kilby tells it,

[The Heffalump] is a large and important animal which has been hunted by many individuals using various ingenious trapping devices.... All who claim to have caught sight of him report that he is enormous, but they disagree on his particularities. Not having explored his current habitat with sufficient care, some hunters have used as bait their own favourite dishes and have then tried to persuade people that what they caught was a Heffalump. However, very few are convinced, and the search goes on.[2]

Kilby and others, when being completely serious, noted that the word *entrepreneur* derives from a French verb, *entreprendre*, meaning to undertake. However, over time, the noun form, *entrepreneur*, developed and was used to refer to someone who would undertake a business venture that had a special feature: The venture imposed *personal financial risk upon the person who chose to undertake it*. Consequently, willingness to assume risk became a defining feature of the entrepreneur. (More on this crucial aspect of entrepreneurial character below.)

After noting these historical mileposts on the road toward understanding entrepreneurs, Kilby stated: "At first glance then, we may have the beginnings of a definition of entrepreneurship. However, detailed study of both the literature and actual examples of entrepreneurship tend to make a definition more difficult, if not impossible."[3] Thus, what I did with my classes and will now do with you is present the most salient defining features of entrepreneurs and entrepreneurism, without an overarching grand schematic that purports to integrate them.

As I considered this problem I realized that not having a proper definition of terms is a blessing in disguise for you. Given that there are no universal, one-size-fits-all definitions of entrepreneur, you are able to be entrepreneurial without conforming to a stereotype or fitting into a template. While some aspects of the myriad existing definitions of entrepreneur are crucial—Schumpeter's, below, being the prime example—there's enough wiggle room in how entrepreneur is defined to enable anyone to claim that self-definition for him- or herself.

Wild Spirits Who Improve Upon the Status Quo

Another contribution to the study of entrepreneurship came when the famed English philosopher and political economist John Stuart Mill defined this process as "the founding of a private enterprise."⁴ The weight of Mill's opinion is doubtless why today's conventional wisdom holds that an entrepreneur is a business builder of any stripe.

Our understanding of what entrepreneurship actually is took a quantum leap forward from Mill's perspective when Austrian-born American economist and political scientist Joseph Schumpeter claimed that the innovation and technological changes developed by a nation's economy come from the entrepreneurs or, as he called them, "wild spirits." He coined the term *Unternehmergeist,* German for entrepreneur spirit, and asserted that "the doing of new things or the doing of things that are already being done in a new way"⁵ was the core contribution to the economy made by entrepreneurs.

Academics who've studied Schumpeter's work maintain

that his view of entrepreneurs is that they initiate innovations in established businesses in order to satisfy unfulfilled market demands. Thus, they hold that Schumpeter defines entrepreneurs as innovators who implement change within markets. Yet in keeping with his notion of entrepreneurs as wild spirits it is important to understand that Schumpeter *actually claims* that entrepreneurs are the agents of *creative destruction*—a theory of economic innovation that refers to the "process of industrial mutation that incessantly revolutionizes the economic structure from within, incessantly destroying the old one, incessantly creating a new one"[6] or "the doing of new things or the doing of things that are already being done, in a new way."

If you add to Schumpeter's theories what another Austrian-born American management guru and author, Peter Drucker, says about the entrepreneur—"The entrepreneur always searches for change, responds to it, and exploits it as an opportunity"[7]—I feel you have all of the academic insights about the Heffalumps of the business world that you need.

What you do not have, and what you must ultimately acquire in order to be able to act entrepreneurially, is a gut-level feel for the modus operandi of the entrepreneur coupled with as much information as you can gather about what an entrepreneur is like as a person. Ideally, you will end up with an understanding of what makes entrepreneurs tick that will enable you to spot one one hundred yards away, and say, "Yup, I can tell by the way he's acting. That's an entrepreneur."

Risk? What Risk?

While it's good to have a gut-level feel for things, the one drawback to that type of understanding is that the objects of your feeling may not share your opinions about them. In my work with entrepreneurs I have never, ever heard one agree with the notion that a hallmark of an entrepreneur's character or personality is that he or she has the courage to initiate business ventures that are fraught with financial risk, which the French and Mill maintained.

Instead, I believe that the hallmark of entrepreneurs—the folks Schumpeter called wild spirits—is that they are just that: wild or, more accurately, unsocialized insofar as having learned to squelch, suppress, or exert control over their feelings, particularly those that pertain to their belief in their abilities, because doing so is the appropriate or politically correct thing to do. It is for this reason that I see defining entrepreneurs as unencumbered, unapologetic risk takers as missing the mark.

What *is* a defining feature of entrepreneurs, psychologically speaking, is that while they do not see themselves risk takers—if you asked an entrepreneur about his propensity to ignore dangers and rush headlong into ventures without seeming to assess risk, he would laugh and call you crazy—their lack of socialization and concern about being PC renders them *ultraattentive to their gut feelings.*

When a person marches exclusively to the beat of his own

drummer, ignores consensus opinions, and mocks or scoffs at the status quo, it may appear that he is risk prone, but in fact that is no way akin to risk taking. Instead, what you see is that the internally (gut) governed entrepreneur knows what he wants, trusts he can get it, feels he should (deserves to) get it, and won't stop striving until he does get it. Where's the risk in acting in accordance with that train of thought? Entrepreneurs are simply obeying their gut feelings and satisfying their hunger to achieve what they want!

Moreover, as Aristotle said, "The angry man is aiming at what he can attain, and the belief that you will attain your aim is pleasant." It is clear that at the start of their careers most entrepreneurs are angry about something or at someone but never turn the anger they feel inward, which would cause them to suffer depression. Instead, *they are energized by anger*; in fact, they flaunt it. They operate in accordance with the pleasant belief that they will attain the aims their anger points them toward because they know how to convert anger into fuel that impels them toward goal attainment. That's not risk taking; that is *supreme confidence*.

This is almost precisely what Cloyd E. Marvin told Daniel Goleman, writing for the *New York Times*[8] in 1986, when he was a director of Harvest Ventures in Menlo Park, California, a venture capital company where Marvin interviewed hundreds of would-be entrepreneurs each year. According to Marvin, "The typical entrepreneur is absolutely sure he cannot fail. Even if he has failed before, he's convinced it won't happen next time—*he only sees the side of the bread with the jelly on it*" (emphasis added).

According to Goleman, that sort of supreme self-confidence is but one of the positive traits coursing through the veins of a typical entrepreneur. Added to the mix are healthy doses of messianic fervor and visionary obsession. As Goleman reported more than thirty years ago, and it is no less true today: "To those who study entrepreneurs, the successful ones are surprisingly alike, mavericks though they may be, with similar emotional pasts and similar skills…[and] *such an intense flame burning inside*" (emphasis added).[9] That flame, in conjunction with being predisposed to not being intimidated by risk or impediments to success, is what accounts for why, if an entrepreneur sees an opportunity that appeals to her, she assumes psychological responsibility for attaining success or enduring failure without hesitation or fear of stepping on toes as she does so.

> There is no "I" in team, but there is an "I" in win.
>
> —Michael Jordan

Another hallmark of the entrepreneurial character is that they crave autonomy and insist upon not being controlled by anyone or anything. Entrepreneurs don't just do what others suffer trepidations about doing without giving their actions a second thought; they do what they want to do on their own terms, without tolerating interference. Why? Once again, they trust themselves implicitly and assume that they won't fail.

One researcher interviewed by Goleman virtually quoted Schumpeter when he said, "The entrepreneur is the wild man in an organization....He pushes the rules to the breaking point. He hungers for a free range; he feels stifled in any organization except his own."[10]

I'll Show Him/Them

In all the years I've worked for entrepreneurs as a psychotherapist and coach or as a consultant to their businesses, the one component of their character that I've found most unique and influential in terms of guiding their behaviors in all realms of life, not just on the job, is what Goleman referred to as an "intense flame burning inside." Actually, more telling than the flame itself is the agent or agency that ignites this flame. You see, a significant percentage of the people who embark upon entrepreneurial journeys, acting with supreme self-confidence, appearing to be impervious to risks, and demanding independence from any form(s) of guidance and/or control do so to achieve outcomes that enable them to make good on their dominant emotional drive: "I'll show him/them."[11]

My personal definition of an entrepreneur, the one I feel best captures the personality of this maverick, is

The entrepreneur has no need to invent anything; all he or she must do is improve upon the status quo in a particular business arena or market. But in order to do that, the would-be entrepreneur must be impassioned and see no impediments to actualizing his or her dream. Above all else, those who thrive as entrepreneurs get lost in their work, sometimes going days without "normal meals," subsisting on the dietary fuel that can be derived from snack foods and caffeinated beverages. Why? Not money, not social status, not power, but to prove to the world that they are, unequivocally, the sharpest knife in the drawer.

Where does this passion come from? The zeal to show the world evinced by entrepreneurs emanates from a deep-seated desire to avenge a hurt or right a wrong. Benjamin Franklin's zeal came from a desire to say to his abusive brother, "Look, you SOB, I beat you at your own game." Virtually all of Steve Jobs's closest associates claim that the trauma of discovering that he was abandoned by his birth parents and a burning desire to show them how wrong they were for doing that to him was the defining feature of his life. (Jobs denied this.) And of course, John Walsh wanted, with an intensity I cannot come close to articulating, to express contempt and hatred to the entire population of criminals who have destroyed the psychological well-being of families forced to live with the pain of having a child of theirs murdered.

The research that Daniel Goleman did for his *New York Times* article on entrepreneurs supports this contention. Specifically, he reported that the I'll show him/them attitude I see as a universal attribute of entrepreneurs was most often a derivative of early (childhood) conflicts with the father of the entrepreneur, but an older abusive brother can serve just as well. Dr. Harry Levinson, the brilliant management consultant, gave Goleman an ultra-Freudian explanation of why entrepreneurs develop their hallmark I'll show him/them attitude: the Oedipal rivalry gone bad. Although this view is dated and ignores roughly 50 percent of today's entrepreneurs—women—Levinson did make one accurate and incredibly important observation:

> There is a smoldering anger that fuels the son's rivalry with the father.... That anger shows up in the entrepreneur's dogged intensity to succeed, holding on, no matter what, coming back from failure to try again and again.[12]

If you qualify Levinson's remarks by noting that the entrepreneur's smoldering anger can be born of any narcissistic injury or self-threat, including, but not limited to, the loss of a loved one, interpersonal abuse (particularly spousal), physical abuse (particularly from intimates), and what Maslow noted is the reason any person would be driven to run away from a job—"being treated as an interchangeable part, as simply a cog in a machine," which yields rage owing to the feeling that someone has cut off half of your growth possibilities—then I feel you can understand the impetus for initiating most entrepreneurial journeys: revenge seeking, payback, or "showing" the party who caused you significant psychological pain.

An Entrepreneur Who Showed Them but Good

If I scared you, above, into fearing that you, a loving, live-and-let-live kind of person who adheres to "Always forgive your enemies; nothing annoys them so much," the advice that Oscar Wilde offered, could never generate the bile needed to fuel an entrepreneurial journey, I apologize. Please do not assume for an instant that the program outlined in the previous several chapters of this book is designed to turn you into the human equivalent of a junkyard dog. Most often, the I'll show him/them flame that fuels passion in entrepreneurs is lit by a spark that is relatively benign in the grand scheme of things,[13] not from horrific trauma such as the one John Walsh endured.

For example, what would you say if I told you that one of the world's most valuable companies got its start when the founder was on a date with a girl who unceremoniously dumped him? Please note: This was the founder's girlfriend, not his spouse, and when you are a nineteen-year-old college student like this kid was, getting dumped by someone you are dating happens with the same regularity as overpartying in your dorm and oversleeping the next day. The only aspect of this entrepreneur's life that augmented the trauma of getting dumped by his girlfriend (insofar as fueling his intense flame is concerned) was that it seemed as though he had a medium-to-large-sized chip on his shoulder born of a desire to demonstrate to the university he attended, and others, that he was an IT wizard/superstar.

If you responded, "That sounds like the guy who created Facebook," you would be 100 percent correct, if you accept the Hollywood version of how this corporation came into being.

In the film *The Social Network*, a biographical drama about Facebook and its founders, the opening scene depicts a life-altering moment for Mark Zuckerberg, at the time the movie opens a nineteen-year-old sophomore at Harvard University.[14] On a date with his exasperated girlfriend, an undergraduate student from Boston University who is doing nothing to hide her frustration with her beau's dissociative narrative, Zuckerberg ignores her nonverbal cues and rambles on about nothing of interest to her. She grimaces at him, and in the movie finally blurts, "Dating you is like dating a Stair-Master." With that she dumps him, and dejected, Zuckerberg heads back to his dorm.

Once back in his room Zuckerberg copes with his crushed ego by filing a blog entry on LiveJournal that consists of making a disparaging comment about his ex; he allegedly says that she is a "bitch." What follows that moment of revenge-seeking, in essence, is this: Zuckerberg, still smarting from being dumped, creates a website based at Harvard University called Facemash that enables visitors to rate photos of female students that Zuckerberg stole from other databases in the university system. (While not shown in the movie, it is worth noting that the website allowed the rating of both male and female students.) Although he was punished by Harvard for doing this, Zuckerberg's entrepreneurial zeal drew the attention of two Harvard upperclassmen, Cameron and Tyler Winklevoss, who invited him to work on a social dating network for Harvard students.

What happens next gets ever murkier, but for some reason after agreeing to work with the Winklevoss twins Zuckerberg teams up with a different friend to build a different social networking website. You know how the story ends: Zuckerberg creates Facebook and becomes the world's youngest billionaire.

When I said, "Zuckerberg creates Facebook," I did not misspeak, but in truth, the concept of a face book is almost as old as Harvard University itself. Long before anyone alive today can recall, universities were distributing, at the start of every academic year, directories (face books) consisting of students' photographs and names to help students get to know one another. Actually, by the early 2000s, many of those face books (by then published online) included advanced features (adopted by Facebook) such as password protection and detailed biographical information. And students could upload and enter information and photographs of their choosing to augment what the university's face book offered.

Writing in *The Harvard Crimson*, Harvard's student-run newspaper, in 2004, Alan J. Tabak noted,

> When Mark E. Zuckerberg '06 grew impatient with the creation of an official universal Harvard facebook, he decided to take matters into his own hands.
>
> After about a week of coding, Zuckerberg launched thefacebook.com last Wednesday afternoon. The website combines elements of a standard House face book with extensive profile features that allow students to search for others in their courses, social organizations and Houses.
>
> Zuckerberg's site allows people with Harvard e-mail addresses to upload their pictures and personal and academic information. Just as with the popular website Friendster, which Zuckerberg said was a model for his new website, members can search for people according to their interests and can create an online network of friends.[15]

Several aspects of this perspective on Zuckerberg's entrepreneurial journey should be noted so you can understand what exactly it is that entrepreneurs do and don't do.

Anger—a substantial amount of it—appears to be what sets Zuckerberg's entrepreneurial journey in motion. The creator of *The Social Network* provides evidence that Zucker-berg was "out for revenge" against the girl who dumped him when what is now Facebook was first conceived. Responding to a commenter who said she was disappointed in the "lack of a decent portrayal of women," the movie's screenwriter, Aaron Sorkin, wrote,

> Believe me, I get it. It's not hard to understand how bright women could be appalled by what they saw in the movie but you have to understand that that was the very specific world I was writing about...Mark's [Zuckerberg's] blogging that we hear in voiceover [in the movie] as he drinks, hacks, creates Facemash and dreams of the kind of party he's sure he's missing, came directly from Mark's blog...I used Mark's blog verbatim. Mark said, "Erica Albright's a bitch" (Erica isn't her real name)....*Facebook was born during a night of incredible misogyny. The idea of comparing women to farm animals, and then to each other, based on their looks and then publicly ranking them. It was a revenge stunt, aimed first at the woman who'd most recently broke* [Mark Zuckerberg's] *heart (who should get some kind of medal for not breaking his head) and then at the entire female population of Harvard* (emphasis added).[16]

While I cannot be certain about the genesis of Zucker-berg's entrepreneurism, given what has been written about him and presented in *The Social Network*, it could be said that he followed Schumpeter's guide to *creative destruction*—the doing of new things or the doing in a new way of things that are already being done—verbatim. Here's what the *Harvard Crimson* article about Zuckerberg reported to substantiate this contention:

> Lisa H. Feigenbaum '04 said that she joined thefacebook.com because it provided an open alternative to the password-protected House facebooks.[17] "If there was a situation where you needed to identify someone for an organization or a meeting, it would be very helpful," she said. Zuckerberg said that the most innovative feature of the site is that people can search for other students in their classes so that they can branch out to form friendships and study groups.[18]

In addition to revenge, Zuckerberg seemed to be driven by an urge to show the administrators of Harvard University he was smarter than they were. This, at least, is what Zuckerberg told *Harvard Crimson* reporter Alan J. Tabak, whose article about the new Facebook website was subtitled "*Facemash creator seeks* new reputation *with latest online project*" (emphasis added). In his article, Tabak quoted Zuckerberg: "Everyone's been talking a lot about a universal face book within Harvard...I think it's kind of silly that it would take the University a couple of years to get around to it. I can do it better than they can, and I can do it in a week."[19]

But that was then. More recently Zuckerberg seems to be motivated by something else—a drive to use his vast wealth to make a positive (and, I would venture to guess, a long-lasting) difference in the world. On December 2, 2015, most major news outlets reported that Mark Zuckerberg and his wife, Priscilla Chan, MD, announced that they will put 99 percent of Mark's Facebook shares into a new philanthropy project focusing on human potential and equality. The announcement came in the form of a letter to the couple's newborn daughter.[20]

Prior to this monumental gesture—Warren Buffett said when he got word of the announcement, "Mark and Priscilla are breaking the mold with this breathtaking commitment"[21]— Zuckerberg gave evidence of the fact that although Facebook may have had misogynistic beginnings, its founder quickly evolved into a mature entrepreneur who can proudly boast a surfeit of healthy narcissism. When he was twenty-six years old—seven short years after posting a hate-filled entry on his LiveJournal blog that maligned the girl who dumped him— Zuckerberg signed the Giving Pledge, an initiative that came into being as a result of conversations that Bill and Melinda Gates and Warren Buffett had with major philanthropists, which invited the world's wealthiest individuals to commit to giving more than half of their wealth to philanthropic efforts over their lifetime or in their will.

Zuckerberg is an extremely positive example of how a person who was hurt can initiate an "I'll show him/them" entrepreneurial venture, have it become wildly successful, and not become hubristic. How and why? Dr. Pricilla Chan is a big part of the how, and the why—this is informed guesswork—were Mom and Pop Zuckerberg. At some point in time I'm certain they told their son, as the Beatles advised, "Money can't buy you love" ... or happiness, self-esteem, and a host of other closely related positive feelings.

What *does* enable you to experience love in an extra-special way (because it is superimposed on a *healthy hunger for eustress* that you are actively gratifying), is not being hubristic. Once you understand this, you are well on your way to turning a sense of purpose into career satisfaction.

Turning Entrepreneurism into Happiness

While I am 100 percent of the opinion that Mark Zuckerberg is a prototypical entrepreneur in the healthiest sense of the term, I fear you might be asking, "So he's giving away the lion's share of his money. He's no Benjamin Franklin when it comes to being generative...." If you did you'd be accurate despite how much a part of the fabric of our daily lives Facebook has become, for most.

On the other hand, if being entrepreneurial in the manner Franklin did it has a special appeal to you, allow me to suggest that you heed what Steve Jobs, a man who is on everyone's Top Ten Entrepreneurs of All Time list, had to say about being entrepreneurial:

Unless you have a lot of passion about [an entrepreneurial venture], you're not going to survive....So you've got to have an idea, or a problem or a wrong that you want to right that you're passionate about; otherwise, you're not going to have the perseverance to stick it through. I think that's half the battle right there.[22]

So, commit yourself to righting a wrong, *any* wrong—albeit one a tad more significant than getting dumped by a girlfriend—and you will likely find yourself doing something that is both fulfilling and entrepreneurially rewarding. If wrongs are something that, at the moment, you would rather not focus on, then simply think about a group you identify with—ethnic, gender-based, religious—and ask what you can do to help fellow members solve their problems. This is an ideal tack to take if you view yourself as perennially seeing glasses as half full (versus half empty), and it satisfies the *Qui bono?* issue given that by helping in-group members you cannot help but move toward achieving eudaemonia.

And don't fear that you have to do something heroic to be impactful, generative, and psychologically rewarded. Your help can be as simple as teaching almost anything, or assisting in more diverse tasks—from transportation to translation—than you can imagine. All that you should avoid, because it will not yield eudaemonia, is writing a check to a charity and concluding that you have done enough. Yes, charity is a boon to those in need, but I'm trying to help you do good and feel good simultaneously. Don't stop tithing to worthy causes, but after doing so, teach, mentor, coach—that will put you on the track toward entrepreneurial gratification because as you immerse yourself in addressing what others need to make them whole, your creative juices will flow with more intensity than you can imagine.

CHAPTER 7

The Devil Is in the Details

For the things we have to learn before we can do them,
we learn by doing them.
> —Aristotle, *The Nicomachean Ethics*

You don't learn to walk by following rules.
You learn by doing, and by falling over.
> —Richard Branson

The quotes above, made 2,300 years apart, convey a message that is irrefutable. As a parent, coach, or advice book author, you do all you can to help your charges do things the right way, yet nothing can prevent them from falling on their butts while they undergo the process of authentic learning.

I know this to be true and accept it, but what bothers me is that some people will fall, and while sitting on their butts, have a real tough time figuring out what to do next. Often, like a rat in a Skinner box, they'll struggle through a sequence of trial-and-error learning responses and ultimately end up being okay. But to the extent possible I want to preempt the need for you to go through that sort of struggle when you implement the Three-C Program that follows. That's why this chapter was written.

Candidly (and in fairness to you), many of the topics I discuss in this book are very complex and cannot become integrated into your way of viewing the world as automatically as, say, learning that a chocolate-covered banana tastes better than either chocolate or a banana alone. Tasting a chocolate-covered banana isn't remotely a religious experience, but if you're like me, after your first bite of that treat you'll be hooked.

In stark contrast, there is no chance that after learning all the reasons why expressing anger is good for your health (if done properly) and that holding anger in is deleterious to your health, you will instantly turn into a person with the ability to be assertive in an ideally balanced manner—not too tough, not too mild. Going from insight to action is just one of the challenges you will have to surmount when you initiate the Three-C Program I've designed to enable you to turn passion into purpose and career satisfaction.

What follows are two examples of the best cause-driven entrepreneurial endeavors programs I am aware of, created by people who actually suffered from the problem they are seeking to redress. If you were to design an enterprise comparable to either of these after mastering the Three-C Program,

I would be as elated for you as you would be for yourself. I say these are the "best" entrepreneurial responses to anger because the founders of these programs suffered tragic loss and could have sought justice the old-fashioned way—an eye for an eye—but did not. Because they did not, and because they had to do something with their rage or they would have imploded, they converted it into adaptive, pragmatic, I'll show him/them passion that became their purpose in life. Above all else, what these people did is take anger and convert it into the fuel that enabled them to find career satisfaction and achieve eudaemonia to the extent possible after having their hearts broken.

On May 3, 1980, in Fair Oaks, California, Cari Lightner was walking to a church carnival with a friend when she was struck, and ultimately killed, by a drunk driver. The aftermath of that event for the victim's mother, Candy Lightner, was incomprehensibly traumatic, but when the police officers who were dealing with the perpetrator—a man who had earlier been arrested for drunk driving—told Ms. Lightner that the driver likely would receive little punishment for killing Cari, she was transformed.[1] Lightner became enraged. She decided to channel her anger and grief into fighting drunk driving. "Death caused by drunk drivers is the only socially acceptable form of homicide," she told *People* magazine. So, four days after Cari's death Lightner started up a grassroots organization to advocate for stiffer penalties for drunk driving. She quit her job and used her savings to fund Mothers

Against Drunk Drivers (later known as Mothers Against Drunk Driving, MADD).

Before a drunk driver murdered her daughter, Lightner claimed she was totally disinterested in politics. "I wasn't even registered to vote," she told *People* magazine. Yet after enduring an unimaginable tragedy, Candy Lightner was indefatigable in her quest for social reform. Once she decided to channel her anger into the passionate pursuit of raising awareness about drunk driving and its consequences, Lightner was a human dynamo. She hounded California governor Jerry Brown on a daily basis until he launched a commission on drunk driving (to which Lightner was appointed), and, later, owing to her status as a leading activist on drunk driving issues, President Ronald Reagan appointed her to the National Commission on Drunk Driving in 1984.

Through MADD, Lightner helped get new anti–drunk driving legislation passed in several states as well as nationally. One of the MADD's most significant accomplishments was spearheading the movement to raise the legal drinking age to twenty-one. Because she was an excellent role model, Candy Lightner's activism inspired her daughter Serena to form the group SADD—Students Against Drunk Driving.

In 1985, owing to a conflict with MADD's governing body over alleged improprieties, Lightner left the organization she founded. Nevertheless, she never stopped her inspirational work as a social activist and speaker. In addition, in 1990 Lightner wrote the book *Giving Sorrow Words: How to*

Cope with Grief and Get On with Your Life, an obvious effort to help victims, like she was, cope as effectively as possible.

A year after Candy Lightner's life as she knew it was totally transformed by the death of her daughter, John Walsh was a partner in a management company that built high-end luxury hotels. He was designing a resort project on Paradise Island, Bahamas, that he saw as being the crowning achievement of an already stellar career, and was doubtless a happy man. Fate intervened, however, on July 27, 1981, to change Walsh's life forever, as noted previously. On that day his son, Adam, was kidnapped and murdered.

Although Walsh was consumed by rage and grief over the loss of his son, rather than seek to personally exact revenge on the man who took his son's life, he channeled his anger into a passion and a purpose he put into practice in an incredibly entrepreneurial way. He did not seek revenge on the criminal who killed his son; he sought to exact a form of socially sanctioned revenge on all criminals by crusading for new laws to protect missing and exploited children and their families.

Moreover, now that he had been gripped by entrepreneurial fervor after successfully campaigning to enact two federal laws designed to achieve those ends, Walsh became even more entrepreneurial: He created a TV program, *America's Most Wanted*, which has helped bring more than a thousand criminals to justice. He also created a line of instructional DVDs to promote child safety and a variety of related products, all with the goals of helping families endure the pain of having a child murdered and helping police put away murderers.

Lightner and Walsh are amazing people. They weren't tutored, told by some expert, "You'll flourish, in the long run, if you convert your anger into passion and become entrepreneurial," but they did so. In fact, their reaction to anger could serve as a prototype of how a person should comply with two key elements of Aristotle's criteria for how to be angry in the appropriate manner:

- Be angry with the right person.
- Be angry for the right purpose and in the right way.

Be Angry with the Right Person

Of all the points in Aristotle's directive regarding the right way to be angry, this point, as I noted above, is by far the most important. Actually, for your purposes, as illustrated by Lightner and Walsh, *being angry with no person in particular is the right person.* By that I mean that although Lightner and Walsh may have felt "I want to kill the person who did this to me, the person who killed my child," they never acted on that feeling. Instead, both grieving parents erased the face of the person who perpetrated the horror against them, considered the perpetrator as part of a class of malignant individuals, and then directed their anger at that class of people in a constructive manner: attempting to stop drunk drivers from ever again doing what was done to Candy Lightner and preventing kidnappers/murderers (and later other criminals) from doing what was done to John Walsh by assisting police in achieving their capture.

Commonsense reasoning—as well as the Bible (Exodus 21:24)—would have justified Ms. Lightner's going to the home of the drunk driver who murdered her daughter and blowing him away with a shotgun. That is what the *lex talionis*—the law of retaliation, an eye for an eye, which claims that the punishment should fit the crime in both kind and degree—would authorize her to do. And had Candy Lightner subscribed to that doctrine and done away with the man who murdered her daughter, she would have doubtless felt great...momentarily.

There is often a feeling of great relief or even joy when you exact retributive justice, regardless of how it is obtained— via physical assault, lawsuits (e.g., for wrongful death, negligence, or related crimes), or even public shaming. However, although prevailing in an action aimed at securing *lex talionis* can feel uplifting, the relief is short-lived and barely palliative at best, and then it's gone. The pain of your loss returns, only now it is worse than before because you wonder, "I avenged the loss, I'm supposed to feel better, but I don't."

This reaction to expecting an "intervention" to have a positive impact on how you feel and discovering that it does not have that effect—it actually does nothing positive for you in a substantive manner—is called a *negative placebo effect*. In addition to accounting for why bogus medical interventions often make people feel worse than they do when they receive no intervention at all, the negative placebo effect represents an empirically validated explanation for why the law of *lex talionis* causes you more harm than good. Here's how a negative placebo effect works.

Traditional, or *positive placebo effects*, are obtained when, for example, a person ingests a pill that cannot have a salutary effect on a problem he is experiencing, yet the intensity of his symptoms diminishes. The positive placebo effect works as it does because the expectations of favorable outcomes harness forces within a person's mind and body that actually bring about imagined outcomes. It's well known in psychology that we can convince ourselves of many things, even that a physical symptom will be relieved if we believe that this particular outcome will come about.

The so-called negative placebo effect occurs when, quite literally, the positive placebo effect boomerangs: Your mind gets prepared to experience a favorable effect or outcome but it doesn't occur; the pill that should relieve a symptom produces no positive consequences. What happens next under these circumstances is that the person seeking relief will most often infer that his disorder is worse than originally imagined.

The reasoning that generates the negative placebo effect goes as follows: "If I felt horrible before the doctor gave me the medicine that was designed to make me feel better, yet

I do not, that must mean that I was really bad off prior to taking the pill. Otherwise, I'm getting sicker; I could be suffering a progressive disorder that grows more severe over time since I feel as bad now as I did before I consumed the curative agent."

Following the law of *lex talionis* can precipitate the most incredibly intense *reverse placebo effect* imaginable: You expect that relief from your anguish will ensue from exacting revenge against the person who traumatized you, but an eye for an eye doesn't give you more than a moment's worth. As Confucius observed, "Before you embark on a journey of revenge, dig two graves." This philosopher understood that you'll need the grave earmarked for you because when the suffering born of your original trauma is compounded by a reverse placebo effect, your anguish is amplified.

With regard to Aristotle's admonition to "be angry in the right way," I hope you see why using anger to fuel a passion or a cause is what he means. This is not simply because *lex talionis* causes more harm than good. The right way to be angry is to channel anger into a cause and sustain that cause, because as you sustain the cause you are invested in—i.e., as you initiate an entrepreneurial journey and it evolves, naturally, into an expanded realm of activities—two positive outcomes result. You experience flow on a regular basis, and the secondary gains or auxiliary rewards that accrue from involvement in a cause you pursue simply because of its intrinsic rewards supplement the eudaemonia you experience.

I've never spoken to John Walsh, so what I'm about to say

is conjecture, but I would bet that, relative to his work in hotel development, the number of days he experienced flow as he was creating *America's Most Wanted* and expanding its activities made the career he had for the six and a half short years that his son Adam was alive feel like being in a Sisyphean hell. I'm not saying that John Walsh was happier after Adam was kidnapped and murdered than he was when Adam was alive; not remotely. What I'm saying is that his work on the project he used to harness the anger he felt in reaction to his son's kidnapping and murder was infinitely more engaging and capable of evoking experiences of eustress or flow than his work in hotel development and management.

This conclusion is easy to reach if you recognize that what he was doing for the memory of Adam was absolutely, 100 percent motivated by intrinsic factors. Entrepreneurial efforts to honor his son were their own rewards. Walsh described his hotel development and management career as rewarding, but I would bet anything that, when Adam was alive, had John Walsh been asked to limit his hotel developmental work to building projects for use by the Habitat for Humanity organization, not luxury facilities, Walsh would have helped, but only on a limited basis (that is, time permitting), and without the experience of flow.

In *The Adventures of Tom Sawyer* Mark Twain observes, "Work consists of whatever a body is obliged to do. Play consists of whatever a body is not obliged to do," which goes a long way toward explaining why entrepreneurs like Alexander Graham Bell could work 24/7 on an idea they feel will be a breakthrough yet could not invest an hour in cleaning the guest room in anticipation of a visit from a family friend. This is Twain's insight: You cannot reward a person into doing anything passionately. If you want engagement in work you must either find a person who is passionate about it or find a person who is in desperate need of money who will do the job, in a barely passable manner, then flee the scene.

An entrepreneurial career has the exact opposite effect on a person. First, an entrepreneurial career is naturally self-propagating. By this I mean it develops new ventures as it matures. If you have ever grown strawberries or seen them grow or can imagine them growing, follow me. As the plant matures it sends out a number of long, leafless stalks called runners that each contain the stuff of a whole new strawberry plant. You cut them off—doing so actually benefits the primary plant since they sap energy from it if not detached—and plant them. Add water, don't fertilize until they grow, some sunlight, and you have more strawberries!

Candy Lightner went through a comparable process. She first campaigned for tougher laws against drunk drivers. People who met her while she was campaigning—not looking for new friends, just doing her lobbying thing—asked her, "Hey, Candy, you're doing the Lord's work. Would you speak to my church, PTA group, Elks lodge, et cetera?" She was serving as a role model for them to understand what community activism is about while she was raising awareness of the dangers of drunk driving. When she was doing that, someone in one of her audiences suggested, "You know, Candy, we should start an effort to raise the drinking age to keep kids from drinking and driving." *Bingo*, another propagation! But even before she gets that initiative off the ground, a police officer who happens to be a member of a PTA group she's addressing asks her after her talk, "You know, my precinct could use your help." *Bingo*, another propagation.

Bottom line, Candy is in a state of flow doing what she can to minimize the damage done by drunk driving, and naturally, without aiming, she is being deluged with rewarding social interactions and learning that her efforts are generative—making the world a better place for the next generation.

Oh, there's a final extra added benefit to this modus vivendi. Recall that Aristotle claimed that eudaemonia is only authentic if you pursue it for life? Entrepreneurship, with its self-propagating offshoots, functions the same way.

Most People, Sadly, Cannot Channel Anger in Adaptive/Entrepreneurial Ways

There is one more aspect of what Candy Lightner and John Walsh did right—actually, in the most ideal manner possible—when channeling their anger into entrepreneurial endeavors that I want to make as salient as possible. It's a detail—wherein the Devil lies—that is a game changer. Fail to grasp this detail or overlook it, and you'll never (a) channel anger adaptively or (b) develop an entrepreneurial enterprise that will enable you to achieve eudaemonia. If you appreciate this detail, respect the need to embrace it, and remain vigilant to constantly appreciating its significance, I have no doubt that you will be able to achieve eudaemonia as Lightner and Walsh did. To help you remember this detail, I dubbed it with a memorable designation: *To channel your anger adaptively, never target it to an entity with a "face."*

Let me explain: Candy Lightner was absolutely 100 percent certain about who killed her daughter while driving drunk. Part of her rage—a large part—stemmed from knowing not only that this man would *not* be punished in a manner that fit the crime he committed, but also, she was told, that there was a better than fifty-fifty chance he would receive a metaphorical slap on the wrist from the judicial system. That, Ms. Lightner had to accept, was the way the court system viewed crimes committed under the influence of alcohol.

If Lightner acted as most people do when victimized in the most horrific manner you can imagine—having a child taken from you—she would have sought to achieve *lex talionis*— as noted above, the law of retributive justice (or retaliation, "an eye for an eye"), whereby a punishment matches the nature of the offense in kind and intensity. Instead, she was able to actively convert her anger into enterprise development because she never went after her daughter's murderer; she never "put a face" (the drunk driver's) on who she was going to "show." She went after anyone and everyone who drives drunk—both genders, all races, all ages. Lightner didn't seek to show someone—an entity with a face. She didn't develop a program that had a delimited target audience. Instead, she sought to show the world what was wrong with drunk driving and what was right with punishing all drunk drivers. Because she didn't seek to "show" something with a "face," she was able to help herself and society in how she harnessed her anger.

On November 10, 2017, a feature film was released about a woman who lost a daughter in a manner that was as brutal and devastating as the manner in which Carli Lightner was killed. *Three Billboards Outside Ebbing, Missouri* ostensibly tells the story of Mildred Hayes (played by Frances McDormand, who won a Best Actress in a Leading Role Oscar for her portrayal), a take-no-crap woman who wants to provoke the local police not to let the rape and murder of her daughter go unsolved. Because seven months after Ms. Hayes's horrific loss, the case of her daughter's rape and murder yields no leads, let alone an arrest of a suspect, she rents three billboards on the outskirts of Ebbing that read, in succession (in a manner designed to shame the police chief), "Raped While Dying," "Still No Arrests," and "How Come, Chief Willoughby?" There is no doubt whatsoever that Ms. Hayes put a very salient "face" on the person she held responsible for thwarting her from achieving justice—and by doing so, compounded her problems as the popular (and terminally ill) Willoughby's social network lined up against her.

Since *Three Billboards* is a made-for-Hollywood movie, it does not address how to channel anger appropriately. Nevertheless, it does present a masterful illustration of how the emotional agony that fuels the drive to seek vengeance is actually augmented, not ameliorated, by striving to achieve *lex talionis*. If Martin McDonagh, the writer-director of *Three Billboards*, intended to demonstrate the validity of Nietzsche's Aphorism 146 from *Beyond Good and Evil* in his film—"He who fights with monsters should look to it that he himself does not become a monster. And if you gaze long into an abyss, the abyss also gazes into you"—he succeeded. He shows how Mildred Hayes grows harder, more isolated, and increasingly embroiled in an ever-widening circle of conflicts as she refuses to abandon her ill-conceived pursuit of justice.

What would I have done to help Mildred Hayes if I lived in Ebbing, Missouri? My only thought—a long shot Hail Mary pass if you will—would be to meet with Mrs. Hayes in the bar she frequented in the movie, give her a copy of *Moby-Dick* by Herman Melville, and urge her to read it. You see, if I was discussing the Mildred Hayes character from *Three Billboards* with friends and wanted a shorthand descriptor for her self-defeating obsession, I would say, "Her daughter's rapist-murderer has become that woman's white whale." Even if you've never read Herman Melville's *Moby-Dick*, one of the most widely studied and best-regarded novels ever written, you are probably familiar with the idiom *white whale*, which is derived from how the protagonist of this novel, Captain Ahab, engineered his self-destruction while seeking to kill the white whale (Moby-Dick) responsible for Ahab's losing a leg.

The woman Frances McDormand portrays in *Three Billboards* could have benefited materially from reading *Moby-Dick* because the book vividly illustrates the self-destructiveness of living out an obsession for revenge, the futility of seeking this form of justice, and how rage takes hold of people in ways that cause them to impute evil to entities that cannot possibly possess or manifest it.

What Melville does masterfully in his book is use the dialogue between the mates on the *Pequod* (Ahab's whaling ship) to deliver commentary and serve as philosophical contrasts to Ahab. My absolute favorite parts of *Moby-Dick* are the tête-à-têtes between Starbuck, the first mate—a very religious man—and Captain Ahab. Here is the key exchange between the two that might have led to break through Mildred Hayes's resistance to abandoning her pursuit of *lex talionis*: Starbuck tries to demonstrate to Ahab that seeking revenge on a white whale is insane since a whale cannot form intent, nor does it act on the basis of emotionality:

> **Starbuck:** "Vengeance on a dumb brute!" cried Starbuck, "that simply smote thee from blindest instinct! Madness! To be enraged with a dumb thing, Captain Ahab, seems blasphemous."

Ahab: To me, the white whale...tasks me; he heaps me; I see in him outrageous strength, with an inscrutable malice sinewing it. That inscrutable thing is chiefly what I hate; and be the white whale agent, or be the white whale principal, I will wreak that hate upon him. *Talk not to me of blasphemy, man; I'd strike the sun if it insulted me.*[2] [Emphasis added.]

Then, again, since Mildred Hayes is a character who does not seem likely to tackle a tome as complex as *Moby-Dick*, I might simply have urged her to consider—as I've urged you to consider—what Confucius had in mind when he asserted, "Before you embark on a journey of revenge, dig two graves." Given the fact that after putting up her billboards, Hayes's life went from horrid to worse than horrid, there is no doubt that Confucius's advice would have rung true. Whether it could have changed Mildred Hayes by pre-empting her self-defeating campaign is something we can never know.

The Path Not Taken by Captain Ahab

Were Mildred Hayes alive and miserable in Ebbing, Missouri, today, I would urge her to do a Google search on Bethany Hamilton and learn all she could about this incredible young woman. Bethany Hamilton didn't lose a leg to a white whale;

she lost an arm to a tiger shark that attacked her the morning of Halloween 2003 when she was thirteen years old, one year after she finished first in the Open Women's Division competition sponsored by the National Scholastic Surfing Association. Soon after Hamilton was attacked and nearly killed by the shark, fishermen caught and killed the fourteen-foot-long predator that maimed her. Was this the revenge Hamilton needed to move on with her life? Not at all. The killing of the shark was irrelevant to her.

Hamilton never sought nor needed *lex talionis*. Actually, the only fight Hamilton fought after she lost her arm was the fight to return to surfing. She was back in the water, preparing to surf competitively, not just for recreation, twenty-six days after the attack. I'm not a surfer, but what I've read about Ms. Hamilton is that if you did not see that she was missing an arm, you would not know that she was maimed when watching her surf. In fact, a year after the extraordinarily traumatic event that nearly took her life, she once again finished first in an NSSA competition.

As a competitive surfer Hamilton has no need to build an entrepreneurial business, but she is pursuing an entrepreneurial journey by devoting a significant portion of her life to motivational speaking, writing, and moviemaking, all to convey the message, "Who cares if you are physically flawed? What matters is what's inside." What I find most admirable about Hamilton is her leadership role in the Beautifully Flawed annual weekend retreat for females between ages fourteen and twenty-five. This event, for girls and women who have lost a limb or limbs, helps attendees bond by following a training program that Hamilton developed to enable female amputees to gain a positive self-image.

Something the Field of Psychology Cannot Explain, but Religion Can

To be wronged is nothing, unless you continue to remember it.

—Confucius

Everything you read about Bethany Hamilton, as well as what you learn about her from the movies she has made, indicates that she was seemingly unfazed by her trauma. Of course, that is not entirely true. How can anyone lose a limb and not be upset at minimum and incredibly disturbed at worst? But to all outward appearances Hamilton was able to move on with an amazing equanimity. How this happened is no mystery at all: Bethany Hamilton is a woman with incredible strength of character that she attributes to her unwavering faith in God.

If you understand people who are as *authentically*—that's the key word—devoted to and trusting in the Lord, you have an important insight into why people who feel this way are more likely to achieve the type of success I describe in chapter 5: Psychological fulfillment as described by Aristotle, Frankl,

Csikszentmihalyi, Lao Tzu, and countless others, born of living well by not acquiring much, save for interconnectedness with people they nurture and receive nurturing from.

You will also understand what happened to Hamilton between being rescued from the shark attack and her hospital stay. Specifically, you will realize that there is no possibility that Hamilton—a beautiful thirteen-year-old stellar athlete at the time she had her left arm ripped off her body, leaving her with a permanent scar—didn't feel angry, out of her mind, bewildered, terrified, delirious. How could she not? However, during the time from the attack to well before her discharge from the hospital, something that was a core component of Hamilton's life for the thirteen years she was alive, apart from surfing, calmed her and actually gave her direction: her faith in God.

When the press became aware of Bethany Hamilton's story—how this poster girl for competitive surfing survived a near-fatal shark attack and returned to her sport to become a champion again—they swarmed her like jackals on a carcass. Hamilton was either too private, shy, humble, or all of the above to warm to this type of attention. When it finally exhausted her she wrote a book, *Soul Surfer: A True Story of Faith, Family, and Fighting to Get Back on the Board*[3] with authors Sheryl Berk and Rick Bundschuh.

Please examine the title of Ms. Hamilton's book carefully. Note the words *faith* and *family*, and consider how they can explain Hamilton's ability to endure, with a serenity that is only available when a belief in a higher power pervades your life, a trauma that could have driven many people crazy. That's *higher power,* not necessarily Jesus Christ, Muhammad, or Buddha. Actually, higher power needn't be based in religion at all. According to Dr. Viktor Frankl, "The more one forgets himself—by giving himself to a cause to serve or another person to love—the more human he is and the more he actualizes himself."

For the forty years I've been professionally involved in psychological studies and practice, I have been astounded, time and time again, at the manner in which authentically religious people are able to face and overcome adversity without acting out angrily, while most of those who lack faith become enraged. Because I am a psychologist first and a student of religions secondly, I explain this by pointing to how religious people either understand the value of *forgetting themself,* or do it naturally because they authentically believe that their self is insignificant relative to a higher power. When you see it occur, you know that those who can forget themselves cannot, or will not, become angry. The reason is simple: Anger—which, you recall, is an *affront to the ego,* not physical pain—cannot burden you if your ego is subordinated to the Lord.

As I've said, my career has always been focused on various aspects of a question that has perplexed scholars since the dawn of time: Why does material wealth fail, with astounding regularity, to enable a person to lead a flourishing life?

My initial attempt to answer that question in book form

resulted in *Time* magazine publishing a Q&A profile of me in 1991 that I mention only because of an answer I gave to a question posed to me that relates to how Bethany Hamilton was ultimately able to flourish.[4] At the time I referred to problems that insider traders like Michael Milken and Dennis Levine were experiencing as the Success Syndrome. The reporter concluded our interview by asking if the Success Syndrome is curable. Here's the exchange (emphasis added):

Q. What's the cure for a bad case of the success syndrome?

A. What's often missing in these people is *deep community or religious activity that goes far beyond just writing a check to a charity.* You don't have to believe in Jesus or Yahweh or some higher being, but *you have to subordinate yourself to a greater cause.* When you do that, you don't take advantage of people, you don't exploit them.

I think everyone who gets a $100,000-plus job on Wall Street should be assumed guilty and sentenced to do community service as a pre-penalty. I can't emphasize it enough. Take your next class of M.B.A.s coming in the door of Salomon Brothers and sentence them to community service with an organization they identify with. Go, be a part of a community. I've seen it work. It's the only antidote for narcissism. Be an Indian, not a chief. Lose your identity in a group. The healthiest people have that commitment.

It is somewhat embarrassing to read that interview today, twenty-seven long years after it was written. I laugh to myself when I see that I was concerned about people on Wall Street who got a $100,000-plus job, when today assistants to analysts and traders earn more than that. I now recognize that "Indian" and "chief" are not PC referents, and I am also aware that no one will leave school and go to Salomon Brothers: The firm is no more.

These embarrassments aside, you can see that I have been steadfast in my belief that the only answer to the question of why money never breeds happiness is that investing in material wealth is antithetical to the process of achieving eudaemonia as the ancient Greeks described it, which is, fundamentally, subordinating one's ego to a cause and investing in service to a community, not hedge funds.

If you believe this, if you understand the incredible strength of Bethany Hamilton, you will doubtless be able to find an authentic purpose and achieve career satisfaction.

The Flourishing Life

The flourishing life is not achieved by techniques. You can't trick yourself into a life well-lived. Neither is it achieved by following five easy steps or some charismatic figure's dogma. A flourishing life depends on our responding, as best we can, to those things uniquely incumbent upon us.

—Epictetus

According to Aristotle, flourishing is a direct result of striving and achievement. At one point in *The Nicomachean Ethics* he defines eudaemonia as "an activity of the soul in accordance with virtue." I've yet to raise this point—and I will not dwell on it—but being active is an invaluable catalytic agent in pursuit of achieving summum bonum. Aristotle repeats over and over that humankind is happiest when we are active: when we are acting in accordance with the common good, but also when learning, socializing, or being deeply involved in exploring aspects of the natural world, such as when a nature lover experiences flow by the ocean, in the woods, or climbing a mountain.

But activity alone is never enough to achieve summum bonum. It has to be a component of a goal-oriented endeavor in the way that Csikszentmihalyi speaks of a healthy, flow-arousing endeavor: not playing the stock market to become rich, but playing the stock market to prove you are the sharpest knife in the drawer.

Epictetus recognized this as well, which is why his quote above is so meaningful. When he states that "a flourishing life depends on our responding, as best we can, to those things uniquely incumbent upon us," he is reminding people that duty, obligations, and the like are of paramount importance in a person's quest to create summum bonum. He didn't say "engage in generativity," but that is subsumed under the concept of honoring obligations. He didn't say, as Viktor Frankl famously did, "The more one forgets himself—by giving himself to a cause to serve or another person to love—the more human he is and the more he actualizes himself," but this, too, is assumed in what Epictetus said since he warns, "You cannot flourish by following five easy steps or some charismatic figure's dogma." You have to invest yourself to lose yourself, and following quick-fix self-help formulas are worthless insofar as achieving that goal is concerned.

Here's my final alert, and I'll use Epictetus to help convey it. You have to be impressed that a man who lived between 50 and 135 CE, someone without the benefit of hundreds of years of psychological research to build upon, had the insight to say, "[You will never live a flourishing life] by following five easy steps or some charismatic figure's dogma." Who exactly do you think he had in mind when he said, "Watch out for those charismatic figures?" You got it: Those narcissists who need cheering sycophants to not let the emptiness in their souls implode like some ancient supernova and who, when they can get away from sycophants, cling as tightly as possible to stars whose brilliance serves their need to "associate with . . . special people" since only they can understand the narcissist (per the diagnostic criteria for Narcissistic Personality Disorder).

You are not a narcissist. I know you do not require constant attention, are not preoccupied with fantasies about success, power, brilliance, beauty, or the perfect mate, and I know that you don't expect special favors.

However, a different challenge lies ahead, which is why the quote above from Epictetus is so crucial. I am about to present you with a very straightforward three-part program for implementing the changes you have learned you need to make. Three points; nothing fancy; nothing at all complex asked of you. You will need to be disciplined and practice various exercises, but nothing arduous.

Why am I telling you this? So you do not confuse what I am presenting with a *fix for what ails you* or *dogma*. Everything you derive from the program that follows comes from *you*. You come up with answers, you come to conclusions, and above all, you will test, retest, and re-retest thoughts and beliefs until you find that what you are doing either fits like a glove or makes you feel in the zone or experience flow.

As Epictetus advised in his final remark mentioned above about a flourishing life, achieving it "depends on our responding, as best we can, to those things uniquely incumbent upon us." A commitment to not underestimate the discipline to do all that lies before you is what is incumbent upon you now. The surprise inherent in doing so is that if you are diligent about working the program with all you've got, you'll feel elated when you are through.

CHAPTER 8

The Three-C Program

If you don't know where you are going, you might not get there.

—Yogi Berra

You have arrived at the upshot of all you have learned thus far—the chapter that will walk you through a process that will enable you to pursue summum bonum, the good life, the experience you once called professional success. Since you now know that "aiming for success" yields hubris and dejection, and you know what it means to derive eustress-like feelings of pleasure from the activities you partake in, in two languages—flow and *Wu wei*—you are nothing if not well prepared to find passions within you or, alternatively, identify a wrong you feel committed to righting, and then converting passion into a purpose—with the result being that you feel that self-actualization is attainable.

Can you believe how far you've come?

I can. You started with an aim—probably to find a job you love—and if I did my job well you lost sight of that aim and simply got immersed in the process of learning stuff. Sometime after you started reading because it felt good rather than reading to advance yourself professionally you realized that bagging the "gotta get ahead" attitude was the only way that professional success would be yours, provided of course that you didn't say that to yourself. But if I can assume that you have, in the main, been reading because you are interested in what you are reading, and then came to this chapter flush with new knowledge, my job is virtually done.

Virtually is the key word. I feel that with some fine-tuning you'll be better able to reach summum bonum, provided of course you know that that is a better place to reach than the Forbes 400, all things being equal.

You're probably thinking, "Where's the how-to program?" and that is an appropriate question; it's coming shortly. But since I'm a true believer in observational learning—you learn better when you "see it done" or "see what you shouldn't do" than via instruction, I hope I can get you immersed in two stories that, between you and me, will teach you the program I've developed for guiding you to career satisfaction without having you realize that they are training you. Then I'll give you the steps and techniques for doing what I am certain you are already thinking about doing, or rehearsing, planning, imagining, in your mind.

I ask you to remind yourself of three truths as you continue your learning experience with me:

- **Learning through experience is invaluable, but you need not literally experience something to learn from it.** Reading about another person's experience, putting yourself in her shoes, and trying to feel what she is feeling as you read about her is one of the best applications of *shoshin*, the Zen Buddhist idea of "beginner's mind," that, I am confident, brought you to where you are right now, and why you learned much of what I will be presenting below without realizing it.
- **Ask questions.** Do not believe you—or anyone else—has definitive answers. Be a doubting Thomas as a means of checking what I have told you in this book. Now, apply that doubt to these final, how-to chapters. Why? Because...
- **Expertise closes your mind.** As Shunryu Suzuki, author of *Zen Mind, Beginner's Mind*, asserts, "In the beginner's mind there are many possibilities, but in the expert's there are few."[1]

That notion—"In the beginner's mind there are many possibilities, but in the expert's there are few"—is really important for you to embrace. If you do so it will be a game changer for you in all aspects of your life. Truly, that attitude will do more to facilitate your being able to find career satisfaction than every existing career guide in print.

Because *shoshin* is such a valuable concept, particularly for your health and well-being insofar as your quest for career satisfaction is concerned, I want to illustrate it for you, presuming, as every bubbie psychologist I know would agree, a picture—even a verbal one—is worth a thousand words.

A successful physician, an obstetrician who was renowned in the major US city where she was schooled and remained to establish her practice, was suffering severe emotional distress for reasons she could not understand. She felt embarrassed to seek counsel in the city where she lived and worked, fearing—irrationally, she knew—that, as a pillar of the community, if she admitted to suffering distress it could make her look weak and untrustworthy to some. Thus, thinking "better safe than sorry," she set off on a journey to find the meaning of life and peace of mind far from her home.

After countless miles of travel across an ocean and many mountain ranges she came to a rural town and the hut of a holy monk. After she introduced herself to the monk and told him of her success, her angst, and her quest, the physician asked if she could be enlightened.

The monk ushered the doctor into his hut and began to serve her tea. As he filled the doctor's cup he did not stop pouring. Although the cup overflowed, the monk continued pouring tea as it spilled onto the table and began dripping onto the floor. The obstetrician watched, dumbstruck, until she had to blurt out, "Stop! My cup is full! No more will go in!" With that, the monk said, "Like your cup, you, too, are full, full of your own knowledge, judgments, and opinions. How can I enlighten you unless you first empty your cup?"

My guess is that this parable has been recounted at least a

million times. Maybe ten million, who knows? It's brilliant, as most Zen parables are, and I consider it to be one of the most valuable components of my toolbox.

Every therapeutic technique I describe and explain to you in the chapters that follow, particularly the relaxation techniques, some of which were in use before Christ walked the earth, are known to others, have been used by others, and—with one important exception—are not my creation. Even the one important exception is only my unique combination of well-known therapeutic techniques created by others. I do not believe anyone else has combined them as I have, but who cares if someone has?

• I have employed every technique described below for decades, as have many others. When different clinicians employ the same therapeutic technique in a variety of contexts for unique reasons, each will add his or her personal wrinkle to it. If you read my description of a technique and it sounds similar to, but not the same, letter for letter, as how a published author described it, please understand that it is human nature to adopt and adapt.

• My hope is that what I just said will lead you to feel free to customize, modify, and personalize all the techniques you read about in this chapter. All roads do lead to Rome if you keep the purpose of the technique in mind. This how-to section is, essentially, a recipe, but if you enjoy being a chef, not merely cooking food to satisfy visceral hunger, you know that recipes should be considered orientations rather than

GPS-generated instructions. For example, whenever I cook and a recipe calls for garlic, I double the amount. Granted, this how-to section is infinitely more important to you than, say, spaghetti carbonara is to me, but I hope you follow my analogy: Customizing aspects of a relaxation program is like doubling the garlic in an Italian dish. Modify at will, but don't omit main ingredients, and you'll be happy with what comes out of your kitchen.

The Three Cs

> Make your work to be in keeping with your purpose.
> —Leonardo da Vinci

Since I'm sure you are wondering what exactly this program I keep referring to is about, let me give you an orientation to it. As I thought of how to help you apply what you have learned thus far to your professional life, it struck me that my instruction naturally fit into three modules. Because my search for a catchy mnemonic to name the program came up dry, I decided that since I could describe each module by using a term that begins with the letter C, I would dub the program the Three-C Program. The Three Cs are:

• **C#1: Calm yourself and control your feelings.** Two words that start with the letter *c*, but since both refer to the same concern I consider them to be one concept. This component of the program is exactly what it says: You learn how to achieve a state of calmness and feelings of being in control. You learn techniques that will relax you, and when you learn to relax and know you can make yourself feel relaxed more or less at will, that knowledge enhances your feelings of self-control.

- **C#2: Convert negative feelings (e.g., anger, a wrong you want to right) into passion.** After you learn to relax, this module of the program will extend that skill to demonstrate how being calm and in control gives you skills that enable you to use negative feelings to your advantage. Specifically, by getting into a calm state and learning to focus your mind like a photographer focuses his lens on an object he wants to capture—and capture is an important notion here—you will be able to convert disruptive emotions into useful passions.

- **C#3: Career planning.** This module has nothing whatsoever to do with traditional career planning as in "get a job." It's 100 percent about discovering what you need to do to pursue your purpose. From a different perspective, you can expect that this module will be your guide to flourishing in pursuit of eudaemonia by engaging in entrepreneurial pursuits. You will not find this module in any advice book, but I will back up the training procedures I provide with examples of people who have used them to achieve the good life.

Since I fear that I may have created some ambiguity in your mind about what lies ahead, what follows are two examples of people who enacted step C#3 of the program flawlessly. One example I describe was a client of mine, and the other is someone I never met or spoke to: He fulfilled the aim of step C#3 naturally!

The reason I elected to describe these men to you is that each of them suffered a trauma that I believe led to the identification of a passion that became their sense of purpose. Before you go off on your own, I want you to feel absolutely certain that what I've described does, indeed, work in the real world.

That said, and for the final time, please do not lose sight of the fact that *you do not need to be traumatized, wounded, abused, or otherwise mistreated to follow the program below, or to benefit from the advice presented in this book.* All you need is to find an intense flame inside, which can come from a variety of sources: anything that makes you hungry for doing the Lord's work. Speaking of the Lord, unless he deems it appropriate to put an end to diseases and natural disasters, it's doubtful they will ever be eradicated, so you can (sadly) rest assured that there are enough cataclysms in the world to provide opportunities for entrepreneurial intervention to everyone reading this book and every one of their BFFs, in perpetuity. You get my point.

The men I describe below found purpose from within, but that doesn't make what they are doing any better, in any way, than what you can do if no inner passion is currently making you hungry to fulfill a purpose. The *why* you find to become your purpose need only be, as Steve Jobs noted, a problem, or a wrong that you want to right. You need not save the world. All you need to do is achieve generativity.

Barry Scheck and the Innocence Project

As I was writing this book, right around the Fourth of July, 2017, most major news outlets had one or more stories about O. J. Simpson's impending parole hearing. As a result of this media coverage I reopened the "trial of the century" in my mind and soon became curious about what happened to Barry Scheck, JD. He interested me for a number of reasons, but the main one was how brutally aggressive he was in defense of his client. You may recall that Scheck was a member of Mr. Simpson's "Legal Dream Team," the DNA expert hired to poke holes in the prosecution's case. And poke he did...with a vengeance!

An article in *Newsweek* that ran in 1995 after Mr. Scheck was done questioning Dennis Fung, the criminalist who worked for the Los Angeles Police Department and was charged with collecting blood and other samples from the murder scene, reported:

> The drama played out last week in Judge Lance Ito's courtroom could have been titled *The Terminator* instead of The People vs. Orenthal James Simpson. The destruction of LAPD criminalist Dennis Fung was so complete that Simpson defense attorney Barry Scheck seemed reluctant to end it.... With his New York accent and even more pronounced New York attitude, Scheck assaulted Fung for five days.[2]

I usually would object if someone substituted "New York attitude" for "mean as a junkyard dog," but the *Newsweek* article's use of the phrase was appropriate. I can still see Scheck's face, menacing and contorted. If he had approached me on the street and glared at me like he glared at Dennis Fung twenty years ago, I have no doubt I would have hit him.

After reading about Scheck, however, were I to meet him today I would, very respectfully, try to hug him. Why the change in attitude on my part? What follows is what I know about Barry Scheck, presented to you from the perspective of someone attempting to demonstrate that by getting in touch with his anger, and feeling a passion because of doing so, Scheck developed a well-articulated and unquestionably generative purpose in life.

Scheck's crowning achievement is undoubtedly the founding, in 1992, of the Innocence Project with his friend and law partner Peter Neufeld. The mission of this nonprofit foundation is to overturn, often by using DNA-based evidence, the convictions of people who have been wrongly convicted of crimes they did not commit. To date, the Innocence Project has helped secure the release of more than 350 victims of judicial injustice. Scheck's passion and sense of purpose are captured in a statement he made about why the work of the Innocence Project benefits all Americans: "Indeed, because every one of us is human and all of us are actors in a fact-finding mission, if just one of us makes an error, jumps to a conclusion, or acts on a false assumption, an innocent man can be condemned to a guilty man's fate."[3]

In chapter 6, I explained Nietzsche's idea of having a *why*—the key to being entrepreneurial. As Nietzsche said, "He who has a why can bear almost any how." Scheck's why came to him no later than his freshman year at Yale when he said "That's not fair" to a system of student deferments enabling young white men to be excused from military service while they pursued a college education, while members of ethnic minority groups were drafted. He had to have said "that's not fair" hundreds of times as a public defender in the South Bronx, since citizens living in low-income communities rarely get legal services on a par with wealthy Americans, and he definitely screamed "That's not fair!" when he cofounded the Innocence Project.

The *how* Scheck engaged in to create an entrepreneurial journey involved keeping his day job with the law firm he and Neufeld founded, teaching at the Benjamin N. Cardozo School of Law at Yeshiva University, and donating his services to the pursuit of justice for wrongly convicted people who probably did not have DNA experts as part of their defense team when they were tried for crimes they did not, Scheck demonstrated, commit. If you are wondering if Scheck is a workaholic, no, he is not. And yes, workaholism is a disease, but to all available outward appearances Scheck has no symptoms of it.[4]

To understand the question "What's up with a guy who works as hard and in as many disparate venues as Scheck does?"—as well as the anticipated concern you may justifiably raise, "I get it, 'stay hungry' means driving yourself to an early grave so you don't *realize* how miserable you are," I say, "Clever but inaccurate." Please think back to our discussion of burnout and recall that the symptoms of burnout that are the consensus favorites among academics include intense negative feelings toward work that breeds exhaustion, apathy, cynicism, despair, feelings of helplessness, and everyone's favorite, ennui.

I assure you, if Mr. Scheck were feeling helpless, apathetic about his work, and suffering ennui, no reporter from *Newsweek* magazine would have said about him, "With his New York accent and even more pronounced New York attitude, Scheck assaulted Fung for five days."[5] I'm from New York City; I "know from" (as we say in NYC) a "New York attitude," the prime example of in-your-face arrogance, swagger, and "I'm the baddest dude around" self-assertiveness on the planet. When this is the sort of self you present to the world, you're not suffering burnout; you are on a high.

Which is the precise feeling that Mr. Scheck derives from his entrepreneurial law career that takes him from the pro bono work he does for the Innocence Project to high-profile cases involving obvious instances of injustice (e.g., the infamous case of three Duke University lacrosse players who were accused of sexually assaulting an exotic dancer and then railroaded by a Durham, North Carolina, district attorney who was ultimately found guilty of criminal behavior), to teaching at the Benjamin N. Cardozo School of Law, and much more. Each and every endeavor that Mr. Scheck engages in that enables him to experience eustress, the high or elation we experience from a job well done.

Csikszentmihalyi made the same argument about being intensely active:

> The best moments in our lives are not the passive, receptive, relaxing times.... The best moments usually occur if a person's body or mind is stretched to its limits in a voluntary effort to accomplish something difficult and worthwhile. Optimal experience is thus something that we make happen.[6]

Attaining flow, according to Csikszentmihalyi, is physiologically arousing: He claims that an optimal experience makes people feel "alert and strong"—what Sherlock Holmes sought from his seven percent solution when he could not attempt to solve "the most abstruse cryptogram or the most intricate analysis." A host of other scientists have noted, when describing a "testosterone high," that the same regions of the brain that respond with pleasure to cocaine are stimulated by surmounting a challenge or doing the goal-oriented activities that create feelings of flow.

One of the most valuable insights to come from Professor Csikszentmihalyi's work is how he debunks the notion "I'll work because I have to, have fun on the weekends, and that fun will offset the crap I do on the job." Erik Erikson, who added to Freud's definition of mental health by noting that we need work, love, *and play* (hobbies and avocations), seemed to suggest that we must "have uplifting experiences" to be mentally healthy, but he didn't really push the issues.

Csikszentmihalyi, on the other hand, does. Csikszentmihalyi contends that a life spent alternating between work that makes us feel trapped in a Sisyphean hell and what most people spend their weekends doing—some form of passive leisure activity, such as being couch potatoes watching football, basketball, baseball, tennis, or reality TV shows—causes them to suffer a dearth of stimulation that does damage to their mental health in general and self-esteem in particular.

It is Csikszentmihalyi's contention that if you engage in activities that produce feelings of flow, you are involved in doing things that preclude feelings of boredom. And as I have maintained in virtually every chapter of this book, boredom, ennui, "been there, done that" is the antithesis of a rejuvenating respite. It is hell. As Fyodor Dostoevsky, the Russian author who examined the lives of convicts in a Siberian prison camp in *The House of the Dead*, notes:

> To crush, to annihilate a man utterly, to inflict on him the most terrible punishment so that the most ferocious murderer would shudder at it beforehand, one need only give him work of an absolutely, completely useless and irrational character.[7]

Let me address the benefits of pursuing a passion from one final angle so you can see why Scheck does as many things as he does and, I hope, determine that if you worked as he did you would experience eudaemonia. When you work because you must, you lose the experience of control over your life, a situation that breeds feelings of despondency. I don't care if you call it a pursuing a passion, flow, or *Wu wei*, when you are engaged in activities that you partake of for the sake of the activity—not to fulfill an obligation, eliminate a d-need (the lower levels of Maslow's hierarchy), or obtain money to pay the bills—you enjoy a variety of self-enhancing, esteem-building, health-promoting feelings. All that nonintrinsically rewarding pursuits—things you do for extrinsic rewards—get you are the tangible reward you sought and nothing more. Worst of all, you get zero psychological gain.

That which is done for intrinsic rewards, flow, or *Wu wei* can be and usually is goal-oriented, but the goal is an *ambition*—a passion to do or to achieve an end, through hard work and determination. For that sort of pursuit to yield eudaemonia its goal must be one that yields generativity. Thus, the entrepreneur whose goal is to be the richest person in Silicon Valley may get what he's after, but he won't be as happy as the IT professional who wants to put an end, once and for all, to spam, since all of humankind will benefit from his work. If he earns a billion dollars for his efforts, not only will he deserve it, but, because he fulfilled his ambition and was generative, he'll also be the happiest guy imaginable.

Aaron's Journey through the Three-C Program

Aaron Schneider (not his real name)[8] contacted me after completing his second year as the principal in one of the more prominent private equity firms in Boston. He was making eight figures plying his trade but was plagued by, and feared he would be crippled by, what he called anxiety. Aaron wasn't anxious in the way most folks are—they have a fear of something "out there" posing a threat to them. There was nothing amiss in Aaron's world: He was the top performer at his firm, his wife and children were postcard perfect, and he was an ideal physical specimen.

What I soon discovered after evaluating Aaron was that his anxiety emanated from within, from thoughts that he had repressed, which meant that he had successfully blocked them from his conscious mind. The problem was that something had happened to Aaron that caused the power of his repression to weaken. Something in Aaron's life was heightening the likelihood that thoughts he'd buried—and wanted to remain buried—would break through to his consciousness. That's what his anxiety was telling him although he didn't realize it: "Look out, Aaron, there are cracks in the dam. That stuff may ooze out. . . ."

In *Inhibitions, Symptoms, and Anxiety*, Freud developed the theory of *signal anxiety*, which explains what happens when the ego cannot deal with the demands of our desires. Specifically, anxiety—a highly unpleasant inner state that people seek to avoid—acts as a signal to the ego that things inside the mind are not going right. In Aaron's case, one trigger that caused his anxiety was instantly recognizable: The work Aaron always assumed would make him feel like a Master of the Universe actually made him feel like a mechanic. He said as much to me: "I'm rich. Big deal. I don't enjoy it. Only my wife and kids benefit from the fact that I work like a day laborer even if it is for eight figures a year."

The question Aaron couldn't answer when he and I began working together was, Why did his feeling like a day laborer trigger anxiety? If you're in a job you hate, you quit, particularly if, like Aaron, you are richer than Croesus. When I asked him to consider that fact Aaron's first explanation involved blaming his wife. He said he was experiencing chronic anxiety, feeling as though he was working as a day laborer primarily because of how his efforts to be a stellar provider were received by his wife. What he told me was, "My [expletive deleted] wife spends money faster than a Formula One race-car driver circles the track at the Indianapolis 500, yet never appreciates my efforts, let alone thanks me. Actually, if she's not spending she's demeaning me, calling me a 'workaholic' or belittling me for not being available to her 24/7. It's a double dose of feeling overwhelming futility and frustration insofar as I cannot please her no matter what I do."

That may have been true, but in my experience, it was insufficient cause for chronic anxiety despite being an excellent straw (wo)man for him to attack. Yes, Aaron's sense of responsibility to and love for his family kept him working in private equity, but that loyalty and love were not why he was chronically anxious.

When clients do what Aaron did—use straw men or straw women in extremely adroit ways—you have to be adroit to help them. I began to help Aaron discard his misdiagnosis about his wife's being to blame for his anxiety as follows:

"Aaron, your self-definition in the context of our work—what you tell me is wrong with you—is, 'I should feel like an alpha male but I feel like a loser or, your word, day laborer.' If Ruth [what I will call Aaron's wife] were to blame, you would refer to her as 'that uncaring witch' and claim 'she never appreciates what I do.' That would be the statement a man makes when he wants his wife to see him as John Wayne (in the role of Marshall 'Rooster' Cogburn, from *True Grit*), but, instead, she treats him like he is Deputy Barney Fife (from *The Andy Griffith Show*)."

Aaron got the point I was making and then said, "So why is believing I should feel like an alpha male but not being able to do so causing me to feel nonstop anxiety?" As a lapsed Freudian I naturally asked Aaron about his childhood—a great place to look when wondering about anxiety born of thoughts that are repressed—and the moment he began talking about his parents I knew we had the answer we were looking for.

As a child Aaron was chronically angry with his mother, who demeaned Aaron's father for not providing for the family as he should. Aaron's father worked as a high school biology teacher, a low-paying job, particularly back when Aaron grew up. However, in Austria, where Mr. Schneider emigrated from, he was on the brink of entering medical school when he had to flee because of the Holocaust. When Mr. Schneider left his native Austria, he did not immigrate to the USA immediately, like most of his relatives. He had a chance to make good money working for a friend in Switzerland, so he went there, lived a monastic life, and sent money to a slew of family members less fortunate than he. By the time Mr. Schneider made it to America, where he met Aaron's mother, he had no chance of getting into a medical school. In fact, it took him years to master English well enough to teach high school biology.

One would assume that this meant little to Aaron's mother, because in addition to demeaning her husband she would tell her son, "You'll do well for Mama. You'll be a real man and not fail me like your father does." Even someone who never studied Freud could see the Oedipal issues that sort of rant would have on a boy: being told by a mother he wanted to love that he would definitely defeat the father he loved and wanted to see as his ego-ideal.

Before telling you more about working with Aaron, let me give you a peek inside his mind. Long before he met me, Aaron was incredibly conflicted about feeling as angry as he did toward his mother owing to how, in his words, she "castrated" his father. What gnawed at Aaron was that he saw his father as a loving, brilliant man forced to work in a crap job through no fault of his own. Adding insult to the injury of being underemployed, Aaron's father was constantly beaten down by Aaron's mother, a woman he wanted to love but could not fully, owing to how abusive she was to his father. Because Aaron couldn't comprehend and accept his parents' relationship and his reaction to it, he buried his conflicted feelings and kept layering psychological muck on the burial site every chance he had, until the pain he felt was inaccessible to his consciousness.

That worked until the rewards Aaron derived from private equity ceased to lift his spirits. Essentially, when Aaron fell into a Sisyphean hell, he felt—in his mind, at least—exactly the same way he imagined his father must have felt: "I'm an intelligent guy; why am I doing this crap and not being appreciated for trying to be a good provider?" The moment Aaron became aware of this negative identification with his father, his defense mechanism of repression started to falter and memories of the pain he suffered during his childhood (watching his father get demeaned by his wife, Aaron's mother) threatened to break through to his consciousness. That imminent breakthrough was what his anxiety was signaling him to be aware of.

When Aaron was fully cognizant of what triggered his anxiety, the work he needed to do to complete step C#1 of the Three-C Program was far from over. Yes, getting relaxed and gaining insight into his feelings was the beginning, but Aaron understood that he still needed to learn to control how he reacted. In other words, to convert his anger into a passion Aaron would have to free himself from the gut feelings about his father and the treatment he was subjected to that, had his parents been alive, would have prompted Aaron into taking action—telling off his mother, offering support for his father, and urging him to fight back against his mother. The reason you cannot be poised to act out angry feelings and, simultaneously, identify healthy passions is that acting on anger is defensive: it springs into action to protect the ego against a self-threat. To form the basis of an entrepreneurial enterprise that exists to achieve a purpose, a passion must be self- or other-enhancing if it is to have its desired effects. Step C#1 will show you precisely how this is done.

As a preview of step C#1, let me show you the fundamental procedure that will enable you to become cognizant of a passion derived from a stimulus that was once distressing or anger provoking. Fundamentally, what you learn to do is be calm and relaxed when exposed to a once-disruptive stimulus. For Aaron, this meant being able to dredge up memories of his mother "castrating" his father and visualizing (or thinking about) that experience, while in a calm and controlled state. When a person can do this, the toxic stimulus becomes neutral and can be examined without fear—as one might examine a scorpion preserved in amber.

The procedure Aaron followed (as you will, too, in step C#1) is a "poor man's version" of what is known as *systematic desensitization*. Most often used to treat people who have phobias, this technique works according to the principle that you cannot be physically relaxed and mentally anxious, or vice versa, simultaneously. If you are thinking relaxed thoughts, your body will, correspondingly, be relaxed. If you are tense, apprehensive, or fearful, your body may, because it is an instinctual response, trigger the reaction pattern identified by Hans Selye and called the general adaptation syndrome (GAS). As mentioned in chapter 2, GAS involves the systems (adrenocortical and others) that control and regulate the release of adrenaline into our bodies. These organs are hardwired to react to danger with an alarm response that signals the body to mobilize against threatened harm. That's why chronic anxiety causes the same disorders caused by chronic distress: When your mind cries, "Look out, danger ahead!" even if there is nothing out there, your body triggers the GAS.

Systematic desensitization—the high-end version of what I will train you to do in step C#1—works as follows. Say a patient fears snakes. He or she is trained to relax (in the same manner I will teach you to relax) and, in that state, is presented with a series of stimuli related to his phobia that become more and more like the object he fears most—say, holding a snake—over time. Initially, a relaxed patient who is being desensitized would be presented with a nonthreatening representation of a snake, say, a picture of a cartoon snake that is smiling. With practice the patient becomes desensitized to snakes by relaxing and viewing gradually more realistic stimuli—from photos of real snakes, to snakes in cages that are situated far from the patient, to walking up to a caged snake and staring at it. Ultimately, after several sessions—the exact number depends upon the patient—he or she will be able, in theory, to handle a snake.

Your training will not be as intense or rigorous as what snake-phobics go through, but the end is the same: You will learn to be calm and in control when contemplating anger-provoking stimuli, imagining a wrong in society you want to redress (animal cruelty, for example) or contemplating becoming a contributor to a cause (bringing fresh water to regions in Africa that have little or none), actively and not by simply writing a check. When you can bypass your defenses and are able to think about once-distressing situations that have plagued you, you will have mastered step C#1 of the Three-C Program.

In Aaron's case, it took well over a dozen exposures—seeing and hearing, in his mind's eye, his mother "castrating" his father—for him to identify that what was most upsetting about his parents' disordered relationship was seeing his father weak and wounded. Previously, if Aaron spoke of his parents, he would claim, "My mother made life difficult for me ... it was hard to love her when she was so demeaning to my father." But that was not what hurt Aaron the most. Certainly, what his mother did was painful for a boy to witness, but not as painful, Aaron ultimately discovered, as seeing his father weak and wounded—that is, not fighting back. When Aaron used that phrase with me—"weak and wounded"—I knew that some permutation of it would become his passion.

At the very next session it did. I recall barely getting settled in my chair after ushering Aaron into my office when he said,

Steve, I know you might want me to hold off on this decision but I am positive I want to help Jews fight for respect, dignity, and the roles they deserve here in America. Not to "fight against their enemies" in the

Middle East, but right here, where they immigrate. I want to help them fight for their personal development. If my dad knew how to overcome the fact that he fled Austria without college transcripts, knowledge of English, and a host of other impediments to professional success, his life with my mother would not have been remotely as bad as it was.[9]

Aaron concluded his epiphany as follows: He told me that seeing a man like his father who was brilliant but psychologically beaten, he wanted to establish a foundation for Jewish émigrés to the USA who are having difficulties with the process of enculturation; specifically, insofar as finding work that matched their competence levels was concerned. Over the course of many discussions with me and others, Aaron developed an agency for people who need to learn how to play the system—get credit here in America for scholastic achievements from the *old country*, get equivalency degrees, and the like—without jumping through hoops, paying bribes, or failing to get what they needed to advance.

Aaron evinced a strong entrepreneurial streak in achieving his goal. Rather than set up a fee-for-service counseling service, Aaron provided any Jewish émigré from Israel, Russia, or nations that were once part of the Soviet Union, where most Jewish émigrés hail from, with free placement counseling based on the model created by SCORE. If you are not familiar with the mission of SCORE, it solicits volunteer service from retired executives to offer specialized skills training to young, would-be entrepreneurs lacking the resources to hire expert consultants by utilizing the expertise provided by retired executives. Hence, the complete name: Service Corps of Retired Executives.

The premise of SCORE is simple. Volunteers benefit psychologically by mentoring, according to the principle *"it is in giving that we receive."* SCORE and service agencies like it have proved, as survey studies demonstrate, that mentors derive as much if not more psychological and benefits as protégés do from their interrelationship. Which was precisely the point Aaron made to sell his program to help well-trained Jewish émigrés to the States obtain the skills they need to land jobs they would be qualified for in their adoptive homeland were they not impeded by language, paperwork, and lack of a social network to facilitate access to schools and/or appropriate certification.[10] The final aspect of Aaron's program was creating fund-raising events to make it possible to hire staff able to do the paperwork needed to help an émigré obtain licensure in a specialty trade, to file it, and to prepare for appropriate exams, for example.

One closing note about Aaron, apart from saying that he enjoyed a spontaneous remission of his anxiety: He never even considered leaving his private equity firm once he found a purpose. Today, Aaron sits on the boards of many agencies that promote the welfare of Jews in America, although his primary work is still with his foundation and private equity firm.

I hope the examples of Barry Scheck and Aaron give you

a feel for what you will need to do to identify a passion and convert it into a purpose that will provide you with intrinsically rewarding pursuits that will afford you ongoing career satisfaction. There is still, however, work to be done, from my perspective. Now I want to give you chapter and verse of how to get through each step in the Three-C Program.

CHAPTER 9

The First C: Calm and in Control (Step C#1)

If you can change your mind, you can change your life.

—William James

I wrote this book with the following thought in mind for you, my reader: You need to change. It won't be easy, but it will certainly not cause untoward distress. In this chapter, I describe the procedures you can use to learn to be calm and in control of your emotions and thoughts—the first step toward kicking burnout in the butt.

I ask you to keep one thing in the forefront of your mind as you read what follows: The training materials presented below are the antithesis of a one-size-fits-all tool kit. Nothing in the Three-C Program—save for the discussion that follows about why achieving calm is imperative—is presented as a "must do." Instead, it is "If it works for you, do it." This is not my way of abrogating responsibility for teaching you what I know will help you. It's simply the truth.

> The problem with doing nothing is not knowing when you're finished.
>
> —Benjamin Franklin

Getting calm and feeling in control does not result from doing nothing. It results most often from doing something to clear your mind of thoughts that are causing you distress, or doing something to put your body in a tension-free state in order to prevent physical tensions from causing distressing thoughts and additional upsetting feelings. If your body is relaxed, your mind cannot experience distress, and if your mind is relaxed, your body cannot feel tension born of distress. Calm one system, the other follows.

But what, you may wonder, is the big deal about being calm, above and beyond the fact that achieving that state makes us less likely to suffer a stroke, die of a heart attack, or shout, "Take this job and shove it!" with a stack of bills to pay and no fallback employment waiting in the wings? To answer that question—apart from saying, "That's not enough?"—I want you to consider the words Socrates proclaimed immediately prior to his execution: "The unexamined life is not worth living." The simple truth is that those who cannot achieve states of calmness are condemned to an eternity of an unexamined life.

My advice to you is to not simply heed what Socrates said but to embrace the notion that examining your life, particularly your inner emotional life, is an invaluable skill, arguably the most important aptitude you can develop. The techniques that will enable you to do so are presented in the pages that follow. *Actually, one of the most important skills I will describe below is a form of Socratic questioning, a method universally understood as being an ideal means of getting to the truth of things.*

You may wonder why being calm and in control of your emotions is the precursor, the necessary precondition, to living an examined life. Simply because unless or until you are able to look at yourself being yourself and view your emotions with as much distance and dispassion as possible, you will forever be a slave to irrational, overdetermined, automatic thinking and the like.

In *Man's Search for Meaning*, Dr. Viktor Frankl quotes Benedict de Spinoza, the rationalist philosopher who flourished in the mid-seventeenth century, as follows: "Emotion, which is suffering, ceases to be suffering as soon as we form a clear and precise picture of it."[1] This statement is rife with interpretive potential, but let me give you the thrust of what I believe Frankl meant: If we understand our emotions, which are the reactions we have to the events we experience, and if we can bring those reactions under our intellectual/rational control, we can live a flourishing life.

The reason this is so is because once we bring our reactions to "emotion, which is suffering" under control, we cease to be passive entities pushed around by distressing events.

Moreover, if we gain control over our reactions to the things that distress us—recall that the experience of distress is an eye-of-the-beholder phenomenon—we acquire the ability to exert control over decision-making that, unless guided by wholly rational thought, is typically less than optimally effective, and is often counterproductive.

The myriad favorable outcomes born of gaining increased control over our inner world and/or our emotional life all occur as a direct function of how much we understand our feelings. As Francis Bacon famously observed, *"Ipsa scientia potestas est"*—Knowledge itself is power.[2]

Before proceeding I want to reexamine the William James quote that opens this chapter in light of the insights afforded by Frankl, Spinoza, and Bacon. Rather than accepting the statement "If you can change your mind, you can change your life" whole cloth, I suggest you modify it to read, "If you can change *your emotional reactions to events*—particularly those that evoke fear, anxiety, distress, and anger—you will gain the self-control to change your life."

I promise that this is true, and I promise that it is the key to understanding the lessons I present in this book. All that remains is showing you how to do it.

Relaxation Training

While we may not be able to control all that happens to us, we can control what happens inside us.

—Benjamin Franklin

229

Relaxation training is a generic term used for any of the myriad methods, techniques, and procedures that help an individual become calm or reduce noxious states such as anxiety, distress, or anger. *Myriad* is the key word in the preceding sentence. There are scores of different relaxation inductions—methods that train you to become calm—available to you, and all are targeted at the same goal: enabling you to lower your blood pressure, reduce your heart rate, and decrease the concentrations of chemicals in your bloodstream that are secreted when your body experiences a GAS response—that is, when it goes into fight-or-flight mode.

Period.

Early in my career I was affiliated with the unit of the hospital I was based at responsible for all behavioral therapies, from cognitive behavior therapy to biofeedback to relaxation training. The experiences I had there make me confident that I learned plenty of tricks and special techniques designed to help people calm down—enough to enable a bomb squad technician to whistle while he works.

Moreover, I practice what I preach: To keep my congenitally high blood pressure as low as possible I do relaxation exercises in my office using two sixty-gallon fish tanks and one Tibetan (or Himalayan) singing bowl, a copper bowl modeled after those used by holy men in India to improve health since well before 1500 BCE. It's not that I'm too cheap to buy high-tech relaxation tools, too lazy to use them, or too stupid to know what the state-of-the-art stuff is. My singing bowl and fish tanks *are* state of the art! Let me prove this to you.

A few years ago, the British paper *Daily Express* ran a story that claimed, "Aquariums boost your health." Wikipedia has an entry for Aquarium Therapy. What is this all about? The finding—not the most statistically significant one you'll come across, but nonetheless legitimate—is that people who devote a significant amount of time to watching fish moving around in aquariums looking for food (which, essentially, is their raison d'être) enjoy enhanced physical and mental well-being. Specifically, watching fish moving around in tanks can reduce one's blood pressure and heart rate. Why? The rhythmic, almost hypnotic movement of fish is calming.

Parenthetically, speaking of hypnotic movement, the portrayal of a hypnotist as some beady-eyed Svengali swinging a pocket watch in front of your eyes and murmuring, "You are getting sleepy," is all Hollywood hokum, right? Wrong! It can work. The principle that a swinging watch exploits, along with my angelfish hunting for food, is what is known as *eye fixation*, which, in technical terms, is simply concentration coupled with visual focus.

To rid hypnotism of its mystique, know this: It matters not how you concentrate and focus—focusing on a pocket watch on the end of a watch chain, fish swimming around an aquarium, watching trees swaying in the breeze, or watching a hawk circling in the sky—they all work the same way and can yield the same calming effect. Your eyes *do* grow weary, you *do* feel relaxed, and you *do* become more open to whatever vocal suggestions the hypnotist is giving you (or you give yourself if you practice self-hypnosis). Best of all, when you are hyperrelaxed and your mind is open, suggestions can break through and affect your cognitive processes. Thus, if I were hypnotized and received the message "It would be wise to stop smoking," that suggestion would be more likely to get me to give up my one (wonderful) vice than the pain of frozen feet and hands I suffer smoking outside during New York City winters.

Returning to the *Express* article that claims theirs is the first study of its kind,[3] I hate to quibble, but the findings they report have been a staple of the bubbie psychology literature for centuries. When I first began studying stress and burnout in the mid-1980s, a patient of mine, a dentist, told me that his dental school taught him to put an aquarium (or several) in his waiting room. Why? Because the sight of fish swimming around helps patients calm down before they confront the dreaded drill.

Fish tanks are not the ideal relaxation induction for everyone. Some folks find that if you own an aquarium, algae builds up on all the inanimate matter in the tank, and waste produced by the fish sinks to the bottom, forcing you to periodically remove both. If you do not, the potentially health-enhancing benefits derived from watching fish will ultimately be negated by the distress caused by unsightly slime and a horrible stink permeating the area around your aquarium.

But fear not: You can get the exact same benefits from a singing bowl, which is actually a bell that sits, rather than hangs, and provides harmonic vibrations when struck or rubbed around the rim with a padded mallet. The advantage of a singing bowl over an aquarium should be obvious: no feeding little creatures, no cleaning the environment the creatures live in, plus singing bowls are often decorated with interesting designs and come with cute little pillows, in various styles and colors, for them to rest on.

To operate a singing bowl simply assume a comfortable position, strike the bowl, hear the sound, focus on the sound, and ultimately experience lower blood pressure and heart rate.[4] My singing bowl decorates my desk when I am not using it, but I move it to the floor of my office where, while seated on a mat, I use it to help me meditate. I watch my fish when I take breaks from working at my desk: I simply shut down my computer, turn off my phone, swivel my chair, and watch my fish for between ten and twenty minutes. It's that simple, and as effective as anything you can learn from a guru.

Many of you will probably be hungering for more complex techniques to follow so you can experience really deep, deep, deep, relaxation. You may think that my low-tech relaxation inductions are too simplistic to work. Wrong. The kind of meditative prayer that has been practiced in the Catholic Church and elsewhere for thousands of years can be just as, if not more, effective, for some, as guru-produced meditation training programs. Moreover, the sort of meditation that holy men practicing Eastern religions have been doing for thousands of years, as well as Transcendental Meditation (TM), which came out of the Vedic traditions of India, are incredibly popular, highly effective, and well-researched relaxation inductions that are as effective as any modern technique available for putting your body and mind in a calm state.

And since I raised the issue of ancient relaxation inductions, you should know that millions of people the world over use tai chi and Qigong, two integrative systems of body movement, posture, breathing control, and meditation designed to improve focus, spiritual awareness, and martial arts skills in the same way they have been practiced since long before the birth of Christ, with scientifically proven benefits. In other words, advances in relaxation training look and sound as though they would be value-added over ancient, simplistic techniques, but no research studies have shown that they are.

The bottom line is that any and all relaxation-training inductions, from singing bowls to breathing exercises, are designed to enable an individual to achieve two goals:

• To "face" negative emotions and not become overwhelmed by them.

• To learn to control negative emotions either by neutralizing them (by remaining calm in their presence) or by thinking them out of existence (per Frankl's takeoff on Spinoza's insight).

But wait, there's more, as TV pitchmen say. The ultimate, absolutely most important consequence of relaxation training is that it takes people out of self-focus and either takes them into an external focus or, if you use the terminology of yoga, enables them to achieve a state called *moksha*—a liberation from the self. Here is how Csikszentmihalyi puts it:

> The similarities between Yoga and flow are extremely strong.... Both try to achieve a joyous, self-forgetful involvement through concentration...[5]

What should one concentrate on when striving for self-forgetful involvement? Ideally, our focus should be on nothing, but that is a very difficult goal to achieve. The enemy of achieving states of calm is intrusive thought, and that is more likely to occur when you try to empty your mind completely than when you empty it of the detritus of everyday life by focusing on neutral stimuli.

This is why my angelfish and singing bowl work so well for me: They have nothing in or about them that elicits judgments or emotionally charged associations. The sound of the bowl and sight of the fish hold my attention outside of me, and when intrusive thoughts hit me—and they do—I return my focus to the bowl's sound or the swimming fish. But again, any external point of focus will let you achieve the goal of quieting your mind by ridding it of thoughts that arouse it in negative ways *if you practice directing the focus of your attention outside of yourself.*

Which brings me to a crucial point: If you consider the definitions of happiness with an eye toward seeing how they condemn self-centeredness, and then consider what all relaxation training inductions strive for—a focus on the external world or, per Csikszentmihalyi (who has come up with my absolute favorite way of characterizing what you should aim for by relaxing to achieve calm and control) *a joyous, self-forgetful involvement through concentration*—one thing is absolutely clear: *Excessive self-focus is arguably as bad for one's health as excess drug use, overeating, or name your poison.*

This is why my advice to you is that you view relaxation training as an adjunct to Frankl's unique take on actualization found in *Man's Search for Meaning*:

> The more one forgets himself...the more human he is and the more he actualizes himself. What is called self-actualization is not an attainable aim at all, for the simple reason that the more one would strive for it, the more he would miss it. In other words, self-actualization is possible only as a side-effect of *self-transcendence.*[6]

Dr. Frankl would have been elated if everyone in the world would strive for transcendence by following his advice to straightaway "give yourself to causes" or the service of another person. I am positive that you will soon, as you work through this program, determine how you can best do that.

For now, you need to learn to relax and be calm so you can ultimately learn how to gain control of your emotions.

Before I begin training you, I have one final clarifying note: Thus far all the relaxation inductions I've discussed are designed to empty the mind—compel you to focus out of yourself—based on the premise that doing so will yield cognitions and somatic indications of calmness. There is a possibility that for some people who do not tense up in their mind, emptying the mind will not be the best possible relaxation induction. These people, if distressed, may have no relevant thoughts as to why they are feeling the way they do or what caused them to feel "a pit in my stomach," a "raging headache," or "pressure in my neck, ears, jaw—all around my head."

Those descriptors of distress come from people who *somaticize* their negative emotions. When upset, apart from reporting bodily aches and pains, these people will often attempt to allay their negative feelings by sleeping (escaping), if possible, or using one or another mind-altering drug. There is nothing wrong with these people in any sense of the word unless they drink alcohol or abuse drugs to excess. They are simply stylistically distinct from people who, if they experience tension, ruminate, obsess, or construct doomsday scenarios in their mind.

All people—those who experience negative emotions as cognitions and those who experience negative emotions viscerally—need to cleanse themselves of tension and can do so with practice. I raise the issue of cognitive versus visceral experience of tension only to say that if you, for example, know that you have to confront someone with bad news, negative feedback, or the like, and in anticipation of this event your mind is essentially blank but your stomach "is in knots," you feel "nauseated," or your "head is pounding," the relaxation induction below, designated as *progressive muscle relaxation,* will probably be best for you.

Conversely, if you know you will be visited by in-laws who have never and will never treat you as anything other than a kidnapper for marrying their son or daughter, and in anticipation of their visit find yourself tortured by thoughts of how they will demean you, the Relaxation Response below is probably what you will find calms you down best.

Then again, folks who feel knots in their stomachs may love the Relaxation Response and hate the technique that follows. Who cares? Relaxation is relaxation. If it works for you, do it.

Progressive Muscle Relaxation

An anxious mind cannot exist in a relaxed body.
—Edmund Jacobson, MD

Progressive Muscle Relaxation (PMR) is one of the oldest, most well-established, and respected relaxation inductions developed in this nation. The American physician Edmund

Jacobson created it, so you may hear it referred to as Jacobsonian progressive relaxation, as well it should be.[7] Jacobson's model is insightful and elegant. He defined relaxation as becoming "less tense, anxious, or stressed," and he felt a direct route to achieving that goal was to remove muscular tension from your body.

The methodology is simple: Progressing through every muscle group in the body—every group you can voluntarily control, that is—you

- Contract or tense the muscles.
- Relax the muscles.
- Notice the difference between feelings of tension and relaxation, and experience calmness.

Jacobson never claimed that PMR would rid a person of distressing feelings such as anxiety, but he did claim that by feeling relaxed you would be better able to cope with distress, anxiety, and other untoward emotional responses.

It is arguably more difficult to learn PMR than, say, relaxing to the sound of a singing bowl, but not terribly so. Here's how you do it.

Orientation

Allow roughly fifteen minutes to complete the PMR procedure. You should find a comfortable chair for the exercise, preferably a recliner that supports your head. If you cannot find one, a bed will do, but you may fall asleep, which, paradoxically, is ill-advised, since the goal of PMR is to contrast feelings of tension with feelings of release to know what "relaxed" feels like.

Turn off phones and lights, if possible, and put out a Do Not Disturb sign. Do not do a PMR induction after a big meal. Settle into the space where you will be doing the procedure, and as a final preparatory step, breathe as slowly as you can for a while to self-calm and prepare.

Note: As you go through the procedure your goal is to *deliberately focus on, and be as cognizant as possible of, the difference between states of tension and states of relaxation.* This is the raison d'être of PMR: feeling calm by noticing the difference between muscle tension and muscle relaxation. If you gain that awareness and practice regularly, you will be able to spontaneously relax during the course of a day the moment you experience muscular tension.

Procedure

For every muscle group described in the list below, tense the muscle group described. Make sure you can feel the tension, but do not flex or tense the muscle to the point where it comes close to being painful. Just try to achieve tension, hold the flexing for about five seconds, and then, after five seconds, stop flexing and relax the muscle group.

After completing the tension/relaxation contrast for each muscle group, stay where you are for a short while and don't force yourself to jump to alertness. When you feel alert, the session is over.

Muscle Group Relaxation Sequence

The manner of flexing each muscle group is described below. To relax the muscle group, just stop flexing.

- **Hands and forearms:** Clench your hand into a tight fist.
- **Upper arms:** Flex your biceps as if making a muscle.
- **Shoulders:** Shrug both shoulders simultaneously, and imagine you can touch them to your ears.
- **Feet:** Flex your toes toward your face (upward).
- **Front of legs:** Point your toes so that your foot is parallel to your leg.
- **Back of legs:** Flex your feet upward, touch your heels to the floor (or imagine doing so).
- **Thighs:** Stretch your leg straight out, keep your foot relaxed, and then press the back of your knee toward the floor.
- **Derriere:** Squeeze your buttocks together.
- **Stomach:** Tighten your stomach muscles to form a "six-pack" (the bulges of muscle that appear in a supremely fit human abdomen).
- **Lower back:** Press the small of your back against the chair, floor, or bed that is supporting you.

- **Upper back:** Place your arms at your sides and squeeze them against your torso.
- **Chest:** Breathe in, hold your breath, and tighten your chest muscles.
- **Neck:** Two parts: (1) stretch your head back as though you were going to touch your chin to the ceiling; then (2) bend your head forward and tuck your chin down toward your chest.
- **Face:** Three parts: (1) frown, (2) pucker your lips in an exaggerated kiss gesture, and (3) shut your eyes tightly, but do not overdo it.

Letting Go

After a considerable amount of practice—you'll know how much is enough when the contrast between tension and relaxation is profound—you can achieve the benefits of PMR on the go in one of the two following ways:

- If you notice tension anywhere in your body, simply release it by imagining you are doing the release component of PMR. In other words, you can, when you master PMR, skip the *tense* or *flex* part of the exercise and simply release a muscle group to feel a sense of calm. If you are practicing letting-go muscle relaxation you can also let go of specific muscle groups, not your whole body.
- Identify a muscle group that you are exceptionally good at flexing and releasing, and noticing the contrast in. Many

people like to flex their hands into fists since that is a very familiar movement. If you notice that you are thinking tense thoughts, *do not make a fist* (if your hand is your preferred site), just simply drop one (preferred) hand to your side, and let go of the tension in you by releasing it out of your hand. If this sounds useful to you, you should practice it—letting tension flow out of a preferred hand or other muscle group so it is handy (pun intended) should you unexpectedly need to relax. In addition, you can "carry" this relaxation induction with you to the exercises in C#2, to use when achieving in vivo calmness is called for owing to the unexpected emergence of a stressful stimulus.

The Relaxation Response

When you follow the procedure Dr. Herbert Benson developed to activate the Relaxation Response, what happens is that a portion of the brain located in the hypothalamus sends out neurochemicals that counteract those neurochemicals released when our perception of threat or the experience of anxiety activates the GAS (fight-or-flight) response. In addition, the Relaxation Response initiates an automatic quieting of brain activity that leads to a general slowing of bodily functions and feelings of well-being. Over time the Relaxation Response has been shown to have measurably positive effects on disorders caused by distress, including high blood pressure and certain cardiac conditions as well a number of digestive disorders.

Most acolytes of Dr. Benson's who describe his work will say that because the Relaxation Response is innate, we may doubt that it is working; we do not feel major changes coming over us (as with PMR) when we practice it. The thing is, Benson's followers will swear it does work as promised. Since the Relaxation Response is a physiologic response, you do not need to exert much effort to elicit it, and it can be activated in a number of ways, all simple and effective. Believe it or not, it takes more work to activate my singing bowl than to create the Relaxation Response. Specifically, Dr. Benson explains that all you need do to activate the Relaxation Response is:

1. Sit quietly in a comfortable position.
2. Allow your eyes to close.
3. Deeply relax all your muscles. Keep them relaxed.
4. Breathe through your nose. Become aware of your breathing. As you breathe out, utter any soothing, mellifluous-sounding word that does not have meaning to you (in order to avoid stimulation of unnecessary thoughts), or utter a neutral sound silently to yourself. For example, breathe in and then out and say "(your word)," in and out and repeat "(your word)." Benson suggests using "one" as a neutral word. You can use "one," "zing," or "bub," whatever. Just breathe easily and naturally.
5. Continue for ten to twenty minutes. You may open your eyes to check the time, but do not use an alarm. When you finish, sit quietly for several minutes, at first with your eyes closed and later with your eyes opened. Do not stand up for a few minutes.

6. Do not worry about whether you are successful in achieving a deep level of relaxation. Maintain a passive attitude and permit relaxation to occur at its own pace. Note: When distracting thoughts occur, try to ignore them by not dwelling on them and return to repeating your word.

7. Practice the technique once or twice daily, but not within two hours after any meal, since the digestive processes seem to interfere with the elicitation of the Relaxation Response.

When I lived and worked in Boston I met Dr. Benson several times and heard him lecture many times. When he touts his brilliant technique, it seems as if he's giving a nod to the Roman emperor Marcus Aurelius, who said, "If you are distressed by anything external, the pain is not due to the thing itself, but to your estimate of it; and this you have the power to revoke at any moment." You see, according to Benson, "We can't change the stressors in our lives, but doing [the Relaxation Response] for ten to twenty minutes every day will change our reactions to them."

Moving Forward

You have more than enough options, I hope, to begin the process of learning to calm yourself or to become calm. That said, you live in a world that is so tightly integrated by social networks of varying stripes (for example, Instagram, Facebook, LinkedIn, etc.) that if you are (a) very inquisitive, (b) very diligent, or (c) very chatty, you may learn that there is another popular form of relaxation training called *guided imagery* that can be described as learning to become relaxed by visualizing yourself in a relaxing setting and enjoying the feelings that you tell your mind to feel in those settings. The telling is done by an audio recording that you play while comfortably reclining or sitting and that guides you to imagine scenes deemed calming.

A more traditional version of this relaxation induction involves telling yourself that parts of your body—following the Jacobsonian model—are becoming relaxed; for example: "My arm is heavy...I cannot lift it" or "My heartbeat is steady, regular, and slowing...I feel myself growing calm." As far as I can tell, the variant of this procedure that has people imagine images versus bodily sensations is the more popular.

In the past when I used guided imagery with patients of mine who did not embrace PMR I found that many people with highly associative minds would attempt to listen to and follow the inductions but would often have cognitive associations to the images I presented that consisted of conflicting or negative thoughts. Consider this example of a guided imagery induction and then I will explain what I mean:

Visualize in your mind an image of a tranquil retreat, a place that is yours alone, where nothing can distress you. This place will be your refuge to relax in, a place you can go to so you can leave your cares in your everyday world. This special place may be a beach where you have vacationed or would like to visit for a respite from the world of work. You may make this place a meadow; it can be an isolated mountain lake where there are no inhabitants but you and the natural flora and fauna. If you like, your special place can be a beautiful garden with flowers that are always in bloom. Or you can make your special place where you can go to escape your distress, any place of significance to you where you know you will be calm. Imagine you are in your special place on an ideal summer day—the sky is clear and blue; the breeze is light; the temperature is just what you will enjoy. Do you hear the birds calling? Do you smell the flowers that are all around you? Do you hear the gentle rustle of the trees?

When I used scripts like the one above I was shocked by how often my patients would say things like, "You know, I hate beaches," so they would stop relaxing the moment I mentioned one. Other patients told me, "I'm always miserable in the summer; I'm a redhead; I burn like a shish kabob no matter how much sunscreen I use." Or, the killer, "Flowers and trees in the summer mean I'm sneezing like a lunatic. I have the worst hay fever imaginable."

My conclusion then was that if a goal of a relaxation induction was to empty your mind of negative, tension-arousing thoughts and you pursued that goal by putting stuff in your mind, you ran a significant risk of having what you put in backfire on you if your mind is innately highly associative.

This is why I urge you to strive to achieve states of calm by *emptying your mind* with an aquarium, a singing bowl, the Relaxation Response, or PMR, since none of these techniques engenders associations if you do them properly.

Yes, a dead fish floating in your tank is a deal killer (until you get a net and haul it out), a muscle spasm during PMR (very rare) would have the same effect, and you can drop a singing bowl on your foot while positioning yourself to use it. But relative to guided imagery, none of the techniques I've suggested are remotely as likely to backfire on you.

If you hear about other techniques from friends or though research, feel free to try them; they won't do damage. They may, however, take you away from the task at hand, which is to relax, get calm, and prepare to look at your emotional life from a dispassionate vantage point.

CHAPTER 10

The Second C: Convert Negative Feelings (Step C#2)

To improve is to change; to be perfect is to change often.

—Winston Churchill

This is the moment of truth—the point in time when I must put up or shut up, where push comes to shove, where the rubber meets the road, or as my Army Ranger buddy would say, "Where boots meet the ground."

Actually, that's only sort of true. You see, this is where I describe the process that will enable you to be the psychological Rumpelstiltskin you wanted to be when you began this book. In the fairy tale published by the Brothers Grimm, Rumpelstiltskin is an amazing albeit conniving little imp who spins straw into gold. In this book, you are an amazing reader who is awaiting the secret that will enable you to take anger and spin it into passion. I've got news for you—you have begun to do it already! Simply focusing on anger and its value as fuel—not as your PC friends see it, the cancer of emotions—deep within your subconscious mind you have begun the process we'll formalize below.

Since this is, in all candor, a crucial point in your evolution, I am making a seismic shift to present all material that follows in this chapter and the next in a more didactic form than I have presented material to you thus far. The reason is that there is a great deal of thinking you must do from here on in, and I want you to be able to easily segregate one thought from the next.

So how can we move you forward to find that passion you've been searching for? Here are the steps that remain:

• I will train you in a procedure that is very similar to the relaxation inductions I hope you are using. It has had widespread success helping people achieve self-awareness.

• Once you have mastered the self-awareness training that follows you will be ready to learn a procedure that is a formalized exercise that will convert all the self-talk you have engaged in your entire life into a purpose-focused raison d'être. The procedure will probably feel odd the first time you try it, but most new things do. Practice, and it will feel natural to you in no time.

• Once you have mastered this procedure, I will give you some examples or scripts of how to employ it. What I do not want this training to do is divert you from the fact that entrepreneurs are distinguished from all other living creatures by the "intense flame burning within" them. They turn "I'll show him/them" anger into passion. And they focus on the type of success that Viktor Frankl identified, not the type exemplified by Gordon Gekko.

An Unbiased Self-Perspective: Background

Mind control has been recognized as an important part of mental health since the 1890s. The goal of mind control is to have the reasoning center of the brain, the frontal cortex, dominate the areas in charge of reflexes, emotions, and habitual behaviors like anger. William James, the first Western scientist I am aware of who recognized the value of mind control—Buddhists were touting mind control for millennia before James taught at Harvard—argued that if the frontal cortex is not dominant, a person suffers wandering attention that lets the mind get hijacked.

> The faculty of voluntarily bringing back a wandering attention over and over again is the very root of judgment, character, and will. No one is *compos sui* [master of himself] if he have it not.[1]

Fortunately, you can learn to bring back the wandering mind in countless ways. I just alluded to Buddhism because part of its tradition established more than 2,500 years ago was to deal with the *monkey mind* by meditating. Let me digress briefly to laud the Buddha's genius.

The benefit of learning mind control is a direct outgrowth, as noted above, of what Dr. Aaron Beck's work on negative cognitive schema and CBT taught the world about the value of bringing thoughts under control. But as I keep reminding you, since King Solomon isn't here to do so himself, "What has been will be again, what has been done will be done again; there is nothing new under the sun" (Ecclesiastes 1:9).

The Buddha recognized what Beck was saying about how the mind is regularly beset by automatic negative thoughts and associations, albeit from a purely naturalistic perspective. "Monkey mind" (*kapicitta*) was the term Buddha used to describe this problem—the way human thought patterns are rarely linear or focused and, instead, are easily distracted, regularly moving about or swinging to and fro like a monkey swinging through trees in a jungle. Since much of Buddhist teaching is passed down informally, the monkey mind is pictured in many ways. I first learned of this construct decades ago while working for the National Institute on Alcohol Abuse and Alcoholism (NIAAA). A colleague of mine at the time claimed, "The Buddha said the minds of normal people are filled with drunken monkeys screaming, screeching, and jumping around. Can you imagine what fills the mind of an alcoholic?" But what I learned since then is that regardless of how you characterize the monkey mind, Buddhist tradition is wedded to the conviction that those monkeys running around your brain *can be tamed by meditating.*

The key term above is *tamed*—neither the Buddha nor a legitimate CBT therapist would ever say, "You will rid your mind of negative cognitive schema (drunken monkeys) by this or that technique." They know better. As a friend of mine who is a Buddhist loves to remark every time he visits me from Austin, Texas (since I live on the Pacific Ocean), "You cannot control the waves, but you can learn to surf." I present this background to you so you can understand what CBT and Buddhism have used meditation for: *the taming of the monkey mind*.

That is not *precisely* what your objective should be. Instead, I will instruct you how to use meditation to achieve an inner peace, and you will want to tame intrusive thoughts that you are having about working through a challenging conundrum, *but not to the point where you render them 100 percent docile or inert*, like a stuffed (toy) monkey. Ideally, you will be asking yourself questions like, "How do I make sense of the fact that when I watch television and see a mugging or related crime on *Law & Order*, I become enraged and want to pound those criminals to a pulp?" And so forth.... Keep "distressing" thoughts in your mind, but keep them firmly under your control, i.e., devoid of disruptive affect.

Mindfulness Training

If you have a conversation with any well-read person these days—someone with even a passing interest in the mind and/or mental health who is not a practicing Buddhist—and you were to say, "I am being driven crazy by thoughts about [fill in the blank]," the odds are quite high he or she would say, "Well you must try mindfulness training." (If the person you were talking to was a Buddhist he or she would describe scores of different meditative procedures to you.) You see, mindfulness training in 2018 is what transcendental meditation (TM) training was fifty years ago when the Beatles traveled to Rishikesh in northern India for a private session with Maharishi Mahesh Yogi at his ashram.

After the Beatles returned from being trained by the Maharishi, circulated pictures of themselves with the Maharishi around London and the USA, lauded the Maharishi, included Indian-themed music in their recordings, and sang the praises of TM everywhere they went, if you were not meditating from 1968 to 1978, you would have likely felt as out of place as someone wearing bell-bottom jeans and Birkenstock sandals to a Hollywood awards ceremony.

Fast-forward to today and you'll find TM has been supplanted by mindfulness as the au courant means of achieving control over disruptive thoughts. Professor Ellen Langer, aka the Mother of Mindfulness, has, on occasion, defined mindfulness as "sense of situational awareness."[2] Elsewhere, Langer has a slightly different take on the phenomenon: "We become mindful when we turn off our autopilot and start to pay attention to our situation. It is a conscious awareness of our context and of the content of our thoughts, in which we link context and thought patterns together."[3]

Mindfulness is too popular, too talked about, and definitely too ill defined for its own good. One indicator of how embedded the notion of mindfulness is in our culture is that while I was writing this paragraph I stopped to do a Google search of "mindfulness." The result? About seventy-nine million entries.

In the service of being as informative as possible but not writing with my monkey mind about mindfulness, here is an excerpt from an exhaustive review of the subject by Vago and Silbersweig. If you want to move beyond what I am presenting here, I urge you to read their report.[4]

Let me underscore this point: I have no vested interest whatsoever in how you train yourself to focus your mind, tame disruptive thoughts, learn to focus on useful thoughts, and sharpen your self-awareness. If you do not like the technique that follows, *please* never forget the maxim *De gustibus non est disputandum*, Latin for "In matters of taste, there can be no disputes." Find a technique for cultivating mindfulness that suits your taste. It will get where you need to go, which is preparing to talk to yourself in a constructive, self-analytic manner.

In the last two decades, the concept of mindfulness as a state, trait, process, and intervention has been successfully adapted in contexts of clinical health and psychology, especially with relation to... targeting emotion dysregulation. Operationalizing mindfulness has been somewhat challenging given the plurality of cultural traditions from which the concept originates.... Generally speaking, there are two models for cultivating mindfulness in the context of meditation practice—a 2,500-year-old historical model that is rooted in Buddhist science and a twenty-five-year old contemporary model...[but both share an interest] in reducing suffering, enhancing positive emotions, and improving quality of life.

Although the contemporary view of the concept "mindfulness" is increasingly becoming part of popular culture, there remains no single "correct" or "authoritative version" of mindfulness and the concept is often trivialized and conflated with many common interpretations. Mindfulness is described as (1) A temporary state of non-judgmental, non-reactive, present-centered attention and awareness that is cultivated during meditation practice; (2) An enduring trait that can be described as a dispositional pattern of cognition, emotion, or behavioral tendency; (3) A meditation practice; (4) An intervention.

In keeping with the notion articulated by Vago and Silbersweig, above, that mindfulness as "a temporary state of non-judgmental, non-reactive, present-centered attention and awareness that is cultivated during meditation practice"—a very scientific way of rephrasing the Buddha's prescription for taming the monkey mind—this is precisely what I will now train you to do.

Achieving an Unbiased Perspective through Candle Meditation

Preparation

• Begin the process by assuming an attitude of *shoshin*— the beginner's mind. If you prefer, tell yourself you will keep an open mind. What you cannot do is judge yourself during your attempt to cultivate mindfulness. If you keep the feeling that you are *eager to learn*, eager to discover what this state of being will unearth, you will be pleased with the results.

• Mindfulness is an ongoing practice. There is no actual getting there, so prepare yourself to view it as a daily ritual.

• Get yourself comfortable. Now you can begin...

Meditation

Follow the steps in the script below until you do not need to refer to them and can achieve mindlessness without guidance.

Step 1: Have a clearly defined, stable, consistent focus for your attention. The sensation elicited by involuntary breathing is the most commonly recommended focus (see next inductions). I use a scented candle, but an unscented one would be ideal as well. Here's why: Most mindfulness inductions use natural bodily processes as anchors to hold one's focus so mindfulness can be practiced whenever you are awake. That is an ideal. To begin, I advise that you use a more tangible anchor that you're free to retire as your familiarity with mindfulness grows. If you agree, that is, if you will use a candle as an anchor during your meditation procedure, please do the following:

- Make sure you are in a dimly lit room.
- Light a candle and position it at eye level or slightly below. Do not look down at the candle and do not look up at it. Focusing either up or down will prove to be uncomfortable.
- Be seated, comfortably and naturally. You can be in a chair or sitting cross-legged on the floor. You need not assume a lotus position or any other formal posture.
- Make sure you are at a distance where the candle is not too bright.
- Once all this is arranged, *simply stare at the flame and allow what you see to fill your mind.*

Step 2: Continue to focus on the candle. Your mind *will wander, as will your eyes…at first.* This is 100 percent normal and to be expected. That said, do your best to return your focus to your candle/anchor, and try as best you can to concentrate only on the process involved in achieving mindfulness.

Step 3: Try to relax as you focus. The inductions that follow will facilitate this. The letting-go exercise described above (at the end of the progressive muscle relaxation section) is an ideal way of self-calming if you are disturbed by distracting or intrusive thoughts.

Step 4: Be keenly aware. If you feel drowsy, this is not mindfulness. You want to be experientially active while focusing on the candle flame and your experience of it. Watch the candle flame move. Enjoy its natural variations in intensity. Look at variations in the color of the flame, blue to red. Enjoy the experience.

Step 5: Gather your insights. When you have thoughts that are related to passion(s), either hidden beneath anger, from wrongs you want to right, or a totally novel desire that will enable you to achieve generativity, PLEASE DO NOT ATTEMPT TO BLOCK THOSE THOUGHTS. Instead, treat those types of thoughts as insights. Take the thought from your mind and drop it in in your Useful Thought Bucket (please come up with your own name for this repository) and return your focus to your anchor.

Your Useful Thought Bucket

The Zen master and world-renowned authority on Zen Buddhism Shunryu Suzuki noted,

> When you are practicing Zazen meditation do not try to stop your thinking. Let it stop by itself. If something comes into your mind, let it come in and let it go out. It will not stay long. *When you try to stop your thinking, it means you are bothered by it.* Do not be

bothered by anything. It appears that the something comes from outside your mind, but actually it is only the waves of your mind and if you are not bothered by the waves, gradually they will become calmer and calmer.... Many sensations come, many thoughts or images arise but they are just waves from your own mind. Nothing comes from outside your mind...." (emphasis added)[5]

I find it amazing that Suzuki Roshi ("Roshi" is an honorific meaning "highly venerated teacher" that this Soto Zen monk was known by when he lived) had an insight about meditation that is so germane to its use in the lives of Westerners today, yet that is one of the beauties of Buddhism: its timelessness. You will help yourself in myriad ways if you follow this great teacher's advice to never, in your meditative exercises, block or censure your thoughts.

I raise this issue and underscore it because if you were using mindfulness training to supplement psychotherapy, particularly CBT where one of the primary therapeutic goals is the cessation of intrusive negative self-schema, you would be undoubtedly plagued by negative thoughts and trained as best as possible to treat all thoughts that intrude during mindfulness training as unwanted disruptions that should be stopped or eradicated.

YOU ARE NOT USING MEDITATION IN THE SERVICE OF PSYCHOTHERAPY. You are in the midst of a process of self-exploration and, as such, your thoughts are invaluable discoveries.

The mindfulness practice you will be doing—just as other people who use mindfulness training for its health benefits do—is designed to help you become more aware of what you are thinking. Specifically, the exercise above will enable you to "watch" your thoughts. The wrinkle I added to it is simply a means of facilitating thought recall. If you use the concept of a bucket that you have in your mind to collect useful thoughts about your search for passion that come to you during meditation, you won't be tempted after a meditation session to ruminate, "Did I recall all that I thought of during my mindfulness induction?"

Then again, as Suzuki Roshi would doubtless agree, no matter what I ask you to do during or after meditation, you would recall important thoughts you had while trying to cultivate mindfulness because that is the way the mind functions.

After you master this procedure—being certain that regardless of what you use for an anchor you do cultivate mindfulness using an anchor—you can use either of these two brief inductions to achieve mindfulness in one step as needed.

A: One Minute of Breathing

Check a watch or clock (ideally, one with a sweep-second hand) and note the time. For sixty seconds, simply focus all your attention on your breathing. Leave your eyes open and breathe normally. Be ready to catch yourself (your mind, your attention) from wandering off. If you wander, return your attention to your breathing. Stop after sixty seconds.

B: Observation

Choose any object in your environment. Take hold of it and keep it in your hands as you direct your attention to be absorbed by it. Just observe it with all your senses. Don't evaluate it, apply it to a task, find uses for it, or judge it relative to other examples of similar objects. Just experience what it is. The goal of this exercise is to be keenly aware of your here-and-now sensations. When this is done correctly, you feel alert and energized, since you are neither constrained by thoughts from the past nor burdened by expectations or demands for the future.

Recap of Mindfulness Self-Awareness Training

Here is a list of the experiences you should derive from the preceding exercises. If you do not, keep practicing. If you do, keep practicing. You cannot overdo a meditative exercise!

• When you achieve mindfulness, your awareness is completely focused on the here and now in an absolutely non-judgmental way.

• Being mindful is a *purposeful focus* that entails attending to the moment and to things just as they are, not projecting into the future, reviewing the past, or allowing a positive or negative judgment to instigate rumination of any sort.

• The catchphrase I came up with to help my clients (since "monkey mind" was already taken) is *Mindfulness is the antithesis of a mind with a "mind of its own."*

• During your training, when thoughts enter your mind, practice the Buddhist principle called *decentering*: developing the capacity to view yourself thinking thoughts from way above you, in a drone, watching yourself. Decentering is arguably the major benefit of mindful awareness since you can think, "Look at me thinking that thought"—not reacting to it, but rather gaining perspective on it.

• *Mindfulness does not involve mounting resistances to thoughts when they occur.* On the contrary, the benefit of decentering when mindful is that you experience the here and now, and if the here and now is a thought, you deal with it by decentering and putting it into your Useful Thought Bucket. Resistance to thoughts would engender feelings of being besieged and actually arouse a host of related negative thoughts. Collecting thoughts gives you a wealth of data about yourself that you can explore in the dialoguing process described below.

Dialoguing with Yourself

Recall the private equity fund manager Aaron who came to see me because he feared he would be crippled by anxiety? To help, I had a dialogue with him. I asked questions, he answered. I asked more questions, he gave more answers. Guess what? It took a while but there came a point when I asked Aaron a question and rather than answering me he responded, "Oh, I get it. I see what you're driving at." While I was querying him, he was talking to himself, answering his own questions, and having a dialogue with himself that paralleled the one I was having with him.

You may have a problem akin to Aaron's—repressing what is plaguing you—or you may simply be wondering what passion you want to pursue or problem you want to redress. Either way, *you need to have a dialogue with yourself.* I will show you exactly how to do that. I won't be with you, but I'm certain if you focus you'll do as well for yourself as I did for Aaron.

I want to take a moment to discuss the process of dialoguing with yourself because, as noted above, one aspect may see a bit odd. It's the physical setting and how you will engage in this self-dialogue process. Once I tell you how to do it I'll describe how to break the ice conversationally.

When I work with patients or clients we usually sit across from each other in two chairs. For you to work with yourself as your client, you will ideally *sit across from you.* This isn't as crazy as it sounds. Actually, what you will be doing is a minor modification of a technique developed by the founder of Gestalt therapy, Dr. Friedrich "Fritz" Perls, and is a mainstay of that school of thought. He called it the Empty Chair Technique. Allow me to explain what it involves.

The premise of Gestalt therapy, above and beyond its obvious allusion to a whole that is greater than its parts, is that in order to make therapeutic progress a patient must integrate the components of his or her whole being, particularly memories and attachments with loved ones—something that can only be achieved if she is acutely aware of her sensations as they come to her in the present moment. Since Gestalt therapists reason that much of a patient's inner awareness deals with people, living or dead, who are not present in the therapeutic setting, a means of bringing them into therapy is to have a patient become engaged with her feelings about a person by seating her across from an empty chair and telling that chair (occupied by a parent, boss, lover, ex-lover, etc.) what she is feeling.

The true value of the chair is for helping clients get in touch with feelings they are having difficulty accessing. If anger toward a parent isn't accessible, putting that parent in the chair and starting a dialogue with him or her is an effective means of drawing the feelings out. Ditto for you.

When Fritz Perls first employed the empty-chair technique he would only have the client communicate with the person who came to occupy the empty chair. As the technique matured, however, Perls would have the client switch roles with the occupant of the empty chair, seat herself in it, and have the person she had been talking to talk to *her* (now in the role of recipient of the input). I note this to reassure you that there is a long tradition supporting my advocacy of dialoguing with yourself after you fill an empty chair with a component of yourself.

In operational terms the empty chair technique works like this:

1. You must be aware of an objective. In your case this will be some variant of "What is the underlying feeling causing me to walk around angry and dissatisfied?" "Is the anger that I am aware of hiding feelings I need to understand?"

2. When your objective—that is, your primary question—is clear, you talk to the you in the chair as though that you understood your distress better than you do.

3. There is no right or wrong way to talk to the chair, provided you probe—for insight, awareness of your inner world, and the like.

4. You want your you in the chair to talk to you with self-talk you might use talking to yourself walking down the street or when asking yourself a question. Another way of thinking about how the you in the chair might talk to you is viewing the person in the chair as a color commentator at a baseball or basketball game you are watching on TV. The commentator is looking on while rendering observations about you that you can hear. The raison d'être of the color commentator relative to the play-by-play announcer is to give you insights about who the player is and/or what the player has been doing: is he in top form, coming back

from the disabled list, or coming back from being with his wife who just gave birth to twins (fatiguing and elating at the same time). Your you in the chair has insights into you. Demand them!

Process Note

When you first use this exercise, it helps a great deal if you visualize your candle/anchor in the chair before you talk to you in the chair. You do not want to dive into a deep discussion with you prior to getting comfortable with the technique. Thus, visualize the anchor/candle in the chair a few times, then assume its place and begin dialoguing.

Dialoguing Dos and Don'ts

You can begin talking to the chair as soon as you are familiar with relaxation inductions and mindfulness meditation is working as described. The reason for waiting for these exercises to yield results is:

- Being calm facilitates talking to the chair.
- Mindfulness meditation will fill your bucket.
- Mindfulness meditation will train you to focus so when you talk to the chair you will (1) listen better than the average listener and (2) be more vigilant to picking up cues that will lead you into profitable lines of inquiry.

Remember: What you are doing when talking to the chair is doing what I did with Aaron, albeit for yourself. A major plus that shrinks-as-interviewers have over, say, TV hosts is that we are trained to be dispassionate—have a clinical ear—and are trained to attend to nuances in a person's language.

Listen to you, and you will find what you are hungry for. What you ultimately want is to find the passions within you that will enable you to stay hungry naturally—keeping you fully engaged in vocational pursuits as well as with friends, family, and significant others in your life.

This will not happen after one conversation; it may take dozens. But ask yourself, "If this gets me out of a Sisyphean hell, never to return, isn't it worth it?" Of course it is.

Above all, be aware of the fact that you will feel odd or strange thinking about talking to yourself sitting in a chair. I noted how well established this technique is within Gestalt therapy circles but want to add that self-talk is a cornerstone of CBT. Above all, you are doing it unconsciously more often than you realize in the same way that every time you see an athlete who errs—a baseball player who strikes out, a beach volleyball player who misses a dig and shouts, "Damn!"—engaging in self-talk. All you will be doing is something that is natural and bringing it to a setting where, because the setting is out of the ordinary, it will initially feel unnatural. I hope this clarifies matters. That said, you will still probably question my sanity the first time you engage in this exercise!

Socratic Questioning

Asking questions is a powerful way to access data in your Useful Thought Bucket or the insights you've gained about yourself since engaging in natural self-talk about what presses your buttons; it facilitates digging within the storage bins of your unconscious to find passion(s). The questions that follow are designed to refer to the following hypothetical nugget I assume you might find in your Useful Thought Bucket: "This [expletive deleted] office is killing me. The air here is so stale it's a health hazard. I swear I'm going to start taking two-hour lunches so I can clear my lungs."

The raison d'être of Socratic questioning is to challenge. An important subordinate goal is to move a conversation toward a goal, in your case, identification of passion(s). That's really all you need to know in terms of background unless it helps you to know that Socrates was so principled, such an ethical human being, that he chose to commit suicide by drinking hemlock rather than compromise what he stood for. If that doesn't warrant a field test of the types of questioning Socrates used to teach his students, nothing does. Here are some examples of how he would delve into your office air-quality issue:

• Who have you shared your concerns with? It strikes me that a "health hazard" is something that the company would want to address.

- Yup; a two-hour lunch. Shrinks call that passive-aggressive behavior. Why not just speak your mind?
- Can you be honest with me: Is it the stale air or the fact that your boss's corner office is five times the size of your cubicle, is not in an open area, and comes equipped with a Do Not Disturb sign that you covet but have no place to hang?

All I can add as you go off on your own to do this exercise is to *not* expect to get a useful answer/response to your questions on your first trial. It may take weeks or months. Also, if you don't find my questions to your liking, use ones you like. All you need to do this right is keep wondering.

Humor

Grandmother always said, "Many a true word is said in jest." Professional psychologists would note that if you learn to laugh at yourself, your righteous indignation will vanish and you can begin to see beneath the surface manifestations of anger much more easily than you did when sitting on your high horse. Moreover, it's a proven fact that using humor when in the midst of trying circumstances detaches you from events, so as you question "you," bringing humor to your chats-with-the-chair will facilitate the process of discerning where your passions lie. For example…

- You're telling me there's a health hazard in your office and you want to flee? Work overtime, get emphysema, and enjoy workman's compensation forever! How about it?

- I feel your pain, I really do. But do you believe that your office is the issue, or is it claustrophobia? Does the elevator ride to and from your office upset you?
- You work in a new office building, so I doubt your contention about the stale air. Try this: Sniff everyone in the cubes adjacent to yours. If you detect a malodorous scent, drop a bar of soap on the guy's desk. Whadayathink?

Be Compassionate to You

The lament we're using as an example could be deemed a really distressing circumstance if the "you" articulating it were more informative. Try caring for the "you" in the chair to see if that doesn't dislodge some information.

- It strikes me that you are feeling put-upon for eight hours every day. Is there nowhere save a lunch in violation of company policy that relieves the angst you feel?
- You and I once flew cross-country in coach. The AC on the plane failed, and when we landed it had to be 100 degrees back in row 18 where we were sitting. I can't believe that office air is causing you this much pain. You see, on our vacation to Boston you were happy as a lark, 24/7, including the time we spent on the plane flying to Beantown.
- You're an Eagle Scout. You went on a two-week trek in the Rocky Mountains. You slept on hard dirt for fourteen days. You cannot be bent out of shape by an office cubicle; you're tough as nails. Wassup?

Finally, Look for Positives

Finally, ask yourself questions as though you care for your well-being, which, of course, you do:

- Have you tried addressing the bad air with anyone? If you do, and if that leads to meetings held outdoors, weather permitting, you become a hero, right?
- Have you considered the fact that people in close proximity to one another typically become more convivial and friendly than people interacting over a distance? I think it's called the propinquity effect. You just got to this job; how about using the fact that you're near folks to make them into friends?
- Don't forget what grandmothers tell us: Necessity is the mother of invention. If you hate your workspace as much as you seem to, I'll bet you'll find a way to leapfrog folks with more seniority than you so you can be promoted to a managerial role and get an office with a door and a thermostat you can control!

In Conclusion...

You've relaxed, meditated, identified problems or angry thoughts, and talked to *you* to dig for issues that evoke feelings of hunger. What I hope is that you want nothing more, at this moment, than to test the procedures described in step C#2. Great!

So, what I end this chapter with is a description of how you transition from data collecting in your mindfulness meditations and talking to the chair to an identification of purpose. This is easier than you think if you keep one caveat in mind: Changing thoughts takes daily practice—*lots of it*. Please believe me: You can change the way you talk to yourself and, consequently, think about yourself, your career, your need to feel good inside versus wealthy. *But you do not achieve that attitude adjustment without work*. Specifically, you must work toward the end of changing yourself day after day after day, until you know you feel a hunger that will fill you in perpetuity.

I've helped scores of people do what you are doing and have had nothing but favorable outcomes. Every person who has asked to work with me because they felt as though they were conscripted to life in a Sisyphean hell has told me, "I found a 'why' you promised I'd find." Some of my clients weren't in love with the first why they identified, and some of my clients found that the why that empowered them had less life in it than they expected. Guess what? They went back to talking to the chair (or me) and discovered that, as I noted above, there are enough wrongs out there in the world to last everyone a lifetime *if you are willing to do the work it takes to answer the question*, "What is right for me?"

To that end, here is a list of answers to the "Now what do I do?" questions I've had asked of me most often. In an ideal world, after several sessions of talking to you in the chair, you should leap up, shout, "Aha!" and tell your spouse or BFF, "I will pick up the cause that died with the death of Ponce de León. I'm forming an exploration club in Florida to search for and discover the Fountain of Youth. Age will never again prevent a person from achieving a flourishing life!" Or some such thing.

But since that may not happen to you, let me try to answer the questions you have about how this process should move to a gratifying conclusion.

FAQ List for Concluding Step C#2 of the Three-C Program

Haven't I been doing this long enough?

Everyone has a different threshold for breaking down barriers to self-insight. If you find yourself saying, "I should be aware of what angers me by now," tell yourself that a CBT therapist would call that a cognitive distortion. STOP. Don't tell yourself when the processes described in this module should conclude; practice them until you feel "Aha!"

What does an Aha! moment feel like?

What does love at first sight feel like? What does the joy you feel in seeing a parent cry because she/he is proud of you feel like? Use the Supreme Court Justice Potter Stewart test: "You'll know it when you feel it." Trust that you will know it.

Should I help the me in the chair when I'm not talking to me?

I'm asked variations of this a lot, such as "I know that I'm bothered by the seniority system here at work—in my business if you have been here since before cell phones you get promoted ahead of younger, more competent people. What should I do?"

What you should do *outside of your meditation room* is always, 100 percent of the time, help *you* in your role as coach, help you in your role as occupant of the chair. If a client tells me that he "hates the seniority system," I wouldn't see that as an aha! moment but, rather, a window into discovering why that person has a very strong entrenched sense of railing against injustice. What I would then do is ask him to read up on agencies like Barry Scheck's Innocence Project.

Paradoxically, you may find yourself hating something because you love it and are seeing it abused. The person who lamented the seniority system may be processing his angst over an awareness of how certain senior colleagues in his company are working themselves into states of exhaustion that imperil their physical health. His "I hate that they get promoted" could be, "Why don't you let these folks have a nice severance package so they won't have to work themselves to death? That job is too strenuous for an old guy."

In other words, your unconscious is complicated, so explore it in the chair, on walks, or use your relaxation/

meditation training to develop a *clear mind that will be receptive to surprise inputs from your unconscious 24/7/365.* The only *should* here is that you should not stop working until you have an authentic aha! moment.

How will I convert a passion into a purpose?

Everyone asks this and the answer is simple: Reread the section that describes my work with Aaron if you do not recall it. If you feel strongly that, for example, incivility is a greater threat to our nation than North Korea's dictator Kim Jong-un, supreme leader of North Korea, you have been bothered by it for years. You hated watching the 2016 presidential debates, you hated watching students at UC Berkeley rioting to block a conservative speaker from coming to their campus, you hated the violence provoked in Charlottesville, Virginia, by so-called White Nationalists and Nazis, and yes, you hate the state of our nation that uses violence to silence horrid entities who advocate Nazism more than you hate Nazism. If that is true, simply iterating all that you hate—if you stick to injustices provoking incivility—you can trust that your self-talk is mulling over solutions.

That is how your conscious and unconscious mind collaborate.

You do not hate incivility, see its deleterious effects, and say, "Ooh, *Judge Judy* is on." You say, "I know that Connie feels as I do. Actually, at the gym Jacqueline went into a rant when some guy called a woman 'fatso.' She doesn't know why political correctness begins and ends inside the walls of a business. I'm going to get together with them." If you talk about your passion to you in the chair, like-minded friends, experts, whomever, if you do a search for insights into what makes you feel passionately you will come upon a purpose. The only caveat to this statement is please DO NOT AIM. Do not tell yourself, "How can I build the next Amazon.com?" That is a tainted thought because it could be a smokescreen for, "I want to be a household name like Jeff Bezos is." TALK. Open your mind—relax, meditate—then talk.

Again, for the final time: If you are angered and you chip away at the detritus that is preventing you from seeing your real anger, once you do break through to find a *why*, your *how* will come along like a puppy that has just left its litter to attach itself to you.

CHAPTER 11

The Third C: Optimize Your Career Plan (Step C#3)

The best way to find yourself is to lose yourself in the service of others.

—Mahatma Gandhi

If this were almost every other advice book about careers—that is, if I were a parishioner in the Confucian Temple of the Big Lie where there is only one commandment, "Choose a job you love, and you will never have to work a day in your life," and I wanted to fulfill a promise to help you with career planning, this is the point where I would help you start looking for love.

That is definitely *not* what is going to happen.

Let me address why briefly so I can take you to the advice that can help you. In a nutshell, to be true to all that I have said to you thus far I could not possibly give you career planning advice consisting of words that were remotely related to "How to get X job, or Y training program, or Z internship." If I said anything comparable to "You can get yourself there," with "there" being an identifiable, tangible goal, that assertion would be a version of "find a job you love" delusional thinking. Nothing like that sort of advice appears here because that sort of advice is tantamount to gentle conscription—the person who is helping you find a job you love guides you to choices he intends for you to make, like used car salesmen walk you around their lots so you can see cars they want to sell you.

This chapter is about helping you actualize the definition of success advanced by John Stuart Mill:

> Those only are happy, I thought, who have their minds fixed on some object other than their own happiness, on the happiness of others, on the improvement of mankind, even on some art or pursuit, followed not as a means, but as itself an ideal end. Aiming thus at something else, they find happiness by the way.[1]

I'll translate: You fix your mind on something that provokes a hunger within you, something you feel passionately about. You follow that passion wherever it leads you. As a result, you will encounter myriad ways of satisfying your basic needs along the way.

I hope I have convinced you that the epitaph that most psychologically gratified people strive for is "She/He did well by doing good." If you yearn to be declared winner of Malcolm Forbes's contest, "Whoever has the most toys when he dies, wins," I fear that is because you skimmed the material that preceded this how-to section, presuming that you could skip ahead to find the answer and then implement it. Sorry.

If, on the other hand, you are intently focused when you read, I assume you are wondering how, given what I just said, I will make good on my promise to help you stay hungry and prevent career burnout. Actually, that's easy if you accept the fact that no one can see into the future and tell you today what will satisfy you tomorrow. What I can do, and have already done, is demonstrate (I hope) that if you have a job today that you feel favorably disposed toward, you will not, as the next year ends, view it in a comparably positive light. Actually, there is no chance whatsoever that in a few years' time you will wake up each morning looking forward to a job you view favorably today. Why? The (dreaded) *seven-year itch* will render that job as unappetizing as reheated fast-food entrees.

If you engage the services of a traditional career planner or a career architect of any stripe—career coach, placement guru, talent management specialist—to help you find a gratifying vocation, it's like going to a matchmaker and asking her to find you a spouse. She may do a bang-up job of identifying someone you'll call a soul mate, but you cannot ignore the fact that the vast majority of soul mates end up dissatisfied with each other or divorced. Thus, through no fault of the matchmaker, the person she identifies as "the one" today won't be "the one" in seven to ten years unless you and "the one" ensure that novel opportunities for experiencing eustress are introduced into the marriage.

If you accept what I just said, then the key—the sine qua non of what you want from a guide to career satisfaction—is not a great job today; in seven years that great job will feel like working in Maslow's dreaded chewing gum factory. To ensure your long-term career satisfaction what you want is a formula for generating opportunities for you to engage in ongoing, varied, and novel forms of eustress acquisition, ad infinitum. This is (if those opportunities are virtuous) what leads to summum bonum. That formula is what I will now give to you in this third and final part of the Three-C Program.

Achieving Summum Bonum

The essence of this formula—the main ingredient of it, if you will—is something I discovered years ago. Presenting that formula was the raison d'être for writing this book. That said, I will present it to you in a way I conceived of not on my own. I discovered it by studying Aristotle's writings. When Aristotle taught at the Lyceum and was asked by his students for some how-to tips they could apply to their career planning, Aristotle invariably responded that the only way to answer the "How do I achieve summum bonum?" question is to observe and study individuals who have already done so. Since I am not hubristic enough to second-guess Aristotle, the career planning guide I've designed for you is presented by illustrating what Benjamin Franklin, the prototype of an American who achieved summum bonum, did to become the most successful—in the *psychological* sense of the term—American of all time.

You see, although Franklin was born into poverty, he believed, with every fiber of his being, that "money has never made man happy, nor will it." But that quotation misses the point: Franklin never aimed to make money nor concerned himself with doing so, but he did so nevertheless. What is most significant about Franklin's life is that he knew, intuitively, that you could not dissociate being a successful person from being a successful professional; in essence, they are one and the same.

As proof of this, despite the fact that Franklin stopped working at the age of forty-two and sold off a business he was established in at the height of his earnings potential, he felt "I have enough (money)." Thus, because Franklin truly believed what he said about money not making people happy, and he wanted to be happy along with being philanthropic—he told his mother that he wanted his epitaph to be "He lived usefully," not "He died rich"—he set off on a path of serial entrepreneurship.

How Franklin succeeded at being a serial entrepreneur, how he was able to come up with new challenges over and over again and ensure that most of his efforts to meet those challenges would be fruitful, is what I will demonstrate to you now. If you study Franklin and model yourself after his example—modifying his modus operandi to suit your style, of course—you will realize that I have made good on my promise to put you on the road toward achieving career satisfaction and, more important, summum bonum.

To underscore and legitimize my decision to adopt the educational style of Aristotle and teach by exemplification, let me explain that what I am doing instead of giving you a recipe for career satisfaction is giving you insight and understanding. Any form of observational learning such as the kind you will experience by attending to how Benjamin Franklin achieved summum bonum is empowering; the knowledge gained from rote learning is more often merely palliative (insofar as it can satisfy a need to get you employed).

What I am striving for in teaching by example is to enable you to *feel* how an authentically successful person's modus operandi worked for him. Once you do, it is simple to shape that modus operandi into what works for you. A wise man once said, "Tell me and I forget. Teach me and I remember. *Involve me and I learn.*" Truly words to live by. Oh, wait... that wise man was Benjamin Franklin! Thus, following his insight into how humankind achieves authentic learning and understanding, I will do my best to involve you in the story of Franklin's career as a serial entrepreneur so you can use it as a prototype of one that you can model your career after.

I fervently believe that summum bonum—psychologically rewarding success—cannot be attained by the quick-fix methodologies that, since Dale Carnegie's *How to Win Friends and Influence People* was published in 1937, have spread through our nation like a pandemic. I'm not knocking Carnegie, per se, just his genre, but it should be clear that Carnegie was a salesman who wanted to sell a formula for success. Actually, Carnegie wanted to sell a formula for success so badly he changed the spelling of his surname from Carnagey to Carnegie so people would associate him with the Scottish American industrialist who was one of the most successful men of all time. Clearly, Dale did something right (from his vantage point), since his astoundingly successful book—more than fifteen million copies sold—is still in print.

The perspective I advocate is that quick fixes fix nothing and that winning—friends or the contest Malcolm Forbes expressed that counts the toys you have amassed prior to your death—is fool's gold. And while this is a minority opinion, it is not as uncommon as you may believe. Many people who have understood what summum bonum is, in reality—an experiential joy born of being connected with humankind versus a transient high born of material wealth—advanced this view I present here long before I did. The Greek philosopher Epictetus, who lived 1,900 years ago, said,

> The flourishing life is not achieved by techniques. You can't trick yourself into a life well lived. Neither is it achieved by following five easy steps or some charismatic figure's dogma. A flourishing life depends on our responding, as best we can, to those things uniquely incumbent upon us.

With the words of Epictetus ever present in my mind, what follows is a description of how Benjamin Franklin achieved summmum bonum. As you read this narrative please do so with the attitude "How can I embrace Franklin's model for achieving personal happiness, intellectual growth, and interpersonal connectedness?" If you do I am confident that not only will you fully grasp how to stay hungry, you will also learn the key to preventing burnout.

Benjamin Franklin: The Prototypic Serial Entrepreneur

Many of Franklin's biographers note that among his countless accomplishments the one that he is often not credited for is pioneering the spirit of authentic self-help in America. Most observers believe that Horatio Alger's novels about young men born to less-than-favorable circumstances who rose, with pluck and persistence, to achieve success ignited America's self-help spirit. Not so. Franklin was the prototype, and when he was established as a professional and wrote his autobiography, that tome, not Alger's work, ignited our spirit of self-determination.

Let me present some of what Franklin did, 100 percent on his own, although his formal schooling ceased when he was apprenticed, at age twelve, to his stepbrother James. Apart from mastering English well enough to write for his stepbrother's newspaper when he was an adolescent and then author countless pamphlets and books, Franklin taught himself Latin, French, Spanish, German, and Italian. He taught himself how to play the guitar, violin, and harp. The printing businesses and offshoots he started developed into a publishing enterprise that put out huge quantities of newspapers and magazines.

When Franklin retired—from being a printer, not from serial entrepreneurship—he turned much of his attention to science. Franklin founded the American Philosophical Society, America's first scientific society, as well as our first science library and museum. Because he regularly crossed the Atlantic Ocean for political purposes, Franklin studied his surroundings. He made measurements that helped chart the Gulf Stream and was a pioneer in the study of hydrodynamics, how water flows around the hulls of ships. As you doubtless recall from seeing when you were in grade school pictures of Franklin flying a kite in a thunderstorm, he was most famous for his experiments with electricity, especially lightning, which provoked his invention of the lightning rod that saved millions of dollars' worth of property in the Colonies, while saving countless lives.

What is less well known about Franklin is that despite the fact that he could have made millions of dollars if he filed patents on his inventions—including that invaluable lightning rod, the Franklin stove, bifocals, the catheter, and other gifts to humankind—Franklin wrote, "As we enjoy great advantages from the invention of others, we should be glad of an opportunity to serve others by any invention of ours, and this we should do freely and generously." Thus, even though his dabbling in science would have constituted an incredibly successful career for anyone who called himself an inventor, when you ask yourself the cui bono question you have to say, "Franklin—because his inventing afforded him eustress."

I noted above that Dale Carnegie was a bestselling author who became wealthy as a result. So was Benjamin Franklin. As a result of starting life as an apprentice printer to his abusive stepbrother James and his ability to constructively harness his "I'll show him" anger, Franklin assumed the vocation of printer, which he used to achieve a healthy resolution of his anger, excelled at this profession, and extended what printing could enable him to do. As a result, the money he amassed from printing and its offshoots made him rich enough that had he lived today he would have made Larry Ellison jealous.

But this iteration of Franklin's accomplishments in business misses the point. Yes, he evinced no overt interest in amassing wealth,[2] but what enabled Franklin to attain summum bonum was that he embodied Erik Erikson's concept of generativity more completely than anyone I know of. The virtue of generativity that guided every single thing that Franklin did in his life—from his role in fathering our nation (he was a signer of the Declaration of Independence), to his diplomatic career, to his founding of the University of Pennsylvania, and so on—is what enabled Franklin to live a flourishing life. He aimed at achieving nothing, per se, just the pursuit of his myriad passions and giving back.

Some of you who have read Franklin's writings or read

about him may object to what I said about his being purely generative and the anti–Dale Carnegie. Chief among your complaints might be Franklin's super bestseller, *The Way to Wealth*, which is still in print. If you said, "Isn't that book just eighteenth-century Dale Carnegie?" I would say no, because its focus is self-improvement, not winning, gaining advantages, or amassing money as ends in and of themselves.

You see, not only did Franklin focus on giving back by not hoarding wealth, he gave back by teaching. Thus, in *The Way to Wealth* Franklin teaches, as he does in his *Advice to a Young Tradesman* (1748). Franklin's way to wealth wouldn't impress Warren Buffett, but fitness experts would praise his notion "Early to bed and early to rise, makes a man healthy, wealthy, and wise." That's the sort of teaching Franklin was committed to, the sort of teaching that is the essence of generativity. Recall that when he defined generativity famed psychoanalyst Erik Erikson said,

> Evolution has made man a teaching as well as a learning animal, for dependency and maturity are reciprocal: mature man needs to be needed, and maturity is guided by the nature of that which must be cared for. Generativity, then, is primarily the concern for establishing and guiding the next generation.[3]

That is the principle that Franklin lived by. In addition to embracing generativity, Franklin had a virtue that is key to entrepreneurial success. What is problematic is that this virtue is hard to define. Whatever you call disposition, Franklin had a surplus of it.

I'm not referring to the fact that he was an abused child who ran away before reaching the age of majority, worked himself silly, and never stopped striving to achieve—those attributes fall under the rubrics of diligence and ambition. What was most unique about Franklin was the ease with which he was drawn to, and succeeded at, turning obstacle into opportunity. Having studied Franklin for decades, I believe this facility was due to his mastery of interpersonal relationships: he was able to turn so many obstacles to his advantage because he knew the value of *teamwork* and the free exchange of ideas.

One of the interpersonal skills Franklin is best known for involves something Dale Carnegie would have envied. When it came to ingratiating himself to people who were once obstacles to him, Franklin was a virtuoso. His technique for winning over former detractors is so impressive that the psychological literature has coined a concept that honors him by having it bear his name: the Franklin effect.

Here's an abridged version of what this effect is all about. Once upon a time, as biographies of Franklin tell it, Ben wanted to ingratiate himself to someone who didn't like him. If you don't understand the psychology of ingratiation you would think that bestowing kindness on the target person you want to win over is the way to go. Not Franklin. Instead of doing something for the man, *he asked the man for a favor*: to lend him a rare book. The man granted Franklin's request, and although he had previously shunned Franklin, the man who loaned him a book became his good friend. Franklin's conclusion: "He that has once done you a kindness will be more ready to do you another than he whom you yourself have obliged."[4]

Interpretations of why this effect works run the gamut from one end of the attitude-and-belief formation spectrum to the other, but that it does work is indisputable. Prior to his death I asked my dissertation adviser, Dr. Edward E. Jones, one of the world's most respected analysts of interpersonal behavior, about the effect. What he told me in his incredibly understated style was, "Yes, it's real," and that I should read his book on the subject of ingratiation (he forgot that I'd read it long before I became his student) where he presents evidence of the fact that "others like us more when we let them do small favors for us."[5]

How can your career pursuits be facilitated by use of the Franklin effect? Quite simply by enabling you to be infinitely better networked than you could possibly be without using it. Let me explain.

In chapter 1 I mentioned social psychologist Elliot Aronson and his work on the so-called gain-loss effect.[6] The Franklin effect is a distant cousin of Aronson's principle. Aronson told us that if you come to expect praise from a person—a doting husband wakes each day, looks at his wife, and, irrespective of how she looks, kisses her cheek and says, "Good morning, my lovely Mona Lisa, the face that has captivated the world!" After years of the same obsequious fawning (cute on a honeymoon, sweet for newlyweds, but obnoxious after a while), Mrs. Mona Lisa will ultimately become sick of being awakened each morning with a catchphrase and yearn for either novelty, authenticity, or both. After seven-plus years of marriage to her doting husband, Ms. Mona Lisa would prefer being awakened by a drill sergeant barking orders than her husband.

Powerful people—those who can actually do favors for you—have one experience in common with Ms. Mona Lisa: People kowtow to them or deal with them according to rehearsed social interactions. A top-of-the-totem-pole occupant rarely hears, "Hey, Mona Lisa—you look hot today!" Forget the impropriety of turning Ms. Lisa into a sex object: Ms. Lisa as CEO has men *and* women address her with deference, and after some time, CEO Lisa longs for authenticity even if it comes wrapped in crudeness. That is, of course, unless a young hustler like Ben Franklin bumps into CEO Lisa and, with the cunning of a fox, figures, "I'll be out of the ordinary and deal with this business leader as though she is merely an intelligent person."

Lisa, of course, is initially offended when Ben says, "Hey, Lisa, got a minute?" not, "Excuse me, Ms. Lisa." But Ms. Lisa is human and softens when Franklin says to her, "I am new to the consulting field and I need some advice. Given that Lisa Advisers is the largest consultancy in Philadelphia and given that I'm looking to be a consultant, I wonder if you might help do for me what no one in my local library could—direct me to an authoritative source on how to be a top consultant?"

Powerful people are not the beneficiaries of honest feedback or interactions as often as you would think, and what makes that situation horrible is they realize people are kowtowing to them. Every powerful person on earth has doubtless read *The Emperor's New Clothes*—excuse me, *should have read*—and knows the moral of the story: Only a young, naïve child who isn't afraid of the king will be honest enough to say to him, "Ah, um, excuse me, but you're naked as a jaybird." Honesty is so refreshing and rewarding to a person who has been fed a steady diet of baloney that the mere sound of authentic feedback is uplifting. Add to this the thought, "That kid has chutzpah, spunk, nerve....I want a kid like that working for Lisa Advisers," and you see why asking for a favor usually gets an "Of course, let me see what I can do for you" response.

If you know that nonnormative interactions can often be ingratiating if they are appropriate—that is, they are for aid in advancing your knowledge or expertise, not asking for money—you understand why the Franklin effect is invaluable. You open the door to making a new friend and you get priceless knowledge or insights that can promote your ability to grow.

Even when he was young Franklin understood these things (which is why, I assume, he got an effect named after him). Here's what I mean: Franklin grew up dirt-poor, the fifteenth of seventeen children. His formal education ended at age ten. He was apprenticed to a stepbrother who abused him physically and emotionally and, in all honesty, no one can explain why Franklin decided that he would educate himself and get even with his stepbrother by showing him, as he did, rather than beating his brother to a pulp. What is more astounding is that beyond his self-guided academic education, Franklin taught himself to be sociable when most kids who get beaten like Franklin was are doing time in prison.

Franklin invested himself in being able to win friends in any and every context he found himself in. A story that ran in the *Los Angeles Times* on the three hundredth anniversary of Franklin's birth (in 2006) reported that in contrast to the Smithsonian that had a tribute to him,

> At McGillin's Olde Ale House in Philadelphia, they know best how to honor Benjamin Franklin...with a celebratory toast. "He was a very jovial fellow who would meet at the taverns, discussing the latest John Locke book or scientific breakthrough over a nice pint of beer," [said] McGillin's owner, Chris Mullins. "I don't think you could imagine getting drunk with George Washington, but with Benjamin Franklin? Definitely."[7]

Franklin's ability to relate to people of all stations in life could be called emotional intelligence, but when you view his interpersonal savvy in conjunction with his generativity— he created the Philadelphia Hospital and the Pennsylvania Academy, which, when founded, was the nation's first modern liberal arts college, later renamed the University of

Pennsylvania—you realize that to do great deeds like those and countless others, *Franklin knew the value of finding the wherewithal to integrate diverse groups of people to work, harmoniously, for a common cause.* How else, long before he could do good for America in myriad ways—actually, before there was an America—could Franklin have served as a diplomat, persuading France to aid the Colonies in their war for independence, without the realization that uniting people was of paramount importance in living a flourishing life?

Many people claim that Franklin was the scientist and inventor he was because of his ability to make friends. Today, Franklin would be called the supreme social networker—among the Who's Who of Facebook, LinkedIn, and Twitter. The thing is, Franklin wouldn't be known on these sites for gossiping or gabbing but, rather, for giving and developing—a penchant he evinced in his youth and developed throughout his life. More accurately, Franklin didn't *give* as in *donating*, he *gave* in the sense of seeing something that needed to be done, gathering resources needed to do it, and then spearheading the effort involved in satisfying the need.

This virtue was in full flourish when Franklin was only twenty-one years old. As a young tradesman, he formed a club called the Junto comprised of other artisans who convened for the joint purposes of self-improvement and community development. Not only did the members of Junto share insights and readings, they also addressed countless community needs including, but not limited to, creating a lending library so other Philadelphians could learn as the members of

Junto were learning. They helped launch the city's first police force and first volunteer fire company. And when not being purely generative, the Junto created an insurance company! You see, being generative does not preclude doing well at one's business endeavors. It is actually a catalyst to doing well professionally. Let me amplify this point.

One thing you will learn as you do business over the course of time is it's not *what* you know, it's *who* you know that counts. Okay, there are limits to this: No one will consent to undergoing a dental procedure unless they are certain that the person holding the drill has a DDS or DMD degree. Franklin had all the credentialing he needed to be the most sought-after printer in America, but he never rested on his laurels. In fact, he put his laurels second to his ability to network. For example, when his *Pennsylvania Gazette* was the most popular newspaper in the Colonies, Franklin, at a mere thirty years of age, campaigned to be made clerk of the Pennsylvania Assembly, a mind-numbing chore that Franklin wouldn't have assumed for thousands of dollars a year. But he took it for a pittance because the social networking advantages born of his position were priceless. The connections Franklin made as clerk of the Assembly proved to be invaluable whenever he bid on lucrative government contracts for printing.

If you are an entrepreneur like Franklin was, or if you own/control any business venture, you will soon discover, if you don't already know it, that social skill is your most valuable asset and a lack thereof will be your biggest problem (or kiss of death). Franklin used his interpersonal skills and the attribute of turning problems into profits when it came to dealing with talent. What he did was beyond brilliant.

Recall that Franklin decided to become a printer and designed his I'll show him scenario when he was apprenticed to his brother. As a successful printer in the Colonies Franklin had apprentices of his own that he not only didn't abuse, but rather nurtured. You see, Franklin realized that when his apprentices reached the age of majority they became journeyman printers and were free to leave Franklin's employ to establish businesses of their own. This was potentially double trouble for Franklin since he lost talent and gained competition if his former apprentices could build their own enterprises. Thus, rather than risking that outcome Franklin ingeniously killed two (bad) birds with one stone: As valued and talented apprentices became journeymen he would offer them the opportunity to be set up with their own franchises of Franklin's operation in a city outside of Philadelphia. In this way Franklin held on to valued talent in a split-the-profits type of deal, expanded his market, and avoided having to compete with someone he trained and who, presumably, had the wherewithal to challenge his dominance.

As I hope you see, Franklin kept moving in the direction that "doing well by doing good" moved him, without concern for what he would get as a consequence. What I didn't tell you about—and you don't often read about elsewhere— are the difficulties Franklin encountered along the way. Two reasons this is so are that it makes for bad reading, and more important, Franklin could have coined the maxim "When the going gets tough, the tough get going." Alternatively, he could have laid claim to the motto "Winners never quit and quitters never win." Bottom line, Franklin was adamant about self-imposed discipline. This to me is the final Franklin virtue (which he had a tremendous surplus of) that I feel you must embrace in order to achieve entrepreneurial success, a trait of Franklin's that is today called the Five-Hour Rule.[8]

In his *Autobiography* (which has a lengthy discussion about his daily schedule that will impress you) and elsewhere, Franklin noted that he spent one hour every workday (for a total of five hours a week) devoting himself to reading and studying. In addition, after a week's work, Franklin would critique his performance over the previous five-day period, and if he found himself wanting in any way he would make note of where he fell short and endeavor to rectify the situation.

Winston Churchill, no slouch when it came to statesmanship and diplomacy (although Franklin was far better at these endeavors), had a similar ethos. In one of his diaries the trusted aide to Churchill John Colville noted that Churchill told him, "Each night before I go to bed, I try myself by Court Martial to see if I have done something really effective during the day—I don't mean merely pawing the ground, anyone can go through the motions, but something really effective."[9]

The capacity for critiquing oneself is much more unique than you would imagine, not to mention being far more valuable. You see, when you preemptively note your own faults the feedback you get from others about shortcomings isn't felt as a slight. Instead, any and all feedback is received as having the potential to augment your ability to do good. As such, it can facilitate the process of surmounting the myriad obstacles and impediments we all face in life.

In complete candor, now that I have a surfeit of referrals to my coaching practice, the test I use to screen potential clients—for goodness of fit with me and my methodology—is to determine if the potential clients naturally engage in self-critiquing behavior. That and that alone, I have found, is the single best predictor of succeeding in a coaching relationship. If I'm screening someone and hear him recounting an inter-action where he was told, "Barry, I feel you would be doing yourself a favor if you were to consider the fact that the 360-degree review I conducted found that when it comes to taking credit for good ideas, you are deemed a hog that could win the county fair," and Barry replies, "That's the green-eyed mon-ster speaking—they're all jealous of me," you can be certain that Barry will be mired in the muck for years to come.

Conversely, the person who tells me, "I know I'm doing something wrong since I sense myself repeating patterns of defeat" is not only receptive to constructive criticism, but also poised to change.

More important, however, is that when a person is engaged in self-critiquing behaviors and seeks counsel regarding self-improvement strategies, the inputs she receives needn't be cautious—walking on eggshells—or cheerleading. They can be what constructive criticism is meant to be: construc-tive. Think about how wonderful the world would be if the self-help industry existed to help men like Benjamin Franklin and Winston Churchill: Every bit of advice an expert offered could be presented honestly, not in terms that couched commentary in the style of New Age-y daily affirmations such as, "I deserve good things, I am entitled to my share of happiness. I refuse to beat myself up. I am an attractive person. I am fun to be with."

How refreshing would it be if a person could hear, "Look: More people would want to be with you if you weren't always soliciting praise, which, when asked for, is infinitely less impactful than when received spontaneously." But saying something like that to a person who lacks self-reflective potential and can't assess why or how his interpersonal relationships are failing would devastate him.

Franklin was religious about adhering to daily routines and structured assessments designed to support his strengths and redress his weaknesses. As Epictetus observed, you don't need a charismatic guru's palliatives to do this. If you are following Step C#2 and meditating, and turning what the meditations yield toward a no-holds-barred self-assessment like Franklin did, you'll be shocked at how invaluable it is to deal with others who have your interests in mind and care enough to speak the truth, not pander to you as though you are an infant.

Why am I so concerned that you learn as Franklin did, make friends as Franklin did, network as Franklin did, and grow as Franklin did? If you do not, the opportunities you will have to experience eustress as you embark upon a career devoted to pursuing a passion will be diminished. We find eustress in learning, mastering, and creating, not repeating. And nothing guarantees learning and creating like clubs modeled after Franklin's Junto, open-ended pursuits like John Walsh's *America's Most Wanted*, and other endeavors that are generative and cathartic in the best possible ways.

Junto was a group of artisans gathering to "Do well by doing good." They critiqued each other often because each came to Junto with a receptive mind. They gave to the community that gave back to them in terms of business opportunities and insights. Through that process each artisan grew and gained the confidence for out-of-the-box thinking. Franklin's club and enterprises that focus first on generativity and secondarily on business are the perpetual motion machines of careerism.

Let me be Windex clear about this point: You cannot do your job with acquisitive "Show me the money" or "Give me the credit" attitudes and be able to live your life in a manner that creates generativity, brings you closer to others, and involves you in ongoing opportunities for eustress. Professional and personal are one and the same: You either see success as Benjamin Franklin and Viktor Frankl did—a "dedication to a cause greater than oneself or the by-product of one's surrender to a person other than oneself"—or you do not. You either live like Franklin did—retiring at age forty-two from making money, then spending the next forty-two years of his life making the world a better place to live in for future generations (i.e., being generative)—or you do not.

If there is a barely perceptible whisper in the deepest recesses of your mind that you hear saying, "C'mon...this is a book...this guy isn't sharing his wealth with you...show me the money," do not lose sight of the fact that Benjamin Franklin would have vomited if someone had suggested to him that "Whoever has the most toys when he dies, wins." He attained his tremendous wealth by living according to the ethos "Money has never made man happy, nor will it."

Alternatively, if that voice whispering the siren song of money causes you to feel that there is a quick-fix means of amassing a bundle of it, simply remind yourself of what Nietzsche said: "He who has a why to live can bear almost any how."

You have found one or more whys to live for by following Steps C#1 and C#2 of the Three-C Program. Now you are set to live a flourishing life. Not necessarily one that is impassioned in terms of living every day of your life for a "why," just living with an eye toward making the world better for successive generations will suffice. If you simply commit yourself to focusing on what provokes hunger in you—that is, *your cause*—and value people 24/7/365, you'll discover more eustress than you ever believed possible.

Notes

Introduction

1. When I moved to Los Angeles in 2000 my academic focus shifted from psychiatry to entrepreneurship, and my teaching shifted from residents and interns to MBA candidates. Whenever I quoted this proverb to a B-school class I would invariably be told, "Thomas Edison stole that maxim and said, 'Vision without execution is hallucination.'" My reply was "Ecclesiastes 1:9: 'What has been will be again, what has been done will be done again; there is nothing new under the sun.'"

Chapter 1: Why Sooner or Later Everyone Wants to Scream "Take This Job and Shove It!"

1. "State of the American Workplace," Gallup, updated 2017, http://news.gallup.com/reports/199961/7.aspx#aspnetForm.
2. Named after Sisyphus, a figure from Greek mythology, whose punishment for offending the gods was being forced to roll an immense boulder up a hill, watch impotently as it came rolling back down, and then be forced to repeat the entire process over and over until the end of time. Sound familiar?
3. Adams, Susan, "Most Americans Are Unhappy at Work," *Forbes,* June 20, 2014, https://www.forbes.com/sites/susanadams/2014/06/20/most-americans-are-unhappy-at-work/#185aae2a341a.

4. Adams, Susan, "Unhappy Employees Outnumber Happy Ones by Two to One Worldwide," *Forbes,* October 10, 2013, https://www.forbes.com/sites/susanadams/2013/10/10/unhappy-employees-outnumber-happy-ones-by-two-to-one-worldwide/#7db98940362a.

5. Twain, Mark, *The Adventures of Tom Sawyer.*

6. Maslow, A. H., "A Theory of Human Motivation," *Psychological Review* 50, no. 4 (1943): 370–96.

7. In chapters 8 and 9 you will see how Aristotle deserves credit, or at least a footnote, in everything written by anyone who calls him- or herself a "humanistic psychologist." One member of that society, arguably among the brightest, Mihaly Csikszentmihalyi, does credit Aristotle for his seminal ideas and work. What matters, however, is not the footnotes, but the coherence of thought: Great minds, as you will see, do think alike about what is rewarding and what yields happiness.

8. Maslow, "A Theory of Human Motivation," 382–83.

9. Ibid., 375.

10. Aronson, Elliot, "Some Antecedents of Interpersonal Attraction," (1969), in Arnold, W. J. and D. Levine, eds., *Nebraska Symposium on Motivation* no. 17, (Lincoln: University of Nebraska Press, 1969), 143–73.

11. Tennov, Dorothy, *Love and Limerance: The Experience of Being in Love* (Chelsea, MI: Scarborough House Publishers, 1999).

12. Brandeis, Louis D., *Letters of Louis D. Brandeis: Volume V, 1921–1941: Elder Statesman* (Albany, SUNY Press, 1978), 498.

13. I discuss the etiology of white-collar crime at length in Berglas, S., *Reclaiming the Fire: How Successful People Overcome Burnout* (New York: Random House, 2001), 80–94.

Chapter 2: Is There a Useful Definition of *Burnout*?

1. Berglas, Steven, *Reclaiming the Fire: How Successful People Overcome Burnout* (New York: Random House, 2001).
2. Levinson, Harry, "When Executives Burn Out," *Harvard Business Review*, July–August, 1996.
3. Maslach, Christina, "Burn-Out," *Human Behavior* 5, no. 9 (1976): 16.
4. Maslach, Christina, W. B. Schaufeli, and M. P. Leiter. "Job Burnout," (2001), in Fiske S. T., D. L. Schacter, and C. Zahn-Waxler eds., *Annual Review of Psychology* 52 (2001), 397–422.
5. Bakker, Arnold B., Patricia L. Costa. "Chronic Job Burnout and Daily Functioning: A Theoretical Analysis," *Burnout Research* 1, no. 3 (December 2014), 113.
6. Freudenberger, Herbert, *Burn-Out: The High Cost of Achievement* (New York: Anchor Press, 1980), xv.
7. Maslach, Christina, *Burnout: The Cost of Caring* (Englewood Cliffs, NJ: Prentice Hall, 1982).
8. Maslach, Christina, S. E. Jackson, and M. P. Leiter, *MBI: The Maslach Burnout Inventory: Manual* (Palo Alto, CA: Consulting Psychologists Press, 1996).
9. Long after I finished this chapter T-Mobile began running a TV ad campaign, 6/29/17, "You're at Home Anywhere with T-Mobile," where a "city" couple is camping, trying to sleep. The woman asks, "Is it too quiet?" The man says, "It's awful," and she boots up an app that plays soothing city noises. You Tube: https://www.youtube.com/watch?v=EhdA8OsawbE.
10. Levinson, Harry, "When Executives Burn Out," *Harvard Business Review,* May–June 1981.
11. Ibid.
12. Ibid.
13. Dollard, J., Miller, N., et al., *Frustration and Aggression* (New Haven, CT: Yale University Press, 1939).

14. "SNCC changed American Politics in Pursuit of Freedom, Bond Says," University of Virginia School of Law, February 2, 2010, https://content.law.virginia.edu/news/2010_spr/bond.htm.

Chapter 3: Anger: The Most Misunderstood Emotion

1. Aristotle, *Metaphysics*, trans. Joe Sachs, 2nd ed. (Santa Fe, NM: Green Lion Press, 1999).

2. Barrett, Lisa F., "The Varieties of Anger," *New York Times*, November 12, 2016.

3. Cannon, Walter B. *Bodily Changes in Pain, Hunger, Fear, and Rage* (New York: Appleton, 1929).

4. The fact that the amygdalae activate us to perceived threat as they do, instinctually, is further proof that we cannot eradicate anger.

5. Herzberg, Frederick, "One More Time: How Do You Motivate Employees?" *Harvard Business Review* 46, no. 1 (January–February 1968) 53–62.

6. Herzberg, F., *Work and the Nature of Man* (Cleveland: World Publishing Company, 1966).

7. Herzberg, F., "One More Time: How Do You Motivate Employees?" *Harvard Business Review* 65, no. 5 (1987).

8. Maslow, Abraham H., *Maslow on Management*. (New York: Wiley, 1998), 16.

9. Ibid., 62.

10. Apperson, George Latimer, *The Wordsworth Dictionary of Proverbs* (Ware: Wordsworth Editions, 2006), 283.

11. Tice, Dianne M., and Roy Baumeister, "Controlling Anger: Self-induced Emotion Change," D. M. Wegner and J. W. Pennebaker, eds., *Handbook of Mental Control*, (Englewood Cliffs, NJ: Prentice Hall, 1993), 393–409.

12. Vygotsky, Lev S., *Thought and Language,* trans. A. Kozulin. (Cambridge, MA: MIT Press, 1986).

13. Nowhere in this brief overview of depression do I address that a prominent cause—some say the major cause—of this disorder is a biochemical (serotonin) imbalance. The reason is that the focus of this book is on job-induced problems and their prevention, not mood disorders.

14. Seligman, M. E. P., *Helplessness: On Depression, Development, and Death* (San Francisco: W. H. Freeman, 1975).

15. Beck, Aaron T., *Cognitive Therapy and the Emotional Disorders* (New York: International Universities Press, 1976).

16. Beck, Aaron T., A. John Rush, Brian F. Shaw, and Gary Emery, *Cognitive Therapy of Depression* (New York: Guilford Press, 1979).

17. Abramson, Lyn Y., Gerald I. Metalsky, and Lauren B. Alloy, "Hopelessness Depression: A Theory-based Subtype of Depression," *Psychological Review* 96, (1989) 358–372.

18. Janoff-Bulman, Ronnie, "Characterological versus behavioral self-blame: Inquiries into depression and rape," *Journal of Personality and Social Psychology* 37, (1979) 1798–1809. See also: note 17.

Chapter 4: Do Get Mad, Do Strive for Authentic Happiness

1. "Richest Americans in History," *Forbes,* August 24, 1998, https://forbes.com/asap/1998/0824/032.htm.

2. Tebben, Gerald, "Patriotic Printers: Benjamin Franklin, Genius in Everything, Printed Paper Money," *Coin World,* October 18, 2015, https://www.coinworld.com/news/paper-money/2015/10/patriotic-printers--benjamin-franklin--genius-in-everything--printed-paper-money.all.html.

3. Freud, Sigmund, *Civilization and Its Discontents,* trans. James Strachey (New York: W. W. Norton & Company, 1930), 11.

4. Steinbeck, John, *America and the Americans* (New York: Viking, 1966), 330.

5. DeAngelis, Tori, "Consumerism and its discontents," *Monitor on Psychology* 35, no. 6 (June 2004), 52.

6. Kasser, Tim, *The High Price of Materialism* (Cambridge, MA: MIT Press, 2002).

7. Niemiec, Christopher P., Richard M. Ryan, and Edward L. Deci, "The Path Taken: Consequences of Attaining Intrinsic and Extrinsic Aspirations in Post-College Life," *Journal of Research in Personality* 43, no. 3 (June 2009), 291–306.

8. Tuttle, Brad, "Psych Study: When You're Bummed, You're More Likely to Buy," *Time*, May 7, 2010, business.time.com/2010/05/07/study-low-self-esteem-makes-you-more-likely-to-buy-luxury-goods/.

9. Sivanathan, Niro, and Nathan Pettit, "Protecting the Self Through Consumption: Status Goods as Affirmational Commodities," *Journal of Experimental Social Psychology* 46, no. 3 (May 2010), 564–570.

10. Tuttle, "Psych Study," *Time*.

11. Baumeister, Roy F., Laura Smart, and Joseph M. Boden, "Relation of Threatened Egotism to Violence and Aggression: The Dark Side of High Self-Esteem," *Psychological Review* 103, no. 1, (January 1996), 8.

12. Rodgers, Joann E., "Go Forth in Anger," *Psychology Today*, last modified December 17, 2017, https://www.psychologytoday.com/us/articles/201403/go-forth-in-anger.

13. Ibid.

14. Tavris, Carol, *Anger: The Misunderstood Emotion* (New York: Touchstone/Simon & Schuster, 1989).

15. From *The Complete Works in Verse and Prose of George Herbert: Volume III, Prose* (1874), edited by the Rev. Alexander B. Grosart, printed for private circulation.

16. Nye, Russell B., ed., *Autobiography and Other Writings by Benjamin Franklin* (Boston: Houghton Mifflin, 1958), 10.

17. Ibid., 17.

18. Ibid., 18.

19. Ross, W. D. ed., *Aristotle: Selections* (New York: Scribner, 1938), 224–230.

20. Erikson, Erik, *Identity: Youth and Crisis* (New York: Norton, 1968), 138.

Chapter 5: How to Achieve *Summum Bonum*: How to Be Happy

1. Csikszentmihalyi, Mihalyi, *Flow: The Psychology of Optimal Experience* (New York: Harper & Row, 1990), 1.

2. I had to bone up on the *Nicomachean Ethics* even though my undergraduate minor was philosophy in order to prepare this section of chapter 5. Most of what I use comes from Kemerling, Garth. *The Philosophy Pages*, Britannica Internet Guide Selection, and Parry, Richard. "Ancient Ethical Theory," in Edward N. Zalta, ed., *The Stanford Encyclopedia of Philosophy* (Stanford, CA: The Metaphysics Research Lab, 2004), both of which I highly recommend to anyone interested in putting meat on my bare-bones presentation of Aristotle's invaluable work.

3. Recall that, in chapter 6, I state that Benjamin Franklin was one individual who could achieve summum bonum, the good life.

4. Freud, Sigmund, *Civilization and Its Discontents* (New York: Norton, 1961), 23.

5. Maslow, Abraham. H., "A Theory of Human Motivation," *Psychological Review* 50, no. 4 (1943), 370–96.

6. Self-Determination Theory (SDT) is not an explanation of why people defiantly proclaim "Nobody tells me what to do." Instead, it is a theory akin to Herzberg's notions about what motivates people. SDT, like Herzberg's "two-factor theory," distinguishes between different types of motivation based on what gives rise to an action and differences in the perceived quality of an action owing to what prompts it. The most basic distinction drawn by SDT is between intrinsic motivation (doing something because it is inherently

interesting) and extrinsic motivation (doing something because it leads to a reward or some independent outcome). Research demonstrates that only behaviors that are intrinsically motivated yield long-term positive feelings and a sense of initiating them because one "wants to"—i.e., self-determined behavior. See Deci, Edward. L., and Richard. M. Ryan. *Intrinsic Motivation and Self-Determination in Human Behavior* (New York: Plenum, 1985).

7. Csikszentmihalyi, *Flow*, 6.
8. Mill, John Stuart, *Autobiography* (London: Penguin, 1873), 117.
9. Frankl, Viktor, *Man's Search for Meaning* (New York: Touchstone/ Simon & Schuster, 1984), 12.
10. Franklin, Benjamin, Letter to Joseph Huey, 6 June 1753; published in Albert Henry Smyth, *The Writings of Benjamin Franklin*, vol. 3 (New York: Macmillan Co., 1905–1907), 144.
11. Dunn, Elizabeth W., Lara B. Aknin, and Michael I. Norton, "Spending Money on Others Promotes Happiness," *Science* 319, no. 5870 (March 21, 2008), 1687–1688.
12. Seligman, Martin E. P., *Authentic Happiness* (New York: Free Press, 2002).
13. Many writers who use this story call it "The Wise Woman's Stone."
14. Schor, Juliet. B., *The Overworked American: The Unexpected Decline of Leisure* (New York: Basic Books, 1993).
15. Goleman, Daniel, "The Strange Agony of Success," *New York Times*, Business Day, August 24, 1986.

Chapter 6: Entrepreneurism: The Secret to Happiness?

1. Blackwell, Elizabeth, "Rich or Not, Entrepreneurs Are Happiest in Study," The Street, September 12, 2012, https://www.thestreet .com/story/11721398/1/rich-or-not-entrepreneurs-are-happiest -in-study.html.

2. Kilby, Peter, "Hunting the Heffalump," *Entrepreneurship and Economic Development* (New York: Free Press, 1971), 1–40.

3. Kilby, "Hunting the Heffalump," 1–40.

4. Mill, John Stuart, *Principles of Political Economy with Some of Their Applications to Social Philosophy* (London: John W. Parker, 1848).

5. Schumpeter, Joseph A., "The Creative Response in Economic History," *Journal of Economic History* 7, no. 2 (November 1947), 149–59.

6. Schumpeter, Joseph A., *Capitalism, Socialism and Democracy* (New York: Harper & Brothers, 1942), 82–83.

7. Drucker, Peter F., *Innovation and Entrepreneurship: Practice and Principles* (New York: HarperCollins, 1985), 28.

8. Goleman, Daniel, "The Psyche of the Entrepreneur," *New York Times Magazine*, February 2, 1986, https://www.nytimes.com/1986/02/02/magazine/the-psyche-of-the-entrepreneur.html.

9. Ibid.

10. Ibid.

11. Please note: If you don't have an "I'll show him/them" feeling now, this in no way precludes you from discovering that one exists within you and has been suppressed or that you can "find one" by identifying a cause or issue that has irked you for a while but, for myriad reasons, is something you haven't invested in redressing. This notion is explained in greater detail in chapter 8.

12. Goleman, "The Psyche of the Entrepreneur."

13. Anyone reading this book has enough motivation within to succeed, a judgment I make owing to the fact that you're reading a book about taking charge of your professional life, not a book promising that "connecting with nature" will make you a star—and need not worry about finding a mechanism to ignite your "intense flame burning inside."

14. According to Aaron Sorkin, who wrote the screenplay for *The Social Network*, the events portrayed in the movie are gleaned from the online blogging of Mark Zuckerberg. Those "diaries," so to speak, are what Sorkin used to understand what Zuckerberg thought or felt at various points in the time during which he developed Facebook. Zuckerberg did not participate in the development of the movie.

15. Tabak, Alan J., "Hundreds Register for New Facebook Website: Facemash Creator Seeks New Reputation with Latest Online Project," *Harvard Crimson*, February 9, 2004.

16. Finke, Nikki, "Aaron Sorkin on 'Social Network' Women," *Deadline/Hollywood*, October 16, 2010, deadline.com/2010/10/aaron-sorkin-on-social-network-women-76206/.

17. At Harvard, nearly all undergraduates live on campus, in dormitories, for the first year, and in the upper-class Houses—administrative subdivisions of the College as well as living quarters (inspired by residential college systems at Oxford and Cambridge) that provide a sense of community in what might otherwise be a socially chaotic and administratively daunting university environment.

18. Tabak, "Hundreds Register for New Facebook Website."

19. Tabak, "Hundreds Register for New Facebook Website."

20. Abutaleb, Yasmeen, "Facebook's CEO and Wife to Give 99 Percent of Shares to Their New Foundation," Reuters, December 2, 2015, https://www.reuters.com/article/us-markzuckerberg-baby/facebooks-ceo-and-wife-to-give-99-percent-of-shares-to-their-new-foundation-idUSKBNØTKSU620151202.

21. Ibid.

22. The Computerworld Smithsonian Awards Program Oral History Interview, "Advice for Future Entrepreneurs," April 20, 1995.

Chapter 7: The Devil Is in the Details

1. The specific data points I use regarding Candy Lightner were gleaned from Biography.com.
2. Melville, Herman, *Moby-Dick, or, The Whale* (New York: Harper and Brothers, 1851), 38–39.
3. Hamilton, Bethany, Sheryl Berk, and Rick Bundschuh, *Soul Surfer: A True Story of Faith, Family, and Fighting to Get Back on the Board* (New York: Simon & Schuster, 2004).
4. Behar, Richard, "The Bigger They Are, the Harder They Fall" *Time*, (November 4, 1991), 14, 16.

Chapter 8: The Three-C Program

1. Shunryu Suzuki, *Zen Mind, Beginner's Mind* (New York: Weatherhill, 1970), 21.
2. Miller, Mark, "A Powerful, Damaging Cross," *Newsweek*, April 23, 1995.
3. "Barry Scheck Biography," A&E Television Networks, last updated July 15, 2016, https://www.biography.com/people/barry-scheck-011316.
4. Berglas, Steven. "Treating Workaholism," in R. H. Coombs, ed., *Handbook of Addictive Disorders* (New York: Wiley, 2004), 383–407.
5. Miller, "A Powerful, Davaging Cross."
6. Csikszentmihalyi, Mihalyi, *Flow: The Psychology of Optimal Experience* (New York: Harper & Row, 1990), 3.
7. Dostoyevsky, Fyodor, *The House of the Dead* (Mineola, NY: Dover, 2004), 17.
8. The account of Aaron Schneider is as true as possible to the events that occurred when he worked with me, save for any and all data that would enable someone to identify him.
9. For the record and in case you are wondering, I disagreed with Aaron's conclusion: Given his father's passivity and his mother's

narcissism, the dynamic between the two would have been identical. Rather than claiming that as a teacher her husband was a "poor loser," if Aaron's father had become Dr. Schneider his mother would have lamented his decision to specialize in pediatrics, not plastic surgery, usually a far more lucrative specialization. That said, my job was to help Aaron find a passion, not conduct a psychoanalysis, so I did not discuss his "insight" further but simply asked him what lay ahead.

10. For reasons of protecting Aaron's privacy, I have disguised his identity and won't discuss his agency, similar to—but not entirely—the example I've provided.

Chapter 9: The First C: Calm and in Control (Step C#1)

1. Frankl, Viktor, *Man's Search for Meaning* (New York: Touchstone Books, 1984), 95.

2. Bacon, Francis, *Meditationes Sacrae* (1597).

3. Winter, Stuart, "Fish Really Are Good for You—and We Don't Mean Eating Them. Aquariums Boost Your Health," *Daily Express*, July 30, 2015, https://www.express.co.uk/news/nature/594653/Fish-aquarium-boosts-health-relaxing-effect.

4. Landry, Jayan M., "Physiological and Psychological Effects of a Himalayan Singing Bowl in Meditation Practice: A Quantitative Analysis," *American Journal of Health Promotion* 28, (May 1, 2014), 306–309.

5. Csikszentmihalyi, Mihalyi, *Flow: The Psychology of Optimal Experience* (New York: Harper & Row, 1990), 105.

6. Frankl, *Man's Search for Meaning*, 133.

7. Jacobson, Edmund, *Progressive Relaxation* (Chicago: University of Chicago Press, 1938), and Jacobson, Edmund. *Modern Treatments of Tense Patients* (Springfield, IL: Thomas, 1970).

Chapter 10: The Second C: Convert Negative Feelings (Step C#2)

1. James, William, *Psychology: Briefer Course* (New York: Harper Torchbooks, 1961), 424.
2. For the most comprehensive review article about mindfulness that I am aware of, see Vago, David R. and David A. Silbersweig, "Self-awareness, self-regulation, and self-transcendence (S-ART): A Framework for Understanding the Neurobiological Mechanisms of Mindfulness," *Frontiers in Human Neuroscience*, http://doi .org/10.3389/fnhum.2012.00296.
3. Langer, Ellen, *Mindfulness, 25th Anniversary Edition* (New York: DeCapo Lifelong Books, 2014).
4. Vago and Silbersweig, "Self-awareness, Self-Regulation, and Self-Transcendence (S-ART)."
5. Shunryu, Suzuki, *Zen Mind, Beginner's Mind* (New York: Weatherhill, 1970).

Chapter 11: The Third C: Optimize Your Career Plan (Step C#3)

1. Mill, John Stuart, *Autobiography* (London: Penguin, 1873), 117.
2. Benjamin Franklin was no ascetic—he loved a good time that included good food, good wine, and hordes of friendly people. What he had no need for was ostentatious display or "hoarding" of any sort.
3. Erikson, Erik, *Identity: Youth and Crisis* (New York: Norton, 1968), 138.
4. Franklin, Benjamin, *Autobiography* (London: J. Parson's, 1791).
5. Jones, Edward E., *Ingratiation: A Social Psychological Analysis* (New York: Appleton Century Crofts, 1964), 200.
6. Aronson, Elliot, "Some Antecedents of Interpersonal Attraction," in Arnold, W. J. and D. Levine, eds., *Nebraska Symposium on Motivation* 17 (Lincoln: University of Nebraska Press, 1969), 143–173.

7. Italie, Hillel, "Ben Franklin: A Man of Many Facets," *Los Angeles Times*, January 15, 2006, articles.latines.com/2006/jan/15/news/adna-ben/5.

8. Writing in *Inc.*, Michael Simmons provides an exceptional discussion on the subject. Simmons, Michael, "Why Constant Learners All Embrace the 5-Hour Rule," *Inc.*, September 1, 2016, https://www.inc.com/empact/why-constant-learners-embrace-the-5-hour-rule.html.

9. Gilbert, Martin, *Winston S. Churchill, Volume 6: The Finest Hour, 1939–1941* (Hillsdale, MI: Hillsdale College Press, 2011), 758.

Index

About the Author

Dr. Steven Berglas has worn a number of professional hats—including research scientist, psychotherapist, consultant, executive coach, and author—during various phases of a career that has been devoted to understanding the negative psychological consequences of work in general, and burnout in particular.

Dr. Berglas's professional career began at Harvard Medical School, where he was awarded two successive Career Scientist Development Awards from the Alcohol, Drug Abuse, and Mental Health Administration to develop his model of success-induced alcoholism. Dr. Berglas simultaneously served on the faculty of Harvard Medical School's Department of Psychiatry during the terms of these awards, and thereafter at McLean Hospital, where he specialized in studying and treating narcissistic disturbances. During Dr. Berglas's almost thirty years at Harvard Medical School he also maintained a private psychotherapy practice.

Dr. Berglas moved to Los Angeles in 2000 to study successful business leaders and the factors that precipitated their burnout. He was an adjunct professor at USC's Marshall

School of Business, where his academic foci were cures for success-induced burnout, burnout prevention, and entrepreneurial psychology. Dr. Berglas retired from clinical practice after leaving Boston for Los Angeles and shifted his focus to an executive-coaching practice, where he applies his knowledge of behavioral and psychodynamic psychiatry to designing interventions that foster the success of C-level executives at risk for, or in the process of, derailing.

Dr. Berglas holds a BA, cum laude, Phi Beta Kappa, with high honors in psychology from Clark University and a PhD from Duke University, and he completed a two-year postdoctoral training program in social psychiatry at Massachusetts Mental Health Center/Harvard Medical School.